D1594292

Problems and Perspectives in Irish History since 1800

Problems and Perspectives in Irish History since 1800

Essays in honour of Patrick Buckland

D. George Boyce and Roger Swift

EDITORS

FOUR COURTS PRESS

This book was set in 10.5 on 12.5 pt Ehrhardt
by Mac Style Ltd, Scarborough, N. Yorkshire, England for
FOUR COURTS PRESS LTD
7 Malpas Street, Dublin 8, Ireland
Email: info@four-courts-press.ie
and in the United States for
FOUR COURTS PRESS
c/o ISBS, 920 N.E. 58th Avenue, Suite 300, Portland, OR 97213.

A catalogue record for this title is available from the British Library.

ISBN 1-85182-759-5

Printed in Great Britain by
MPG Books Ltd, Bodmin, Cornwall.

Contents

Notes on contributors

D. GEORGE BOYCE is a Professor in the Department of Politics at the University of Wales, Swansea.

PHILIP BULL is a Senior Lecturer in the Department of History at La Trobe University, Melbourne.

MERVYN BUSTEED is a Senior Lecturer in the Department of Geography at the University of Manchester.

CHRISTINE KINEALY is a Senior Lecturer in the Department of Historical and Critical Studies at the University of Central Lancashire.

ALAN MEGAHEY is Vicar of Leadenham, Lincolnshire.

MARK McGOVERN is a Senior Lecturer in the Centre for Studies in the Social Sciences at Edge Hill University College.

FRANK NEAL is Professor of Economics and Social History at the University of Salford.

ALAN O'DAY is Fellow in Modern History, Greyfriars, University of Oxford; and Visiting Fellow, Rothermere American Institute, University of Oxford, 2002–3.

SHAUN RICHARDS is Head of Research and a Professor in the Department of English in the School of Humanities and Social Sciences at Staffordshire University.

ROGER SWIFT is Professor of Victorian Studies at Chester College.

Introduction

D. GEORGE BOYCE AND ROGER SWIFT

This volume of essays pays tribute to the enormous contribution to the development of Irish Studies in Britain made by Professor Patrick Buckland, director of the Institute of Irish Studies at the University of Liverpool from its foundation in 1988 until his retirement in 1997.

Patrick Buckland's research and publications established him as a leading authority on the history of Irish unionism and Northern Ireland.[1] He took his degree at Birmingham University, and then completed an MA on 'The Irish Question in British politics, 1910–14'. This was no ordinary MA; it comprised three volumes, was based on detailed research, especially on the little-used Austen Chamberlain Papers in Birmingham University Library, and offered a wholly new interpretation of the subject. It was a model for all his subsequent work, which was marked by the most thorough, original research; a vast reservoir of enthusiasm; and a deep commitment to Irish History. He then spent the session 1965–6 at Queen's University, Belfast, where he began his PhD research under the supervision of Professor J.C. Beckett. These two men – so unalike in their personalities – immediately struck up a fruitful and friendly relationship. Patrick Buckland enjoyed his year in Queen's. He was the inspiration behind the establishment of an informal 'Irish Studies' group, which, supported by other postgraduates working in Irish History, held seminars in places as diverse as his own flat, Professor Beckett's house, and the Linen Hall Library. These occasions were notable, not only for their academic content, but for their conviviality. Unfortunately for Queen's, Patrick Buckland returned to Birmingham to a research fellowship which enabled him to complete his PhD thesis; it was thus that he rescued the Southern unionists from anonymity, making them a subject for scholarly enquiry.[2] He also made a significant contribution to our knowledge

1 See, for example, Patrick Buckland, *Irish Unionism 2: Ulster unionism and the origins of Northern Ireland, 1886–1922* (Dublin and New York, 1973); Patrick Buckland, *A history of Northern Ireland* (Dublin, 1981); Patrick Buckland, 'Irish Unionism and the new Ireland', in D. George Boyce (ed.), *The revolution in Ireland, 1879–1923* (London, 1988), pp 71–90; Patrick Buckland, 'A Protestant state: Unionists in government, 1921–39', in D. George Boyce and A. O'Day (eds), *Defenders of the Union: a survey of British and Irish unionism since 1801* (London and New York, 2001), pp 211–26. 2 Patrick Buckland, *Irish Unionism 1: the Anglo-Irish and the new Ireland, 1885–1922* (Dublin, 1972); Patrick Buckland, 'The Southern Irish Unionists, the Irish Question, and British politics, 1906–1914', *Irish Historical Studies*,

and understanding of the development of devolved government in Northern Ireland,[3] of the role of politicians in this process,[4] and of the origins and significance of the Northern Ireland Question in British politics.[5]

Patrick Buckland's great achievement, however, lay in the establishment and leadership of the Institute of Irish Studies at Liverpool. On 16 December 1991, in her address to the Institute of Irish Studies at the University of Liverpool, Mrs Mary Robinson, the president of Ireland, congratulated the University on its initiative in establishing the Institute of Irish Studies as the national centre for the development of the study of Ireland in Britain. She also stated that she was 'deeply impressed by the standards of excellence of the director, Dr Patrick Buckland, and his staff, and by their success in dramatically raising the profile and image of Irish Studies here in this country and developing an Irish Studies dimension within the British education system'.[6] Patrick Buckland fully deserved this public accolade, for his vision, enthusiasm, determination, energy and unswerving commitment to the cause of Irish Studies had been integral to the establishment and subsequent development of the Institute at Liverpool University in the immediate aftermath of the Anglo-Irish Agreement and on the recommendation of a survey commissioned by the University Grants Commission in 1986. As the first teaching and research centre of its kind in Great Britain, the Institute sought subsequently to foster the academic study of Ireland, past and present, and of the relationship between Britain and Ireland, and to promote the educational aspirations of the Irish community in Britain, with a view to increasing understanding and respect between the people of Ireland and the United Kingdom.

President Robinson spoke also in her address of the great challenge which faced Irish Studies for the present generation, namely 'the challenge of commending a diversity, a richness and variance of culture, when often a singleness or narrowness of interpretation is more welcome and coherent'. This was a challenge from which Patrick Buckland never shirked; from the outset, he believed passionately that Irish Studies should form an integral part of the educational system in Great Britain, not least because the study of Ireland, and Ireland's relationship with the wider world, including Britain, addressed issues of intellectual interest and contemporary concern, including multi-culturalism, democratic change and economic development. Thus he was determined that

xv, 59 (1987), 228–55; reprinted in Alan O'Day (ed.), *Reactions to Irish nationalism* (London, 1987), pp 365–92.   **3** Patrick Buckland, '*The factory of grievances*': *devolved government in Northern Ireland, 1921–39* (Dublin, 1979).   **4** Patrick Buckland, *James Craig: Lord Craigavon* (Dublin, 1981); Patrick Buckland, 'Carson, Craig and the partition of Ireland, 1912–21', in Peter Collins (ed.), *Nationalism and unionism: conflict in Ireland, 1881–1921* (Belfast, 1994), pp 75–89.   **5** Patrick Buckland, *The Northern Ireland Question, 1886–1986* (Historical Association, London, 1987).   **6** *British Association for Irish Studies Newsletter* (Spring 1992), 2–3.

teaching and research within the Institute should be broad-based, including studies not only of aspects of Irish History, Anglo-Irish Relations and the Irish Diaspora, but also of the Irish Language, Irish Literature and Drama, and Celtic Art. This philosophy duly informed the development at the Institute of wide-ranging research programmes, which drew on links with Irish Studies associations in Britain, America and beyond, of innovative interdisciplinary and multidisciplinary MA and BA degree courses in Irish Studies, and of extramural educational provisions, including public lectures, for the local community. It was also reflected in the establishment of a Joint Education Programme in Irish Studies, a collaborative enterprise between the British Association for Irish Studies, staff at Liverpool University, teachers in schools and colleges, and representatives of the Irish community in Britain, which sought to raise the profile of Irish Studies in British schools. Under the auspices of this unique programme, a wide range of teaching materials, informed by National Curriculum criteria, were developed for use in primary schools, new A and AS level syllabuses in Irish History and Literature were validated by the Joint Matriculation Board, and a series of national conferences and seminars for teachers and students were instituted. In this context, it is perhaps fitting that the contributors to this volume of essays include some of the Institute's original staff who shared, with Patrick, those heady if hectic early years, namely Roger Swift and Christine Kinealy (as director and deputy-director of the Joint Education Programme respectively) and Mark McGovern (the Institute's first PhD student, supervised by Patrick). Fifteeen years on, and despite the cessation of similar initiatives elsewhere in the university sector, the Institute of Irish Studies continues not only to thrive but also to reflect the ideals of its first director.

The essays presented in this collection, penned by distinguished scholars who have worked with Patrick Buckland during his career, seek to provide new perspectives on a range of themes and issues integral to contemporary debates in modern Irish history. As such, they focus on aspects of nineteenth and twentieth history. This is a period in which research has developed significantly over the last several decades, because of the release of new material, both official papers and private collections; and because of the publication of key sources, such as the diaries of W.E. Gladstone and Thomas Jones. One of the most significant aspects of this development has been the deep interest in Irish history on the British side of the Irish Sea, as reflected in these chapters. This has been due in no small measure to the work of Patrick Buckland and the Institute of Irish Studies in Liverpool. Individual scholars have also contributed to this, in universities as diverse as Hull, Stirling, Swansea, North London, Birkbeck, Oxford and Cambridge. The uncertain and at times fraught nature of the British-Irish relationship, and of Northern Irish politics, has in no way jeopardised this project; indeed, in many cases it has quickened interest in it. Not the least notable aspects of this volume is the willingness of historians to move from the grove of academe, to step back from what Tom Paulin characterised as 'Brahmin' – like mentality and yet to remain true to their profession and to the unforgiving demands of the historical method. Recent research and publications are reflected in the essays and the detailed notes and references that accompany them. These exemplify several main advances in Irish history writing: emigration and the Irish experience in Great Britain; the nature and impact of the Union with Great Britain; nationalism and unionism, especially in their cultural developments; and the complex nature of the Anglo-Irish relationship, and the way the peoples of the Islands have deeply influenced each other, even when their relationship has been a less than satisfactory one. The reader will also note that several of the essays in this collection – by Busteed, Swift, Boyce and Richards – straddle the disciplinary boundaries and, as such, perhaps recall Patrick Buckland's own commitment to interdisciplinarity in his work at the Institute of Irish Studies.

Alan O'Day begins with a survey of Ireland under the Union. He challenges the view that Ireland was of marginal importance to Great Britain and to England in particular, citing not only the impact of Ireland on British politics and the rise and fall (usually fall) of British governments, but also the impressive and radical legislation passed by the British parliament to reform Ireland, the better to retain her in a United Kingdom whose very existence as a nation-state and imperial power seemed threatened by Irish nationalism. He concludes, however, that the passing of this axiom, which amounted to a kind of fundamental law, to be succeeded by the tendency of contemporary British politicians to exclude 'national minorities or inconvenient places', is likely to shape British policy towards Northern Ireland: 'Loyalty and even a common experience of war was an insufficient cement; there must be an "imagined community" as well.'

Mark McGovern traces the way in which the siege of Derry in 1689 became 'the most enduring and evocative historical myth of Irish Protestant and Ulster unionist political culture'. He explains how the siege changed and shifted its meaning, depending on the circumstances in which Irish, and especially Ulster, Protestants found themselves. There was always a tension between the siege as part of the glorious history of Britain – the destruction of divine right and Catholic tyranny – and the siege as integral to a local sectarian conflict, disliked by those in Britain who did not want the 'Glorious revolution' of 1689 confused with sectarianism. Ulster Protestants, for their part, experienced the tension arisng from the fear that– as in 1689 – they would be given only half-hearted support from their English compatriots. The embedding of a 'siege mentality' in Unionism is a development whose significance can hardly be exaggerated.

Christine Kinealy explores in detail another celebrated incident in nineteenth century Irish Protestant political life: the 'battle' of Dolly's Brae, in Co. Down, in 1849, when Orangemen and 'Ribbonmen' fought a pitched battle whose repercussions were to have a resonance far exceeding that of the incident itself. It provoked accusation and counter-accusation about the right of the Orange Order to march where it would, and the role of the government and the forces of law and order in arbitrating between the contending parties. Here, siege was replaced by another significant word in Ulster politics – invasion – invasion by the enemy of one's own territory.

The experience of the Irish in Britain is as important for nineteenth-century Irish studies as that of the Irish in Ireland. Three chapters address this theme. Frank Neal studies the impact of the English Poor Law and the Laws of Settlement and Removal, 1819–79, on Irish migrants, showing how British legislation saw fellow-subjects of the crown as semi-aliens to be removed back to their 'own country'. He concludes that the impact of these laws were softened by their less than stringent application. Mervyn Busteed examines the Irish migratory experience from another angle: that of the changes in Irish identity brought about by the experience of living in Great Britain, while at the same time the immigrants carried with them important notions of Irish identity, and especially of Irish political aspirations. Busteed uses street ballads to compare the mystical, millennial ballad style with the more rational one of citizenship rights. A mixture of guilt and nostalgia, and also adjustment and the ability to state an ironic social comment and criticism, not merely of British society, but of the Irish migrant community itself, reveal the complexity of this experience. Roger Swift uses little known material to analyse Thomas Carlyle's thoughts on the Union between Great Britain and Ireland, showing how his prejudice against the Irish (Catholic) people did not lead him to conclude thereby that the Union should be dissolved. On the contrary, Britain could not afford to lose control of an alien people – however alien they might indeed be – in her proximity. Her duty was to govern, maintain order and bear the burden of her great world mission: to civilise – even to civilise the Irish.

Philip Bull explores a different way of working out a satisfactory relationship between Britain and Ireland, through the ideas of Isaac Butt, founder of the Home Rule movement. Butt hoped to mobilise nationalism in Ireland, not to undermine the Union, but, by means of a moderate adjustment in the constitution, to place the Union on firmer ground. He places Butt's embarking on the Home Rule trail in the context of Gladstonian efforts to reform the Church of Ireland and the terms of land-ownership in Ireland. Gladstone's 'loss of steam' in reforming Ireland gave Butt the opportunity to launch his Home Government Association to take up where Gladstone left off, and to 'sustain a basis of civil order threatened by the demise of Gladstone's mission'. Alan Megahey explains how different this kind of reforming mission appeared to the Protestants, and even to Presbyterians (despite their radical past and indeed radical present). He shows how the different conditions prevailing in Ireland made for a rupture between Irish nonconformists and their brethren in Great

Britain – despite the marked anti-Catholic views of many, if not most, British nonconformists. Home Rule would not mean Rome Rule in Britain; but it would in Ireland. British nonconformists replied that Home Rule and the releasing to power of the Irish democracy would overturn the already existing power of the Roman Catholic Church, and thus end, not begin Rome Rule. The different perceptions of what it meant and means to be Protestant in Britain and in Ireland could hardly be better illustrated.

The final two chapters embark on an exploration of cultural themes arising from the Anglo-Irish relationship. Shaun Richards traces the attempts by Irish dramatists, from Sean O'Casey to the present day, to assert, deny, or – more recently – objectively explore the dominant political traditions of Ireland; and in so doing to raise questions, not only for their audiences, but for historians, who would draw a distinction between 'collective memory' and history (which often challenges that 'memory'). He shows that imaginative work and history are not always very far apart; some recent playwrights, notably Sebastian Barry, seek, like the historian, to give 'all Irish histories their allotted space; even those whose desired outcomes ran counter to that of the dominant national desire'. Thus, while history remains a preoccupation to the Irish theatre, its politics are now 'the politics of multiple experiences, rather than those of narrow and competing nationalisms'. George Boyce looks at the idea of Celticism and the Celtic hero as a recurring theme in Irish nationalism in the nineteenth century. He shows that it was not, however, confined to nationalism, but was taken up and used by the three main groups whose interaction make up the history of modern Ireland: Protestant, Catholic and Dissenter. Representatives of all these groups have deployed the Celtic past, and especially the Celtic hero figure, as the best means of staking their claim to be integral to Ireland, and (in the case of modern Ulster Protestants) to be integral also to the history and culture of Great Britain. Yet this use of Celticism has not, on the whole, served its advocates well: on the contrary, it has almost invariably returned to plague its inventors, compromising, undermining or frustrating their search for roots and thereby for legitimacy.

Taken together, these chapters explore a wide and complex range of issues addressed by historians of nineteenth- and twentieth-century Ireland and Anglo-Irish relations. While not of course comprehensive, they illuminate important aspects of what has over the past forty years amounted to a major reassessment of British as well as Irish history, culture and politics: a reassessment in which Professor Patrick Buckland has played his own, major, part.

Ireland and the United Kingdom[1]

ALAN O'DAY

> The Prime Minister ... reaffirms that they will uphold the democratic wish of the greater number of the people of Northern Ireland on the issue of whether they prefer to support the Union or a sovereign united Ireland ... the British Government ... have no selfish strategic or economic interest in Northern Ireland ... They accept that such agreement may, as of right, take the form of agreed structures for the island as a whole, including a united Ireland ... They reaffirm as a binding obligation that they will ... introduce the necessary legislation to give effect to this ...
>
> [Downing Street Declaration, December 1993]

This expression of United Kingdom policy by the then prime minister John Major must be one of the more remarkable pronouncements in modern British history. Not only did it reiterate that the territorial integrity of the nation-state is malleable, but he proposed that the fate of national territory rests in the hands of the people of one part of it alone, and at that merely the 'greater number' of those residing there. Previously official declarations, themselves in marked contrast to the status of the rest of the United Kingdom, referred to, or implied, the necessity of a majority not just the 'greater number'. Major's position may owe something to Ernest Renan's dictum that 'a nation's existence is ... a daily plebiscite' but except in the wake of actual or imminent military defeat, there must be few precedents for a powerful nation willingly adopting the proposition that a portion of its territory can cede itself to another state, solely on the basis of an ephemeral headcount.[2] If nothing else, this invitation to breed is an ingenious means to reverse negative population growth in post-industrial society though it is doubtful that many countries will emulate the example.

No other part of the United Kingdom occupies indeterminate status as part of the nation-state; as Major affirmed, the Union between England and

1 An early version of this paper was given at the Institute of Irish Studies, Queen's University, Belfast. I am grateful for the suggestions offered on that occasion and especially to Timothy Bowman for his comments. Col. Helen O'Day once more encouraged my endeavour and the editors offered useful guidance. 2 Quoted in Umut Özkirimli, *Theories of nationalism: a critical introduction* (Basingstoke and London, 2000), p. 35.

Scotland is forever. Major's Conservative Party was the mainstay in defending the legislative Union between 1886 and 1914; it rejected Gladstone's doctrine that a local plurality, no matter how large, in favour of local legislative autonomy in Ireland was a sufficient basis to grant home rule. A.V. Dicey, *England's case against Home Rule* (1886) underpinned the case for preserving the Union even if Ireland democratically declared for its dissolution.[3] As one Tory succinctly declaimed in 1886, 'one Throne, one law, and one Parliament'.[4] Gladstone, of course, argued that a domestic legislature for Ireland did not spell separation but would enable the Catholic Irish to identity fully with Great Britain and the empire. His Liberal successor as prime minister, Lord Rosebery, though, in 1894 enunciated the doctrine 'that before Irish home rule is concluded by the Imperial Parliament, England as the pre-dominant member of the Three Kingdoms will have to be convinced of its justice and equity'.[5] The Conservative F.E. Smith possibly adumbrated Major's stance when in 1910 he was ready to countenance 'Home Rule All-Round' as a means to get rid of 'a dead quarrel for which neither the country nor the [Conservative] party cares a damn outside of Ulster and Liverpool'.[6] Present-day Ulster unionists may be forgiven for a touch of paranoia when British governments equivocate about their membership of the United Kingdom, when oaths of allegiance to the state and official symbols are removed or made optional, but the home secretary, David Blunkett, calls upon Asians to become more British, and, for him, classes about, and ceremonies of British citizenship are flavour of the season.

Perhaps it is pedantic to insist upon political consistence above expediency but the contradiction between the position of Northern Ireland and other parts of the United Kingdom raises tantalising questions about the British perception of Ireland past and present. During the nineteenth century doubts about Ireland's place and permanence within the nation surfaced to be sure but the context, level of interest and motives were far removed from the current situation. The transformation in British outlook begs for exposition. The transition is easier to locate in time – the beginnings of the 1920s – than ascribe to a simplistic causation. If by-and-large the question being posed receives modest contemporary notice, it had sustained airing in the great age of the construction of a United Kingdom.[7] It merits reflection now for what is implied about the nature of the Anglo-Irish connection and the formation of the United Kingdom nation-state along with its future prospects.

3 A.V. Dicey, *England's case against Home Rule* (new imp.; Richmond, Surrey, 1973), pp 34–46, 67–72, 282. 4 *Parliamentary Debates* [*PD*], 306 (18 May 1886), c. 374. 5 Quoted in the Marquess of Crewe, *Lord Rosebery* (London, 1931), vol. 2, pp 444–5. 6 John Campbell, *F.E. Smith, first earl of Birkenhead* (London, 1983), p. 222. 7 E.g., Alan O'Day, 'Defending the Union: parliamentary opinions, 1869 and 1886' in D. George Boyce and Alan O'Day (eds), *Defenders of the Union* (London, 2001), pp 90–111.

The objective here is to gaze into the prism from a slightly different angle. The aim is fourfold: to consider the record, in many ways an impressive record of British involvement in Ireland; to inquire why a particular, mainly critical, assessment of that record informs the literature; to consider reasons for intense British concern about Ireland; and finally to place the British obsession in the context of some theoretical constructs. This last constitutes the less developed portion of a hitherto widely disseminated story in which George Boyce's, *The Irish Question and British politics, 1868–1996*, is a key text.[8] The present story study is a footnote to that work, differing in emphasis on the beginning of intense British involvement, and, in some measure, about the reference-point of the governing elite's interest in Ireland. Literature on nationalism generally focuses on processes by which national units emerge; writings on state-building and citizenship tend to begin from another point on the compass, identifying the successful or in some instances futile efforts to inculcate a common identity while those on imperialism look at large countries during a stage of mainly external expansionism. To the extent that the United Kingdom fits these paradigms, it is through analyses of representative institutions and the rise of democracy, overseas expansion and core-periphery or exploitive relationships. The rise of Irish nationalism is viewed as a national/religious challenge to a dominant British state, a state that is alleged to have been insensitive to the distinctive traditions and yearnings of its neighbour. Traditionally the Anglo-Irish connection is characterised as two dimensional: a dynamic assertiveness of Irishness and relatively static Britain responses. To put it another way, Irish nationalism initiates change and was proactive while Britain reacted to these demands.

The typical rendering can be inverted. Ernest Gellner, Benedict Anderson, E.J. Hobsbawm and Miroslav Hroch, among others, representative of the modernist analysis of nationalism, afford insights that reveal the leaders of strong centralising national constructs as the initiators and peripheral peoples as reactors.[9] Gellner – most notably his *Nations and nationalism* – emphasises the effect of industrialisation on ethnic consciousness which arises in reaction to the threat of modernisation and centralisation.[10] Benedict Anderson observes that ethnic communities are necessarily 'imagined' in the sense of linking groups of people together who have not had and can not anticipate having direct physical acquaintance with one another. This he insists only happens when modernisa-

8 D.G. Boyce, *The Irish Question and British politics, 1868–1996* (2nd ed.; Baskingstoke and London, 1996). 9 See Jim MacLaughlin, *Reimaging the nation-state: the contested terrains of nation-building* (London, 2001). This study asserts that nation construction in both Catholic Ireland and Unionist Ulster is attributable to the 'organic intelligentsia', that is local religious, educational and cultural elites, it gives the traditional perspective a fresh colouration. He is critical of the big-state perspective of these and other writers. 10 Ernest Gellner, *Nations and nationalism* (Ithaca, NY, 1983).

tion reaches the stage where communication, notably print, allows disparate peoples to imagine themselves having a common bond.[11] National conscious- ness in geographical peripheries as a response to the a modernising aggrandis- ement of metropolitan cores is now established in the literature on nationalism though it is less frequently applied to Ireland. But from such a vantage point British national leaders can be seen as proactive formulators of a United Kingdom nationality and Irish nationalists responding to this incursion by counter-appeals to a unique identity of their own. In Dicey's words, the Union 'is favoured no less by the current of English history, than by the tendencies of modern civilisation'.[12] What emerges then is two separate dynamics running along separate but parallel paths which ultimately converge only to collide. This inversion affords an explanatory framework for the intense involvement of Britain in Irish matters and the precipitous decline in interest after 1921 which can be expressed as a dialectic leading to a synthesos, the practical effect of which was closure of the project for a United Kingdom inclusive of Ireland.

Irish and United Kingdom nationalism were fashioned in a common caul- dron though the impetus for each differed. This is to sustain Linda Colley's theme that British identity was formed out of hostility to the 'otherness' of Catholicism but to suggest a more nuisance picture.[13] Michael Billig observes that nationalism is not the preserve of the periphery but is the ideological means by which core nation-states are reproduced. For this process he coins the term 'banal nationalism' by which Billig means the continual 'flagging', or reminding, of nationhood.[14] This is to challenge Colley's assertion that Ireland

> was rarely able or willing to play a satisfactory part in it ... Ireland's rela- tionship with the empire was always a deeply ambiguous one ... Ireland was cut off from Great Britain by the sea; but it was cut off still more effectively by the prejudices of the English, Welsh and Scots, and by the self-image of the bulk of the Irish themselves, both Protestants and Catholics.[15]

In contrast, it is urged that Ireland very much played its part albeit not always in ways compliant with British expectations. Even Irish Protestants were in vital respects 'marginal Britons',[16] but there was also a profound reality noted

11 Benedict Anderson, *Imagined communities: reflections on the origin and spread of national- ism* (London, 1983), pp 46–7, 102. For another angle on the modernisation theme, see Joan Vincent, 'A political orchestration of the Irish Famine: County Fermanagh, May 1847' in Marilyn Silverman and P.H. Gulliver (eds), *Approaching the past: historical anthropology through Irish case studies* (New York, 1992), pp 75–7.   12 Dicey, *England's case against Home Rule*, p. 283.   13 Linda Colley, *Britons: forging the nation, 1707–1837* (London, 1995), p. 8. 14 Michael Billig, *Banal nationalism* (London, 1995), pp 5–9.   15 Colley, *Britons*, pp 8–9. 16 D.G. Boyce, '"The marginal Britons": the Irish', in Robert Colls and Philip Dodd (eds), *Englishness: politics and culture, 1880–1920* (London, 1986), pp 230–53.

by Declan Kiberd that the Irish and British identity fed on one another.[17] The unresolved nature of Irish nationalism (and unionism) created dysfunctions which continue to circumscribe development across Ireland. The common fund of ideas and language with the ideological assumptions contained therein both obscured and modified the rhetoric of nationalisms, moderating Seamus Deane's appraisal that the

> final incoherence that has always characterised the relationship between the two countries, the incoherence that comes from sharing a common language which is based upon different presuppositions. The failure of language to accommodate experience, the failure of a name to fully indicate a place, the failure of lovers to find the opportunity to express their feelings, whether in words or deed, are all products of this political confrontation.[18]

The present over-arching argument is that the concept of a British or United Kingdom state being forged was fundamentally a top-down phenomenon, a notion fostered by an elite with its central apparatus at Westminster. This is not to prelude the influence of other forces, local, cultural and alike. Nevertheless, the cockpit of state formation in the case of the United Kingdom was anchored in the political and administrative apparatus of Westminster. Following Hobsbawm, the key phase came during an age of bourgeois-capitalism running from approximately the 1820s to the late 1860s. The mass democracy of post-1867 Britain was less persuaded by a nation-building exercise that included Ireland. This indifference required time to be absorbed by an elite which still held to older, almost atavistic attitudes about an all-British Isles nation.

The time-lag was reflected in two political outlooks. Gladstone and Liberals came to believe that British nationality would be preserved by limiting the drive toward a centralised, bureaucratic state for all parts of the nation. It advocated a de-centralised state which could cater for unique wants. When introducing the Government of Ireland bill, Gladstone insisted: 'The principle that I am laying down I am not laying down exceptionally for Ireland.'[19] Later in the 1886 he contended:

> What is no less likely, and even more important, is the sense of nationality, both in Scotland and in Wales, set astir by this controversy may take a wider range than heretofore. Wales and even Scotland, may ask herself, whether the present system of entrusting all the affairs to the handling of

17 Declan Kiberd, *Inventing Ireland* (London, 1995), p. 2.   **18** Seamus Deane, *Brian Friel: Plays One* (London, 1996), p. 22.   **19** *PD*, 304 (8 Apr. 1886), c. 1081.

a body, English in such overwhelming proportion as the present
Parliament is and must probably always be, is an adjustment which
does the fullest justice to what is separate and specific in their several
populations.[20]

This transition can be found in the Irish Church Act, 1869, which by differen-
tiating Ireland from the rest of Great Britain, through ending the formal link
between church and state reversed the trend toward uniformity. Unionists,
though, took exception to this diagnosis, insisting on the organic unity of the
nation. In 1886 Lord Hartington, a dissident Liberal, objected to Home Rule
because, 'we may have not only different laws in Ireland from those which
prevail in England and Scotland; but laws found on totally different principles
and administered in a totally different spirit'.[21] Later Sir Edward Carson, leader
of the Ulster Unionist Party, answered his own rhetorical question, 'What is the
object of the United Kingdom? As I understand it, it is that all parts of that
Kingdom should be worked together as one whole; under one system, and with
the object that the poorer may be helped by the richer, and the richer may be
stronger by the co-operation of the poorer.'[22] In the aftermath of the First
World War many unionists adopted a Gladstonian view. Ironically, the Liberals,
a party more comfortable with democratisation dropped Irish matters earlier
than the Conservatives, still in many ways an elite party. By the early 1920s their
respective attitudes converged, driven by popular indifference to Ireland.

This paradox receives notice indirectly from Reinhard Bendix who contends
that the British state was exceptionally capable of facilitating the civic incorporation of the workers, that once done 'lower class protest may progress from a
demand for full citizenship within the prevailing political community [the
United Kingdom] to a demand for a change of this community in order to make
full citizenship possible'.[23] While he sees this as a reason for the decline of
support for socialism, the logic of Bendix's argument is that the outcome can
also be for the realignment of the national state and of those entitled to belong
to it to accord with this new ethic. This hypothesis appears to be supported by
intermittent opinion polls that reveal popular indifference considerably
outruns the that of Westminster politicians to present-day Northern Ireland.
Whereas, Ireland was hotly contested between British parties before 1914, the
so-called bi-partisan approach since the late 1960s rests on a firm bedrock of
public apathy.

20 W.E. Gladstone, *The Irish Question: I. The history of an idea. II. Lessons of the election*
(London, 1886), p. 20.   21 *PD*, 305 (10 May 1886), cc. 615–16.   22 Quoted in John
Kendle, *Ireland and the federal solution: the debate over the United Kingdom constitution,
1870–1921* (Montreal and Kingston, 1989), p. 143.   23 Reinhard Bendix, *Nation building
and citizenship* (rev. ed.; Berkeley and Los Angeles, 1977), p. 86.

BRITAIN'S IRISH OBSESSION

If the Irish have become, to use the meaning of George Boyce's telling phrase, 'marginal Britons' in the contemporary United Kingdom, their place was more entrenched in an only partly democratic nineteenth century Great Britain. Gladstone confirmed this centrality when in the wake of the Fenian uprising he professed 'I am oppressed day and night with the condition of Ireland, with the sad and painful spectacle it exhibits to the world.'[24] Intensity of interest in Ireland was not a momentary aberration but a constant pre-occupation signalled by Gladstone's oft quoted pledge, 'my mission is to pacify Ireland', which Boyce suggests 'marked the definition of the Irish Question in its modern form: for it crystallised the Peelite policy of attempting to modify, while at the same time maintaining the Union between Great Britain and Ireland'.[25] For much of Ireland's existence under the Union (1801–1921) the particulars of the Irish Question were far from consistent or universally self-evident, at least to the British politicians charged with providing answers. At some points the Irish Question appeared as a religious issue, that is, rights for Catholics and their Church while at other moments, it revolved around access to land or some other matter: but always, to quote Boyce, Britain 'assumed that it would be able to control and regulate the destinies of the lesser partner. These tensions were present in Anglo-Irish relations until the formation of the Home Government Association in 1870; but they became acute with the rise to power of Charles Stewart Parnell ...'[26] Adding to this picture Phillip Bull suggests that the Land Act of 1870 opened a period when 'British political leaders, members of Parliament and a wider circle of opinion-formers [began] to grapple with an Irish problem within the context of a sustained and systematic attempt to understand distinctively Irish perspectives'.[27] Boyce notes that the vigorous involvement was impelled by 'the recognition that Ireland required what Disraeli called a "Revolution" effected through English policy, and the difference between what England could consent to, and Ireland be contented to receive, was the essence of the Irish Question in British politics'.[28] After 1886 the Irish Question was synonymous with the self-government or the national demand, though that too, always contained a degree of ambiguity. Thus, at one level Irish concerns were part of most British controversies and nearly all literature on nineteenth-century Ireland is about the Irish Question broadly defined.

From a quantitative perspective alone, no other area of policy between 1869 and 1914 absorbed so much parliamentary time – not the problem of poverty,

24 Quoted in H.C.G. Matthew (ed.), *The Gladstone diaries* (Oxford, 1982), vol. 7, p. 158. 25 Boyce, *Irish Question*, p. 18. 26 Boyce, 'Marginal Britons', p. 230. 27 Philip Bull, *Land, politics and nationalism: a study of the Irish land question* (Dublin, 1996), p. 54. 28 Boyce, *Irish Question*, p. 129.

not social reform, not the economy and perhaps even more surprisingly not military. imperial or foreign affairs.[29] In view of the close connection between the British Establishment, the empire, foreign office and the numerous military officers propping up the benches of the houses of parliament the time allocated to these areas compared with that given to Ireland is astonishing. Wales and Scotland, in contrast, scarcely got a look in. The Irish were loath to associate their claims with those of Wales and Scotland. At the turn of the twentieth century Douglas Hyde and Patrick Pearse both showed interest in fostering pan-Celt connections but their individualistic enthusiasm occasioned controversy in their own ranks. When Hyde proposed to attend the Pan-Celt Conference planned for 1900 in Dublin the committee of Coiste Gnothe informed him that they 'would be sorry that any of their members should give time or money to an enterprise that could not help the Irish language'.[30] Ireland's primacy in British political culture can be illustrated briefly. For instance, at the close of the parliamentary session in 1881 during which the Irish Land Act of that year was passed, Edward Hamilton, Gladstone's private secretary, jotted down in his diary, 'the unparalleled session terminated yesterday – 'the one or single *Bill* session' as it is facetiously, and may be truly, called'.[31] In the short parliamentary session of 1886 the Gladstone's home rule proposal consumed sixteen days; to cite R.C.K. Ensor's assessment, it was 'debated at very high levels of eloquence and argument'.[32] In 1893 the second Home Rule bill was introduced in February and received its third reading on 1 September by which time it had occupied the house of commons for 85 sittings. In the house of lords where the bill was swiftly dismissed it succeed in bringing 'together the largest muster of peers on record'.[33] Between 1912 and 1914 Ireland's future, particularly that of Ulster, brought the nation near the brink of internal conflict, so close, in fact, that George Dangerfield subsequently cites Ulster resistance, abetted by Tory connivance, to an all-Ireland Home Rule regime as one of the leading ingredients of 'The Strange Death of Liberal England'. It is not necessary adopt Dangerfield's doomsday scenario in order to conclude that Ulster resistance precipitated a major crisis.

Under the Union there was no dearth of official commissions, parliamentary legislation, controversy or literature on Irish questions. As Edward Norman notes, between 1810 and 1833 alone there were 114 Royal Commissions and 60 select committees on Irish matters.[34] According to him, 'the development of

---

29 See, Alan O'Day, 'The Irish problem' in T.R. Gourvish and Alan O'Day (eds), *Later Victorian Britain, 1867–1900* (Basingstoke and London, 1988), pp 229–49.   30 Quoted in Ruth Dudley Edwards, *Patrick Pearse: the triumph of failure* (London, 1977), p. 31.   31 Dudley W. Bahlman (ed.), *The diary of Sir Edward Walter Hamilton, 1880–85* (Oxford, 1972), vol. 1, p. 161.   32 R.C.K. Ensor, *England, 1870–1914* (Oxford, 1938), p. 98.   33 H.C.G. Matthew, *Gladstone, 1875–1898* (Oxford, 1995), p. 211.   34 Edward Norman, *A history of Ireland* (London, 1971), p. 14.

Ireland was so strikingly redirected by the Union ... that it is possible to assign to 1800 a real significance which rarely attaches to a particular year ...'[35] Continuing, he maintains, 'a modern [Irish] nation was created'. The impact extended to the whole of the United Kingdom for 'the effect of the Irish debate was central to the entire structure of the Constitution'.[36] He points out that important innovations such as the introduction of dispensaries for the sick in each county in 1805; creation of lunatic asylums in 1817 and provision for their inspection by sanitary officers in 1819, state finance for emigration from over-crowded districts in 1823 and 1825, establishment of the Board of Public Works in 1831, the National Board of Education in 1831, the Tithe Composition Act, 1832, the Church Temporalities Act, 1833, legislation for a national police in 1836, the Tithe Act, 1837, the Poor Law, 1838, Municipal Corporations Act, 1840, the Charitable Donations and Bequests Act, 1844, Maynooth College Act, 1845 and legislation for foundation of the Queen's Colleges, 1845 peppered the legislative agenda of the first fifty years of the Union. The list does not end there; in 1836, for example, the Royal Commission on Irish Railways laid the corner-stone of modernised transport. For the nineteenth century as a whole, important measures pertaining to Irish land holding were passed in 1816, 1826, 1849, 1860, 1870, 1881, 1882, 1885, 1887, 1888, 1891, 1896, 1903, 1909 while enactment's for agricultural labourers became law in 1883, 1885, 1886, 1891, 1892, 1896, 1903 (part IV of the Land Act) and 1906. Major commissions to investigate the conditions of Irish land were appointed in 1844, 1879, 1880, 1887 along with the land conference of 1902. Few British cabinets enjoyed relief from the Irish land problem or indeed from any of the other constituent parts of the Irish Question.

Other significant legislation in the post-1869 years included acts for intermediate education, 1878, university education, 1879 and 1908, abolition of fees in national schools and compulsory attendance for children between age 6 and 14, 1891, local government, 1898, and, of course, more controversially the several measures designed to deal with social and political unrest.[37] Nor were these the only proposals or pieces of legislation that took up space in the parliamentary timetable; there were many more lesser and unsuccessful matters. The frequently voiced claim of nationalists that Ireland was ignored by parliament does not stand up to inspection and their contention that Westminster-made legislation failed to take adequate account of Irish peculiarities fares only a little better. The latter argument could be applied in equal measure to Scotland and Wales, indeed, to regions of England. Furthermore, many general parliamentary acts applied to Ireland as well as the rest of Britain. This list includes franchise and

35 Ibid., p. 29. 36 Ibid., p. 51. See, also, Donald H. Akenson, *The Irish education experiment: the national system of education in the nineteenth century* (London, 1970), p. 388. 37 See Virginia Crossman, *Politics, law and order in nineteenth-century Ireland* (Dublin, 1986), appendix.

election legislation, among these being the important Acts of 1884, 1885 and 1918. (There were separate acts for Ireland in 1832, 1850 and 1868). Much of the Edwardian social welfare legislation, such as the Old Age Pensions and Children's Acts, 1908 and the National Insurance Act, 1911, were instrumental in changing the face of Ireland. Ireland, too, received generous consideration by house of commons committees and during Question Time, perhaps being the subject of a quarter of queries put to ministers in the years after 1880. Numerous parliamentary and royal commissions examined the state of the country. Yet, it was not simply the time of the house of commons that was devoured by Irish affairs. Perusal of opinion journals like the *Nineteenth Century* or the *Fortnightly Review*, examination of the contents of newspapers, and the mass of political cartoons such as those appearing in *Punch*, *Vanity Fair*, and the now largely forgotten, *St Stephen's Review*, the last sporting the craftsmanship of Tom Merry, attest to the place of the Irish Question in British national life.

At first sight this absorption must seem very curious indeed. Ireland was a relatively remote backwater. And, unlike India, Ireland's contribution to Great Britain's economic well-being was modest though certain industries such as shipbuilding, engineering and textiles, concentrated in the North were an exception. As noted already, Ireland attracted vastly more attention than Wales or Scotland though its economic resources overall were scarcely commensurate with, say, the coal mines of south Wales or the industrial output of the Clyde. She had few precious natural resources and her large agricultural sector was a growing embarrassment in the later Victorian years when the bounty of North America and elsewhere flowed into the British market. Nor was Ireland a place where hordes of British emigrants flocked; they went elsewhere; instead Irish migrants flooded into Britain where they were a somewhat disruptive element, especially in mid-century, adding yet another aspect to the ever-enlarging debate about Ireland. Although there was some concern about Ireland's strategic location at Britain's backdoor, this in reality was no more than a minor distraction. Belgium and northern France had greater military significance and were a good deal closer to London.

The high level of interest in Ireland in the late Victorian era could be seen as the result of Irish disaffection, of the need to ward-off the menace of nationalism, of the power wielded by an Irish Party under Parnell and his successors, or simply the consequence of benevolent or malevolent actions of Englishmen. But this obsession was not a dike which burst spilling into late Victorian political culture or the influence of an enlarged democracy. A similar catalogue can be compiled – has been compiled – between the Union and 1868. Boyce dates this fascination to 13 February 1844 when the house of commons began a nine-day debate on a motion by Lord John Russell, who spoke to the theme that 'Ireland is occupied not governed'.[38] But this, too, is rather belated for the

---

38 Boyce, *Irish Question*, p. 1.

Catholic Question had convulsed British politics between 1801 and 1829: Robert Peel in 1827 declared that it was 'mixed up with everything we eat or drink or say or think'. Even beforehand sectarian clashes revived between 1810 and 1815. British governments routinely are accused of anti-Catholic bias in Ireland and, while this charge can not be dismissed easily, it was never wholly accurate, at least in intent. Peel was scarcely less hostile to Orangemen, and for much the same reasons as he opposed the Catholics. In October 1813 he wrote to Lord Liverpool, 'we feel it, I assure you, a most difficult task when anti-Catholicism (if I may so call it) and loyalty are so much united as they are in the Orangemen, to appease the one without discouraging the other'.[39] In July the following year he noted of the annual Orange celebrations, 'if they meet as yeoman, and offer just cause of offence to their Catholic brethren, and we do not interfere to prevent it, we are in fact little less than a party to it'.[40] To him it seemed a society 'not under the control of the Government'.[41] This outlook was not confined to Peel. In 1825 both the Catholic Association and the Orange organisation were curtailed by the Unlawful Societies Act and legislation in 1832, 1838 and 1844 curbed party processions inciting sectarian violence. Erich Strauss, a rather neglected Marxist historian, more than half a century ago, anticipated Norman, pointing out:

> From the time of the Union Ireland's influence in Great Britain became so much more intimate that it changed its character: it was, in fact, the most powerful influence ever exerted by a colony on an imperial power since the cultural penetration of the Roman empire by Greece ... Irish problems and the Irish people became one of the most powerful factors in British public life, from parliament down to the inarticulate and politically semi-conscious movement of the submerged masses.[42]

In his estimation:

> The record of the Irish Question in the imperial parliament during the first half of the nineteenth century was ... [that] it directly overturned Pitt's long administration in 1801, the Ministry of All the Talents in 1807, Lord Grey's government in 1834, Sir Robert Peel's first administration in 1835 and his second administration in 1846 ... It set in motion

39 Quoted in Norman Gash, *Mr Secretary Peel: the life of Sir Robert Peel to 1830* (London, 1961), p. 146. See Hereward Senior, *Orangeism in Ireland and Britain, 1795–1836* (London, 1966), pp 194, 284. 'Orangemen represented a distinct interest of their own which made them actively oppose any government measures designed to conciliate the Catholic majority in Ireland. They were thus both a barrier to revolution and an obstacle to compromise' (p. 284). Also, Sean Farrell, *Rituals and riots: sectarian violence and political culture in Ulster, 1784–1886* (Lexington, KT, 2000), pp 50, 61, 66. 40 Gash, *Mr Secretary Peel*, p. 147. 41 Ibid. 42 Erich Strauss, *Irish nationalism and British democracy* (London, 1951), p. 70.

the train of events which culminated in the Great Reform Bill of 1832, and it was the proximate cause of the crisis which ended in the repeal of the Corn Laws – the two outstanding social and political measures of British history during the first half of the century.[43]

His affirmation neglects the impact of Daniel O'Connell on the Whigs during the 1830s and the campaign to Repeal the Union in the 1840s. Nor can any analysis omit the substantial success in incorporating the large Irish immigrant population into British society. Its existence was a reminder that the Anglo-Irish relationship was never wholly about Ireland and Britain and indeed became transatlantic in the post-famine decades.

AN UNENVIABLE REPUTATION

The evidence recited here is not new. The level of British involvement in, British concern about, Ireland is documented in general and specialist works. However, the literature is saturated with generally critical assessments of British involvement in Ireland or, as in many recent studies of modern Britain, it tends to be downgraded or ignored, a tendency noted by Boyce.[44] This focus is the consequence of a nationalist-liberal perspective that has animated both the scholarly and public spheres of discussion of Ireland over the last three generations. Yet, it is pertinent to remember in the wider context, as Boyce remarks, 'a study of the Irish Question and British politics represents the point at which two historical, as well as political, traditions intersect. Yet very often historical treatment of Ireland fails to acknowledge this fact'.[45] 'If Ireland was considered historically at all', he comments, 'it was in terms of a troublesome and alien irruption into the British body politic. And whereas Irish historians are reluctant to see their country's history in terms of "questions" and rightly so. British historians find it difficult to see their neighbour's history and relationship in terms of anything else.'[46] Elsewhere he interjects, 'the idea of Englishness had much in common with the idea of Irishness: the desire to misrepresent their unique relationship, to flee from the mutual influences they exerted on each other, and from the reciprocal nature of their history'.[47]

A record of endeavour as outlined might be expected to find historians falling over themselves in obsequious praise. That, it hardly needs, saying is far from the case. John Whyte, *Interpreting Northern Ireland*, reflects the usual dismal appraisal, declaring that 'when all mitigating circumstances had been taken into account, Britain's record in Ireland was deplorable'. More politely

43 Ibid., pp 116–17. 44 Boyce, *Irish Question*, pp 16–17. 45 Ibid., p. 13. 46 Ibid., p. 14. 47 Boyce, 'Marginal Britons', p. 249.

but just as assuredly the *Framework document for Northern Ireland* (1995), for instance, euphemistically states that the British and Irish 'governments recognise that there is much for deep regret on all sides in the long and often tragic history of Anglo-Irish relations'.[48] In the *Times Literary Supplement* in 1998 Martin Pugh accuses 'those who frustrated Gladstone in 1886 and for years afterwards are in a real sense the authors of the trail of blood that leads all the way to the streets of Omagh in the centenary year of his death'.[49] Versions of this assessment reverberate through both general and specialised accounts. Brian Jenkins, *The age of emancipation*, asserts 'one consequence of the delay in conceding Emancipation was the creation in Ireland of a new spirit of nationalism'.[50] Monsignor Ambrose Macaulay's intones of emancipation in the North, 'the gratitude that the measure could have called forth was therefore diminished and sullied by grudging means by which it was enacted'.[51] Seán Connolly in *A new history of Ireland* (1989) issues much the same verdict, raising doubt about potential healing effect of emancipation when it had been delayed for so long. 'Already by 1823', he writes, divisions between Catholics and Protestants had reached a point where the idea of conciliation had become largely irrelevant'.[52] Few episodes have escaped indictment or not been damned with faint praise. Writing on the land measure of 1870, E.D. Steele, supposes that 'in Ireland there are two sets of laws – the English ... and the laws and customs of the country ...'[53] L.P. Curtis, jr, in the early 1960s attempted to rehabilitate Arthur Balfour's historical repute but nevertheless felt obliged to insist, 'toward Ireland the Conservative Party, in general, had displayed a consistently negative attitude'. He goes on to assert, 'compared with the Conservative interpretation of the Irish question, Gladstone's attitude was not only more courageous but farsighted as well'.[54] The biographer of Sir Henry Campbell-Bannerman advises that 'looking back on the long, sad history of our dealings with Ireland, it is difficult to resist a degree of scepticism about our political sagacity or our capacity to deal adequately with the problem on our doorstep which has plagued us for so many years'.[55] Lord Blake in his biography of Andrew Bonar Law in 1955 placed his subject's support for Ulster refusal to be incorporated into an all-Ireland regime between 1912 and 1914 squarely in the dock adjudicating that 'undoubtedly in making a declaration of

48 John Whyte, *Interpreting Northern Ireland* (Oxford,1991), p. 141. 49 Martin Pugh, *Times Literary Supplement*, 18 Sept. 1998. 50 Brian Jenkins, *Era of emancipation: British government of Ireland, 1812–1830* (Montreal and Kingston, 1988), p. 304. 51 Ambrose Macaulay, *William Crolly, archbishop of Armagh, 1835–49* (Dublin, 1994), p. 89. 52 Seán Connolly, 'Union government, 1812–23' in W.E. Vaughan (ed.), *A new history of Ireland, vol. 1: Ireland under the Union, 1801–70* (Oxford, 1989), pp 55, 73. 53 E.D. Steele, *Irish land and British politics: Tenant-right and nationality, 1865–1870* (Cambridge, 1974), p. 17. 54 L.P. Curtis, jnr, *Coercion and conciliation in Ireland, 1880–92* ((Princeton, 1963), p. 27. 55 John Wilson, *CB: a life of Sir Henry Campbell-Bannerman* (London, 1973), p. 69.

this sort Bonar Law was going far to break the conventions upon which parliamentary democracy is based'.[56] John Ramsden's opinion of the Ulster resistance supplied in the official history of the Conservative party is substantially
the same: 'whatever the errors of the Liberals, the fact remains that the
Conservatives were launched on a very perilous course,' he writes. Ramsden
believes that Bonar Law as 'leader of the opposition in Parliament approved
and supported the destruction of both the practice and authority of parliament'.[57] Norman, who might be expected to offer a less condemnatory opinion,
goes so far as to argue that 'the imperial parliament intended to extend to
Ireland the leading benefits of the United Kingdom – the extension of equal
laws ...' but concedes that its good intentions got blown off course by differing
conditions there.[58] And, Boyce, who can not be labelled a hostile observer,
accepts that the Anglo-Irish relationship did not succeed because the Union
'promised much, but was felt by Irish Roman Catholics to give little'.[59]

The Irish aristocracy predictably is similarly dismissed. It is portrayed as a
nuisance, even to Conservative leaders. Andrew Adonis points out that once in
office Lord Salisbury's authority went unchallenged on major questions, Irish
land issues excepted.[60] When he was out of office, 'Irish peers both focused and
organised aristocratic discontent, and their parliamentary strength gave them a
disruptive potential within the Unionist party ...'[61] Furthermore, 'all governments were subjected to regular questioning from the Irish peers ...' with Irish
issues overall accounting for about a third of all questions put to ministers in
the house of lords.[62] The pre-eminent assessment is familiar. While it is unsurprisingly that Gladstone, Whigs and Liberals come off the better, it is also true
that many of the legislative enactment's already identified came from
Conservative governments. It does not stretch credibility to maintain that the
most decisive pieces of land legislation from 1885 were passed by Conservative
governments. Alistair Cooke and Anthony Malcomson made this point in the
introduction to the Ashbourne Papers, noting 'contrary to popular belief, it was
the Conservative party, not Gladstone, that came closest to solving the Irish
problem in the late nineteenth century'.[63]

What small credit accorded to British interventions has come under unsym-
pathetic scrutiny. From one vantage point British involvement is reduced to
'racism'. A distinctly odd exercise in pseudo-science alleges that Victorian eth-
nology 'tended to polarise Englishmen and Irishmen by providing a scientific

56 Robert Blake, *The unknown prime minister: the life and times of Andrew Bonar Law,
1858–1923* (London, 1955), p. 130.   **57** John Ramsden, *The age of Balfour and Baldwin,
1902–40* (London, 1978), p. 85.   **58** Norman, *Modern Ireland*, p. 45,   **59** Boyce, 'Marginal
Britons', p. 247.   **60** Andrew Adonis, *Making aristocracy work: the peerage and the political
system in Britain, 1884–1914* (Oxford, 1993), p. 31.   **61** Ibid., p. 44.   **62** Ibid., 69.
63 A.B. Cooke & A.P.W. Malcomson (compl.), *The Ashbourne papers, 1869–1913* (Belfast,
1974), p. ix.

basis for assuming that such characteristics as violence, poverty, improvidence, political volatility, and drunkenness were inherently Irish and only Irish'.[64] However, to quote this same source, 'slightly more tolerant' Victorians

> assume[d] that the Irish people could still be effectively ruled from Westminster provided that the law was applied in a firm and consistent manner. A small minority of Victorians ... genuinely sympathised with Irish grievances and the Home Rule movement, and these less prejudiced men believed that on the whole Irishmen were no lazier, darker, drunker, or more pugnacious than their own countrymen.[65]

From another angle, Cooke and John Vincent attribute British action in Ireland to the momentary requirements of party and personal ambition. 'For them [Tories], as for Liberals,' they write, 'the Irish question was not one into which practical Irish considerations entered in any detail.'[66] As an explanation, they propose,

> The 'Irish question' was the temporary and particular name given in the 1880s to a continuous and permanent existential problem which party managers inflict upon themselves. This is the task of finding party lines, divisions, and alignments, and then rationalising these for the benefit of that great majority of even their senior colleagues who hold themselves bound by habit, honour, loyalty, and decency to an extentionalist view of party definitions of which they then loyally expect the moral entrepreneurs of the party to evolve for them from their own inner Nihilism.[67]

Equally, Jonathan Parry's demotes Gladstone's Home Rule bill to a sort of intellectual aberration: It was, in his opinion, 'the most convincing demonstration imaginable that his priorities were at odds with those of the mainstream nineteenth century Liberal tradition'.[68]

However, as Boyce observes, it is the growing tendency in writings on modern Britain to depreciate or ignore the Irish dimension that twists the story out of shape most completely. Much of it gives scant recognition to the Irish part in the story, as though the country already had been hived off from the

---

64 L.P. Curtis, jnr, *Apes and angles: the Irish in Victorian caricature* (Washington, DC, 1971), p. 21. This peculiar volume was republished in 1998. In conjunction with it, an imperative reading is S.W. Gilley, 'English attitudes to the Irish in England, 1780–1900' in Colin Holmes (ed.), *Immigrants and minorities in British society* (London, 1978), pp 81–110. **65** Curtis, p. 107. **66** A.B. Cook and J.R. Vincent, *The governing passion: cabinet government and party politics in Britain, 1885–1886* (Brighton, 1974), p. 160. **67** Ibid., p. 18. **68** Jonathan Parry, *The rise and fall of Liberal government in Victorian Britain* (New Haven and London, 1993), p. 302.

genuine history of Great Britain.[69] Ramsden's official history of the Conservative party, already cited, hardly notices the Wyndham Act of 1903 and the devolution crisis of the following year.

IRELAND'S PROMINENCE

The reasons for British involvement in Ireland remains a matter of contention but its sustained level is scarcely in dispute; it is excessively relativist to remove Ireland implicitly or explicitly from the wider United Kingdom story. In 1868 John Morley, later twice Liberal chief secretary for Ireland, outlined the importance he attached to Ireland:

> There is the Irish Question, for example. Underneath the surface of this, and wrapped up in it, are nearly all the controversies of principle which will agitate the political atmosphere of our time. It is a microcosm of the whole imperial question. It is the test of our fitness to deal with the other problems which modern circumstances, pressing hard against the old order of ideas and traditions, is forcing upon our attention. The functions of the state, the duties of property, the rights of labour, the question whether the many are born for the few, the question of a centralised imperial power, the question of the pre-eminence of morals in politics – all these things lie in Irish affairs.[70]

Morley's view is germane and applies to the entire period. The issues raised can be conveniently summarised:

1. Could Great Britain successfully integrate diverse traditions and peoples into a harmonious unitary nation? This had implications for the management of the empire and especially for the position of India.
2. Related to this was whether, in particular, a Protestant country could absorb a Catholic population, especially one whose loyalty was in doubt, not least because many of its spokesmen decried the British connection? While portions of the confessional state were in the process of being dismantled, the position of Catholicism remained uneasy and not beyond controversy.

69 A few examples include, Bentley Gilbert, *The evolution of national insurance in Great Britain: the origins of the Welfare State* (London, 1966); Richard Price, *An imperial war and the British working class* (London, 1972); José Harris, *Unemployment and politics: a study in English social policy, 1886–1914* (Oxford, 1972); Geoffrey Alderman, *The railway interest* (Leicester, 1973). 70 John Morley, 'Old parties and new policy', *Fortnightly Review*, iv, new series (1 Sept. 1868), p. 327.

3. It raised questions about the respective rights of local majorities and minorities at a time when the British political elite was grappling with the implications of democracy.
4. The Irish land question brought to the fore the matter of property rights and the balance between rights of those who owned the land and those who toiled on it.
5. For much of the period the issue of law and order found a special resonance in discussions of Ireland.
6. Because Ireland had a substantial representation in the house of commons the tactics and role of nationalists in political institutions were also prominent.

Like much proffered already, these aspects are convincing so far as they go but at the same time not entirely satisfying. Politicians do not devote such attention to abstract issues no matter how many principles these may raise. Fundamental to the question is the deeply held belief that Ireland was or ought to be part of a unified British Isles kingdom. Peter Jupp observes that, though the duke of Wellington may have failed, nonetheless his intent in the late 1820s was to 'create a new polity in Ireland, one that could be integrated into Britain'.[71] Similarly, Richard Brent notes that the Whigs in the 1830s considered Ireland 'to be an integral part of a grander United Kingdom'.[72] To that end he cites Lord Mulgrave's aim 'to treat the English and Irish as "one nation"'.[73] It was an ambition that remained pertinent over time and across the political divide. This was implicit in Sir Stafford Northcote's observation in 1869, 'England is not for the English, nor Ireland for the Irish ... and to diminish the influence which the one ought to have on the other, will be bad for both.'[74] In 1886 G.J. Goschen intoned, 'our interests, English, Scotch and Irish are all interlaced in a manner, totally different from what is the case between Britain and the colonies ... You cannot treat Ireland differently from England and Scotland without involving yourself in innumerable anomalies and injustices.'[75] Sir Henry James maintained, 'it is not the identity of manufacture; it is the identity of the manufacturing power that makes the unity of a kingdom'.[76] And perhaps most simply, another Tory proclaimed, 'I do not care whether Ireland is one or two nations; at any rate, she is not a foreign nation but an integral part of the British empire.'[77] And, an arch-unionist like Walter Long, might 'be able to accept a measure of home rule which would do not injury to the empire ...'[78]

---

71 Peter Jupp, *The first duke of Wellington in an Irish context* (Southampton, 1997), p. 17.
72 Richard Brent, *Liberal Anglican politics: Wiggery, religion and reform, 1830–1841* (Oxford, 1987), p. 51. 73 Quoted in ibid. 74 *PD*, 194 (1 Mar. 1869), c. 1874. 75 Ibid., 304 (13 Apr. 1886), c. 1466. 76 Ibid., 305 (13 May 1886), c. 916. 77 Ibid., (17 May 1886), c. 1236.
78 Quoted in John Kendle, *Walter Long, Ireland, and the Union, 1905–1920* (Montreal and Kingston, 1992), p. 18.

When chief secretary in 1905 he was determined to 'do my best to administer the government with justice and impartially to all creeds and classes ...'[79] Nor did the story end there; during the First World War a sharp gulf opened between proponents of a United Kingdom and Irish nationalists. French revolutionaries had held that 'the source of all liberty resides essentially in the nation; no group, no individual may exercise authority not emanating from the nation'.[80] The Duties of Man declared, among other items, that 'every citizen owes his services to the Patrie' whenever the law summoned him to defend it.[81] For the British state, the Patrie was the whole British Isles; for Irish nationalists it became delimited to Ireland; and the Irish citizen's duty did not extend to responding to the summons of the law to join the army.

TOWARDS A NEW SYNTHESIS

The work of theorists of nationalism has many facets and at present only brief allusion to these can be made. But, a constituent part of most of the literature is recognition that the nation-state as a completed form is a comparatively recent development, a point underlined from another perspective by Bendix. Modernists equate the concrete manifestations to the revolution in communications which were part of a larger economic transformation. An elite, especially in less advanced communities, began to foster cultural idioms or to invent new ones in the face of the challenges of modernisation; the forces of that same modernisation against which they reacted, provided the means to reach a wider audience and thereby construct 'imagined' communities. Hroch developed a typology to explain the stages of development of national consciousness in small nations and the sequential nature of national movements.[82]

A key ingredients in his and similar analyses is the role of the intelligentsia and of elites in the formation stage. Jim MacLaughlin, among others, points to the role of a local, rather than national, intelligentsia, but the conversion and role of this group properly falls into the latter part of Hroch's second phase, that is, when the purveyors of national ideas expand cultural enthusiasm into a political programme.[83] The third phase in this typology is the incorporation of the masses.

79 Quoted in ibid., pp 25–6.   80 Quoted in D. George Boyce, 'A Great War transition: state and citizen in Ireland, 1914–1919' in D. George Boyce and Alan O'Day (eds), *Ireland in transition, 1867–1921* (forthcoming).   81 Ibid.   82 See Miroslav Hroch, *Social preconditions of national revival in Europe* (Cambridge, 1985); his main themes are reprised in an amended form in 'National self-determination from a historical perspective', in Sukumar Periwal (ed.), *Notions of nationalism* (Budapest, London and New York, 1995), pp 65–82. 83 Also, see T.J. Edelstein, Richard A. Born and Sue Taylor, 'Introduction' in T.J. Edelstein (ed.), *Imaging an Irish past: the Celtic Revival, 1890–1940* (Chicago, 1992), p. xiii; Joep Leerson, *Remembrance and imagination: patterns in the historical and literary representation of Ireland in the nineteenth century* (Cork, 1996), pp 101, 108.

The work of Gellner, Anderson, Hroch and others pertains to emergent, essentially small, nations. But their notions can be applied to large established nation-states as well. The United Kingdom was a new state created in 1801 built on the foundation of older nations, and it, though the most economically advanced society, was undergoing modernisation and for the first time becoming an 'imagined community'. Though Bendix does not treat nation-building in big states, his argument is consistent with it. Accompanying these transformations was the transition of subjects to becoming citizens as part of democratisation. Incorporation of Ireland into the new state posed exceptional difficulties, but interest in the country the period up to the end of the 1860s conforms to an era when an elite sought to come to grips a construction of nation and citizenship. The elite often followed a path in Irish affairs that ran in opposition to the popular will – Catholic emancipation being one such instance. In a top-down process of nation-building, as existed in the United Kingdom project, popular anti-Catholicism was overridden by an elite aspiration to form, if not an inclusive state, at least one in which all groups were incorporated. In this context Colley misses an important clue to the nature of the post-1801 United Kingdom.

The period after 1868 can be equated to Hroch's period of mass mobilisation, that is, when a nation or ethnic group is mobilised for political purposes. The level of interest thereafter remained high until 1914, but the constraints on the formation of policy by an elite was more severe – Home Rule and the Ulster crisis being apt illustrations. In the mass mobilisation phase, though, the opinion of the elite and public sentiment began to coincide. For so long as there remained a sense of United Kingdom nation-building, Ireland was central to the process. However, by the early 1920s, in the aftermath of the war and with Great Britain rapidly sliding into economic crisis, public feeling about Ireland understandably diminished and high level political opinion followed it into apathy. The process, then, is a shift, gradual and then more quick-paced, in the transformation of concern about Irish affairs from initially an elite preoccupation to a democratic policy formation downgrading Ireland's place in the United Kingdom. The essence of the story is that liberal democracy has many outstanding virtues though these apply only unevenly in a nation-building exercise meant to include national minorities or inconvenient places.

To return to the beginning, Northern Ireland for Britons, as the rest of Ireland, is a story of disengagement which began the descent away from being part of the 'imagined community'. Just as the British abandoned their sentimental attachment to Canada (but not Australia) they jettisoned all of Ireland, even the supposedly loyal part. Loyalty and even a common experience of war was an insufficient cement; there must be an 'imagined' common destiny as well.

'A besieged outpost': the imagination of empire and the Siege myth, 1860–1900

MARK McGOVERN

THE SIEGE AND THE EMPIRE

The Siege of Derry of 1689 is the most enduring and evocative historical myth of Irish Protestant and Ulster unionist political culture.[1] The Siege itself was a key moment of Irish history. It was the longest siege ever to take place on the island and it helped pave the way for the Williamite Settlement and the rise of the 'Protestant Ascendancy'.[2] In other words, it had a profound effect on the shape of modern Ireland. However, over time it also emerged as 'myth cycle' for Ulster Protestants. It became an historical touchstone, a narrative told and re-told in different ways at different times and by different people at the same time. Particularly from the late eighteenth century onwards the Siege myth emerged as an imaginative space through which the various (and at times contradictory) currents within Ulster Protestant political consciousness were forged and expressed. The rites, rituals and practices associated with its commemoration became a vehicle through which an Ulster Protestant view of the world, and of themselves, was manifest. This was most clearly evident in the two annual parades that were established to mark the 'Shutting of the Gates' and the 'Relief of the Siege' and in the actions and perceptions of members of the organisation set up in the early nineteenth century to organise these events – the Apprentice Boys of Derry Clubs.

1 This chapter is based upon work undertaken for a PhD thesis that was supervised by Professor Patrick Buckland; see Mark McGovern, 'The siege myth: the siege of Derry in Ulster Protestant political culture, 1689–1939' (unpublished PhD thesis, University of Liverpool, 1994) and 'We have a strong city: politicised Protestantism, evangelicalism and the siege myth in the early nineteenth century', in William Kelly (ed.), *The sieges of Derry* (Dublin, 2001). Since this research was completed a number of works dealing with the siege myth have appeared in print including: T.G. Fraser, 'The siege, its history and legacy', 1688–1889', in G. O'Brien (ed.) *Derry and Londonderry, history and society* (Dublin, 1999); T.G. Fraser, 'The Apprentice Boys and the Relief of Derry parades', in T.G. Fraser (ed.), *The Irish parading tradition: following the drum* (London, 2000); Neil Jarman, *Material conflicts: parades and visual displays in Northern Ireland* (Oxford, 1997); Ian McBride, *The Siege of Derry in Ulster Protestant mythology* (Dublin, 1997). 2 Jacqueline Hill, 'The meaning and significance of the Protestant Ascendancy: 1787–1840', in *Ireland after the Union* (Oxford, 1989).

At any given time a range of ideological and political influences shaped the meaning of the Siege myth. In the late nineteenth and early twentieth centuries one of the most important was the idea and identity of Empire. Crystallising around the issue of Home Rule for Ireland the period from the 1880s to the 1920s constituted a prolonged crisis for the British state. As a result successive British governments adopted a range of political strategies in Ireland, from an initial, grudging and hotly contested support for Home Rule through to the introduction of partition. The changing nature of British political strategy represented a cultural as well as a material challenge to the emerging force of Ulster unionism. This was in large part because unionism was a populist political movement developing against the backdrop of the extension of the electoral franchise and the emergence of modern mass politics. In this context it based much of its appeal on what has been referred to as imperial patriotism or 'imperial collectivism'. 'Imperial collectivism' identified a call for domestic social and economic reform with imperial expansion, and conceived the role of the citizen in relation to the need for authoritarian leadership.[3] The Siege myth came to encapsulate these ideas of identity and political mobilisation. However, there was an acute problem for unionists when the state and 'imagined community' which they argued they were part of suggested that this was not, after all, the case.[4] By the early twentieth century unionism as a hegemonic force was faced with an Irish nationalism which, it argued, was intrinsically alien and inimical and sections of the British ruling elite that were willing to reconstitute the Anglo-Irish relationship as the first step to reforming the imperial state. It was a situation in which unionism became more thoroughly imbued with the consciousness and imagery of siege.

This chapter will examine the relationship between the Siege myth, the imagination of imperialism and the character of unionist ideology through the second half of the nineteenth century as the issue of Home Rule rose to prominence. It will argue that the contradictions of 'loyalty' and 'rebellion' that began to emerge within Ulster unionist ideology in this period were rooted in the material position of an Ulster Protestant community founded as a 'colonial outpost', shaped by the rise of late nineteenth-century industrial capitalism but dependent on an (at times) reluctant and reticent imperial centre. To do so it is necessary to look at two phases and aspects of the Siege culture of this period. First, the way in which the celebration of imperial values developed within the Siege myth from the mid-nineteenth century onward. Second, the relationship of empire, nation and religion in the definition of the 'imagined community' of Ulster unionism from the 1880s until the turn of the century. This analysis may also provide an insight into the position unionists faced during the Home Rule

Crisis of 1912–14 when their social and political realities were increasingly at odds with an identity founded on imperial patriotism.

'A CONTEST BETWEEN NATIONS': MACAULAY, EMPIRE AND
THE SIEGE, 1840–80

Early advocates of an imperial-patriotism laid the foundations of the 'imagination of empire' in the mid-nineteenth century. Like so many others they found the Siege of Derry could become an exemplary model for their point of view. One of the first, probably most important and undoubtedly most well-known of these Siege myth advocates was Thomas Babington Macaulay. Macaulay was one of the most dominant English political and intellectual figures of his day and his *History of England from the accession of James the Second*, published in four volumes between 1848 and 1855 remains the apogee of Whig historiography.[5] The *History of England* was extraordinarily popular and, as one of the most well-read pieces of mid-nineteenth-century English literature, contributed greatly to the rising interest and ever more widespread cultural celebration of the Derry Siege. This was largely because Macaulay made the Siege one of the centrepiece episodes of his work. Although originally intended to cover the period from the seventeenth to the nineteenth centuries, the *History of England* became concerned solely with the 'Glorious Revolution' which, Macaulay argued, had laid the foundation of British industrial and imperial progress.

It was this perspective which made the Siege so central to Macaulay's work, and led him to describe it as, 'the most memorable in the annals of the British Isles'.[6] Indeed, it is probable that no other single text of the nineteenth century influenced the imagination of identity contained within the Siege myth more than did Macaulay's history. Both supporters of the Siege culture of the day and later unionists would cite Macaulay extensively in speeches and sermons dedicated to the Siege myth. 'Since the publication of Macaulay's history', the governor of the Apprentice Boys John Guy Ferguson told the commissioners

4 Benedict Anderson, *Imagined communities: reflections on the origin and spread of nationalism* (London, 1983).   5 The first two volumes were published in 1848 and were immediate 'best-sellers'. Chapter XII, which is concerned with Ireland during the 'Glorious Revolution' and includes a large section on the Siege, formed part of volume III, written from 1849 onwards and first published in 1855 along with volume IV. There were 25,000 advanced orders for these volumes. A final incomplete volume was published posthumously in 1861. For accounts of his life and works see Owen Dudley Edwards, *Historians on historians: Macaulay* (London, 1988); J. Millgate, *Macaulay* (London, 1973).   6 Thomas Babington Macaulay, *The history of England, from the accession of James II* (London, 1849–61), p. 771.

investigating the riots in the city in 1868 and 1869, the pride of Derry Protestants in the Siege had 'been greatly increased'.[7]

As a prime example of Whig historical writing Macaulay's *History of England* was a celebration of the British parliamentary and constitutional system designed, in true Whig fashion, to popularise and inculcate a moral, political, and social value system. In his biography of Macaulay, Owen Dudley Edwards argues that the *History of England* was written to 'train a citizenry for participation in and possession of a future England'.[8] This ambitious ideological project aimed at culturally defining the relationship of citizen, state and empire through the imagery of the past. A social and political authoritarian, who believed that 'the higher and middling orders are the natural representatives of the human race', Macaulay combined this outlook with a desire to promote the idea of a national community through the celebration of popular culture.[9] It was in this vein that he intended his *History of England* to be not only a record of 'government' but also 'of the people', to include accounts of the 'revolutions which have taken place in dress, furniture, repasts, and public amusements'.[10] In line with this approach Macaulay travelled to Derry in August 1849 before writing his account of the Siege. While there he spent two days viewing the walls and collecting the local anecdotes and folk tales that had built up around the Siege culture.

However, as Eric Hobsbawm has argued, mid-nineteenth-century Whig and liberal conceptions of what constituted the 'nation' were marked by 'a surprising degree of intellectual vagueness'.[11] Macaulay sought to establish an idea of the British national community around what has been described as a 'grammar of imperialism'.[12] The aim was to found a sense of identity capable of maintaining domestic stability through the celebration of a distinctive (and supposedly superior) British civilisation that would, in turn, legitimate imperial expansion. A keen advocate of such expansion Macaulay had directly affected its path when, as president for the 'Committee of Public Instruction' in Bengal, he wrote his *Minutes of education*. The *Minutes of education* amounted to a blueprint for the policy of Anglicisation, the cultural accompaniment to British economic and political domination in the Indian sub-continent. Macaulay's *History of England* was intended, therefore, not only to establish the idea of a national memory and a national past, but also to evoke such a memory in the cause of empire.

7 John Guy Ferguson, quoted in *Minutes of Evidence: Report of the Commissioners of Inquiry, 1869, into the riots and disturbances in the city of Londonderry*, House of Commons, 1870, C5, xxxii, p. 157.   8 Owen Dudley Edwards, *Macaulay*, p. 134.   9 E.P. Thompson, *The making of the English working class* (London, 1963) p. 95.   10 Thomas Babington Macaulay, *History of England*, p. 15.   11 Eric Hobsbawm, *Nations and nationalism since 1780: programme, myth, reality* (Cambridge, 1990), p. 24.   12 J. Millgate, *Macaulay*. The phrase Millgate employs in a very localised sense for a particular part of Macaulay's work could perhaps be used in a much wider context to define the processes involved with the ideology of empire.

This perspective very much characterised Macaulay's vivid and emotive depiction of the Derry Siege. The Siege, Macaulay argued, represented less a confrontation between two communities defined by their religious difference than a struggle of nations, conceived as distinctive cultural formations. This is not to say that religion had no part to play. It is clear throughout his work that Macaulay regarded Catholicism as politically undesirable and historically anachronistic. However, the true significance of the Siege for Macaulay was the struggle it symbolised between a morally and culturally advanced civilisation and one which, through its defeat, was shown to be less so. What is evident too, is that Macaulay saw moral and cultural development as a result of national characteristics: 'It was a contest, not between engineers, but between nations; and the victory remained with the nation which, though inferior in number, was superior in civilisation, in capacity for self-government, and in stubbornness of resolution.'[13] Similarly, the 'nation' imagined through the Siege, was explicitly to include all social classes acting in concert.[14] It was also a 'nation' defined not as a group distinctive to the North of Ireland, but a wider national-racial family, an amalgam fused into a single entity by the imagined threat of a shared foe: 'The inhabitants were Protestants of Anglo–Saxon blood. They were indeed not all of one country or of one church; but Englishmen and Scotchmen, Episcopalians and Presbyterians, seem to have generally lived together in friendship, a friendship which is sufficiently explained by their common antipathy to the Irish race and to the Popish religion.'[15] It is therefore 'race', the character of the 'Anglo–Saxon colony', and the relationship of 'race' to the political community of the United Kingdom that above all else defined the imagined collective of Macaulay's besieged.

Such a perspective also meant that Macaulay could be openly critical of the more blatantly sectarian aspects of the Siege culture. For the political relationship of the Union to operate effectively, Macaulay suggested, the abuse of authority by an elite, defined in terms of their religious difference, had to be avoided.[16] Devotion to the secular gods of nation and cultural civilisation (which for Macaulay were the primary means of constituting social and political consensus) made him critical of religion as a form of public and political discourse. Although he had himself been brought up in an evangelical household, Macaulay developed an ideological perspective which saw politicised Protestantism as detrimental to the operation of state authority and 'Britishness' as a dominant, hegemonic identity. Certainly his parliamentary defeat in Edinburgh in 1847 (largely due to the rise of conservative Protestantism in the city) was likely to have heightened this perspective. Two years later, when he visited Derry in order to collect material for his account of

---

13 Thomas Babington Macaulay, *History of England*, p. 772. 14 Ibid., p. 749. 15 Ibid., p. 725. 16 Ibid., p. 750.

the Siege, Macaulay foreshadowed criticism of the 'double aspects' of the Siege parades levelled at the Apprentice Boys by the 1869 Riot Commissioners. He denounced the more obviously sectarian aspects of the marches as, 'faults which are ordinarily found in dominant castes and dominant sects [that] have not seldom shown themselves without disguise at her festivities'.[17]

Nevertheless, the Siege was no mere artefact of the past for Macaulay, it was an idealised mythic model for action, an event quite undiminished in its relevance by the passage of time. The significance of Macaulay's conception of the Siege lay most of all in his conscious desire to promote the Siege culture as an example of how the 'imagined community' of the 'British peoples' should be culturally and popularly remembered through social practice and public display. He described in detail Walker's Pillar, the preservation of relics and other monuments, the burning of Lundy, the nature of the clubs, parades, speeches and sermons of the Siege culture. He argued that the walls were 'to the Protestants of Ulster what the trophy of Marathon was to the Athenians', and pointed out, in no uncertain terms, the ideological role such a series of cultural practices could perform: 'It is impossible not to respect the sentiment which is indicated by these tokens. It is a sentiment which belongs to the higher and purer part of human nature, and which adds not a little to the strength of states. A people which takes no pride in the noble achievements of remote ancestors will never achieve anything worthy to be remembered.'[18] Macaulay was, in essence, advocating the invention of a British national tradition through the Siege culture.

However, Macaulay's was not the only voice promoting the Siege as a narrative of empire. He was joined by a veritable chorus from within the Derry establishment and among the local organisers of the Siege parades in projecting an imperial identity through the Siege myth. Significantly, evangelical clerics were very much to the fore in this process. Sermons, given on the theme of the Siege, had become established as one of the set-piece rituals of the Siege culture and provided an opportunity for clergymen to articulate a particular definition of the moral and political meaning of the Siege myth. Many used this occasion to extol the virtues of empire from the mid-nineteenth century onward. However, for some advocates of the Siege, the significance of nation or empire as the basis of identity was extremely limited, and, in some quarters, regarded as potentially damaging. A number of commentators defined the Siege as an example of Protestant virtue and argued that this should not be confused with, or diluted by any other ideological identity. The fusion of Protestantism and empire, which was to be an underlying characteristic of Ulster unionism, was a matter of process rather than natural conclusion.

17 Ibid., p. 773. 18 Ibid.

For many such commentators, however, there was no contradiction in the construction of a sense of Britishness that was definitively Protestant in character. Among the earliest proponents of British imperial patriotism were the same evangelical Protestants who, in the 1820s and 1830s, promoted the 'Second Reformation' in Ireland.[19] These evangelicals conceived of Britain as having a special relationship with God, imagined as that of the Israelites of the Old Testament, whereby they were ordained to be a world-wide civilising and christianising influence whose Protestant values were enshrined in the constitutional history, and gave rise to the economic prosperity, of the English people.[20] The antithesis of this was 'popery', and particularly the Irish variety, a perspective that gave both 'meaning and direction to the long-standing English anti-Catholic tradition' and 'explained' the poverty and political unrest of Ireland.[21] The imagery of 'God's Chosen Few', and the civilising project of the British empire, found a home in the culture of Orangeism and echoes among the advocates of the Siege myth from the mid-nineteenth century onward.[22]

The concepts of 'empire', the 'British people' and 'patriotism' were also hardly new to Protestant political culture in Ireland, nor to the Siege myth, by the 1850s and 1860s. Yet, they had tended to be expressed only in the vaguest of terms and as peripheral to the 'real' meaning of the Siege, which was predominantly conceived as a defence of essentially 'Protestant' values. Protestantism continued, of course, to be a dominant element in the Siege myth, but it was also now related more precisely to the imagery of 'empire' and 'nation'. For example, preaching in Derry Cathedral for the Relief parade of 1858, the Revd William Beresford (an Evangelical of the Church of Ireland) drew direct comparisons between the values supposedly struggled for in the Siege and those enshrined in an imperial destiny. Beresford defined both the Siege and the empire in terms of a divine mission:

> It is the glorious destiny of Great Britain to send the gospel with all its saving and civilising influences to all other lands, to unite all in one majestic harmony ... We have not only an earthly inheritance of historic lore, lofty reminiscences of traditions of power, honour and wealth ... but the inheritance of hoe and trust in the redemption of our lord and saviour and the manifestation of his spirit ... the spring of unity and concord, of domestic virtue, of intellectual excellence ... these are the inestimable privileges committed to our stewardship as a nation ... these are the

---

19 Mark McGovern, 'We have a strong city'.   20 J. Wolffe, 'Evangelicalism in mid-nineteenth century England' in R. Samuel (ed.), *Patriotism: the making and unmaking of British national identity*, vol. 1: *History and politics* (London, 1989), pp 189–91.   21 Ibid., p. 191. 22 Anthony Buckley, 'The chosen few: biblical texts in the regalia of an Ulster secret society', *Ulster Life*, 24 (1985), pp 5–24.

blessings our God has showered on us in a degree unequalled by all that the world has seen since the days of his favoured people Israel.[23]

Significantly, when Beresford spoke of the people 'as a nation' he did so in terms of both a British and Protestant community to which he saw his Derry Protestant audience belonging. Three years later the Revd William McClure, the Derry Presbyterian minister, eulogised the Siege in much the same vein, arguing that the 'we' for whom it had been fought included not only the 'nation' but also the 'vast colonial empire', which was, consequently, indebted to the Siege for its existence. Further than this, he proposed that patriotic support of the nation was a Christian virtue exemplified in the Siege myth: 'Patriotism is a part of religion, and he who is a true lover of God will be a genuine lover of his country also.'[24] McClure was, however, less specific about the 'country' to which such duty was owed. While loyal attachment to the empire and a British identity were becoming more prevalent elements of the Siege myth (and not only among Evangelical Protestant preachers), there continued to be a certain fluidity in the definition of what constituted the 'nation' that was not restricted to McClure's liberal cast of mind. 'Britishness' was still a highly problematic term. For example, in 1860 the *Londonderry Guardian* described the crimson flag as being 'neither Orange or Green; it is the blood red flag of Old England'. However, this was both an idiosyncratic description and one designed specifically to criticise the presence of a large military and police force in the city for the Siege parade.[25] The editor of the *Londonderry Sentinel*, John Edward Finlay (as far from a liberal as one could find), published an account of the Siege in the same year. Finlay drew a contrast between 'British Protestants' and 'Irish Protestants', even though he also described the walls as a 'sacred enclosure which gave shelter to the British race and the Protestant religion'.[26] For Finlay, in line with the politicised Protestantism that was the basis of the early nineteenth-century Siege culture, 'Britishness' continued to take very much a secondary role to 'Protestantism', and the idea of such a thing as 'Ulster Protestantism' was significantly nowhere to be found. In fact, there was little or no mention of an Ulster identity (or of the Siege as a specifically Ulster cycle) in accounts of this period. Though Finlay certainly argued that, because of the Siege, Derry was 'a sacred spot, dear to memory and ever-kindling by its very name the fire of patriotism', his was a vaguely defined 'British' patriotism. It was also one that (directly contradicting Macaulay) had only a limited meaning: 'The victory has been ascribed to superiority in civilisation, to greater capacity in self-government, to stubbornness in resolution, and difference of race. This

23 Revd William Beresford, *Derry Standard*, 17 Aug. 1858. 24 Revd William McClure, *Derry Standard*, 15 Aug. 1861. 25 *Londonderry Guardian*, 19 Dec. 1860. 26 J.E. Finlay, *The Siege of Londonderry* (Londonderry, 1860), pp 30–1.

may be true, but it is not the whole truth; all these are elements of success, but the main elements were Protestant spirit and divine assistance. These are the elements which cast the brightest halo around Derry'.[27]

Ulster unionist political identity would ultimately ground itself upon a fusion of racial and religious distinction but (while there was undoubtedly an affinity between 'Britishness' and Protestantism) that fusion was neither inevitable nor easy. Certainly there were some versions of the Siege myth which saw patriotism and Protestantism as (at least potentially) conflicting loyalties. In 1871 the prominent evangelical preacher 'Roaring' Hugh Hanna published a pamphlet defending a lecture he had given on the Siege that had been attacked by a liberal Presbyterian cleric, the Revd A. Robinson. Robinson had contended that Hanna was at fault both for over-emphasising the similarities of the Episcopalian and Presbyterian traditions, and for discounting the relevance of racial distinctiveness. Hanna re-asserted his belief that the Siege should, indeed, be seen as a model of identity and action, believing that the 'past speaketh to the present'. Not surprisingly he went on to suggest that the story of the Siege 'advocated Protestant Union in resistance to the growing political power of the Papacy'.[28] However, he also countered the Macaulay-esque theory proposed by his critic, that the Siege had been a battle of nations rather than religions, by citing what he regarded as the erroneous behaviour of the 'Old English' during the seventeenth century:

> The Norman and Saxon origin of the chief migrants should on his [Robinson's] theory have secured their friendship for the immigrants of the plantation. Race should have come to its kindred race. But it did not. The sympathies of race were overruled by the stronger spirit of religious fanaticism, and the Anglo-Irish papists were among the fiercest persecutors of the men who, in Ulster, represented the land of their fathers. The sympathies of race never have opposed a sufficient barrier to the cruelties of intolerant bigotry.[29]

Significantly the populist, demagogic, Orange orator Hanna thus combined his emphasis upon the difference of religion with an implicit distinction drawn between the 'men' of 'Ulster' and the 'chief migrants', the 'Anglo-Irish' of the rest of the island.

In a sense it is the tension between the communal integration of religious division and the imperial integration of the 'British nation', as the basis of identity and political hegemony, that defines the 'double aspect' view of the

---

27 Ibid., p. 30. 28 Hugh Hanna, *Weighed and wanting: an examination by the Rev. Hugh Hanna of a review by Rev. A. Robinson of a lecture on the Siege of Derry* (Belfast, 1871), pp 18–19. 29 Ibid., p. 21.

Siege culture expressed by the 1869 Riot Commissioners. Their report is infused throughout with the rationale of Macaulay, celebrating the Siege as a 'noble exploit of humanity', a 'fine example of fidelity to principle' and of 'unyielding valour'. But they also echo him, almost word for word, when they argue for the ending of all parades in the city on the grounds that they are ultimately, and dangerously, socially divisive.[30] The eyes of the commissioners were trained on (and in) a British polity whose social and economic power base was increasingly ordered through the imagined shared interest of a national tradition. Seen from such a perspective the Siege culture, at one moment a celebration of that very tradition, was at the same time marked by a sectarianism rooted in the particularity of social relations in Irish society. The Siege culture could, therefore, only be regarded as outside their conception of order. Not until the 1880s would large sections of the British ruling class readily identify Ulster Orangeism as at least coming from the same ideological stable as their own imperial patriotism.

THE UNION, PROTESTANTISM AND THE CROWN: THE SIEGE AND IMPERIAL PATRIOTISM, 1880–1900

On 1 November 1883 the nationalist lord mayor of Dublin, Charles Dawson, was due to speak at a meeting in the Corporation Hall in Derry under the auspices of the local 'Catholic Working Men's Institute'.[31] Before his arrival a body of some 500 Apprentice Boys, accompanied by local landed and business leaders and led by John Guy Ferguson, invaded and occupied the Corporation Hall. Despite the presence of several hundred extra police and troops in the city they met with no opposition. Soon afterwards shots were fired from the Corporation Hall at a nationalist crowd and two Catholics were shot dead. Massive rioting ensued for several days and was accompanied by a wave of strikes among Catholic workers in the city. In the midst of the occupation of the Corporation Hall one Vance Macaulay, a Coleraine Orangeman and 'working man of the county', addressed the Apprentice Boys. He argued that they stood for, 'three things which could not be separated ... the Protestant Crown of England and the Bible – (cheers) – Ireland and England – (cheers) – and capital and labour'. The three elements which Vance Macaulay picked out illuminate the character of Ulster unionist ideology and the nature of the Siege myth by the 1880s. The Union, Protestantism and the crown were the foundational elements upon which the cross-class alliance of 'capital and labour' was to be based. While these 'three things' were, in many ways, particular to Ulster

---

30 *Report of the Riot Commissioners, 1869*, p. 16.   31 *Report of the Commissioners of Inquiry into the Riots in the City of Londonderry on 1 Nov. 1883*, House of Commons, 1884, xxviii, p. 13

unionism they also reflected currents of political thought and symbolism that unionism shared with British conservatism in general.

By the 1880s and 1890s mass political mobilisation had led to the growing importance of imperial nationalism. The idea of what was called the 'common patriotism' of the empire, a platform for the mass appeal of English conservatism from the early 1870s onward, was inextricably bound up with the emerging ideology of Ulster unionism.[32] The struggle over Home Rule accelerated this process. It brought into sharp relief the contours of an identity that combined the empire and the Union, Protestantism and the crown, into a cohesive and recognisable ideological perspective capable of establishing a cross-class alliance. In turn, this was given a cultural outlet in the Siege parades. The basis for this fusion of religious distinctiveness, imperial patriotism and the celebration of the monarchy in both Ulster unionism and the Siege culture in the latter part of the nineteenth century was partly the result of political opportunism and even more of major structural changes in Irish society.[33] However, it was also a consequence of changes in the ideological concepts themselves. From the late 1860s onward Irish nationalism was clearly established as a significant social and political force with the rise of Fenianism, the Home Rule movement and the Gaelic Revival. At the same time British imperial patriotism emerged as a strident phenomenon from the early 1870s and was an ideological discourse through which Ulster conservatism, unionism and the devotees of the Siege increasingly came to see themselves. Unionism therefore shared a great deal with British social imperialism. It is worth examining these traits as they were expressed within the Siege myth, not least to illuminate the ideological difficulty facing unionism when the project of an 'Ulster nationalism' was briefly, half-heartedly and unsuccessfully attempted during the crisis years between 1912 and 1920.[34]

The Conservative leader Benjamin Disraeli has been credited with establishing the importance of patriotism in British politics in his Crystal Palace speech of 1872 when (as one commentator put it) he 'discovered the conservative working man [and] the electoral value of imperial sentiment'.[35] The growth of mass political activity and the expansion and consolidation of the empire both fed into the growth of popular imperialism. In this Britain was not unique. Beginning first in France, the concepts of patriotism and nationalism significantly altered in the early 1870s, shifting from concepts associated primarily

32 G.S. Bennett, *The concept of empire: Burke to Attlee, 1774–1947* (London, 1953), p. 262.
33 Peter Gibbon, *The origins of Ulster unionism: the formation of Protestant popular politics and ideology in nineteenth century Ireland* (Manchester, 1975) 34 Ibid., pp 136–7; David Miller, *Queen's rebels: Ulster loyalism in historical perspective* (Dublin, 1978) , pp 108–21. 35 G.S. Veitch, *Empire and democracy, 1837–1913* (London, 1914), p. 58. See also G.S. Bennett, *The concept of empire*, pp 257–8; H. Cunningham, 'The Conservative party and patriotism', in R. Colls and P. Dodd (eds), *Englishness: politics and culture, 1880–1920* (London, 1986), p. 283.

with 'liberalism and the left' into a 'chauvinist, imperialist and xenophobic movement of the right'.[36] This shift impacted upon the character of politics throughout Europe. As the imperial and dynastic power structures of the continent adapted the language and momentum of patriotism into what Benedict Anderson has called their 'official nationalisms', Irish conservatives found in the imagination of British imperial patriotism a counter to the ideological force of Irish nationalism.[37] To a great extent it was the English monarchy that became the focus of this process in British politics, symbolised in the idea of the 'crown' itself. The very constitutional powerlessness of the English crown by the end of the nineteenth century made it, paradoxically, even more crucial as the ritually enhanced centrepiece of British imperial nationalism, a 'symbol of consensus and continuity'.[38] Certainly the crown also emerges as a dominant symbol of the meaning of the Siege myth in the same period. Defending the walls of Derry became centred around an avowed allegiance to the crown. As an ideological symbol the crown became both an idealised reflection of the meaning of the Union and the iconographic representation of the imagined community.

Of course, loyalty to the crown was not new within Protestant political culture or within the Siege myth, where it had invariably been tied to a concept of religious distinctiveness. For example, after the Relief parade of 1867 the Orange leader William Johnson argued that the 'Apprentice Boys have shown today that they are ready not only to pay due respects to the Queen, but also ready, as of old, to man the walls in defence of her throne'.[39] On the same occasion, the preacher of the Siege sermon called upon the Apprentice Boys as 'champions of all Protestant truth, loyal to your Queen, [to] come to the help of the Lord against the mighty'. To some extent the appeal to the symbolism of the crown reflected the importance of the 'Covenanting tradition' within Irish Protestant political culture. This contractarian model of the state-society relationship emerged as the mythologised legitimation of anti-authoritarian and anti-state sentiment in the late nineteenth century and fed into the character of Ulster unionist ideology.[40] Within this ideological tradition the crown (conceived as the symbol of social and moral good) was also disassociated from the mundane exercise of parliamentary power. To support the crown and to oppose the abuse of power by government, were conceived, during key moments of crisis, as the central reason the Derry Siege had taken place. The Siege myth therefore proved capable of legitimating the rejection of parliamentary authority.

36 Eric Hobsbawm, *Nations and nationalism*, p. 121.   37 Benedict Anderson, *Imagined communities*, pp 80–104.   38 David Cannadine, 'The context, performance and meaning of ritual: the British monarchy and the invention of tradition, 1820–1977', in Eric Hobsbawm and Terence Ranger (eds), *The invention of tradition* (Cambridge, 1983), pp 108–32.   39 *Londonderry Guardian*, 15 Aug. 1867.   40 David Miller, *Queen's rebels*, pp 114–21.

However, the growing importance of the crown outside the confines of this tradition and through the imagery of imperial nationalism must also be seen as a factor in its role as a unionist icon. As a symbol, the crown came to incorporate the heightened prestige and profile afforded the imperial monarchy and combined that prestige with a diverse range of meanings. Speaking in Derry shortly before the 1883 riot, for example, Lord Claud Hamilton (a member of the north-west's most powerful landed unionist family) argued that the crown was the very embodiment not only of the Union and Protestantism but also of industrialisation and the imagined mission of empire.[41] Similarly, the Royal visits to Derry by the Edward VII as the then prince of Wales in 1885 and again as king in 1903, demonstrated the growing propensity of the monarchy to take part in public symbolic display.[42] It also provided an opportunity for local unionists and the Apprentice Boys to show their 'loyal' support for the Union and empire. The crown was, therefore, a means to combine an Ulster Protestant identity with this more general imagination of social imperialism.

Similarly, the horizons of the political community in which the Siege culture was conceived continued to be expanded beyond the confines of city and state to endorse the far-flung imperial regime. It became increasingly common during the 1870s and early 1880s for the Siege to be seen as a great moment (*à la Macaulay*) in the 'history of England' and one of the events which marked 'a glorious era in the history of the Empire'.[43] The bicentenary celebrations of 1888 and 1889 allowed this definition of the Siege myth to be given full vent, although the parades themselves were in other ways no more remarkable than in any other year.[44] The *Sentinel* contended that these commemorations were designed for those who 'stand true to Queen and country – that is the United Kingdom and the British empire'.[45] Similarly, during the Shutting of the Gates anniversary in 1888, the canon of the cathedral, who was 'chaplain' both to the 'lord bishop' and the 'Apprentice Boys' argued (with hyperbolic praise of the Siege rare even on such occasions) that:

We are to trace the wonderful dealings of God in the history of our Empire from that hour in which the Gates of Derry were closed ... We

41 *Londonderry Sentinel*, 11 Oct. 1883. 42 *Derry Standard*, 29 July 1903, p. 1. 43 *Londonderry Sentinel*, 20 Dec. 1883. 44 It is worth noting, however, that although the *Sentinel* heralded the bi-centenary celebrations as an 'unprecedented' event the *Derry Journal* described them as a 'tawdry turnout'. While this gulf in opinion is hardly surprising, there was little to differentiate the Siege parades of these years from any other in the level and personnel of attendance, the rites and rituals involved or the political significance which they were afforded. The real significance of the Siege parades at various times owed more to the political environment within which they operated. *Londonderry Sentinel*, 13 Aug. 1889, p. 3; *Derry Journal*, 14 Aug. 1889. 45 *Londonderry Sentinel*, 13 Aug. 1889.

trace all the greatness and the glory which belongs to the British nation to the noble defence of our walls.[46]

Eight months later the bishop of Derry, William Alexander, gave the bicentenary Relief sermon. Alexander was a highly influential clerical figure in unionist circles and a staunch advocate of opposition to Home Rule. His speech gave voice to these political beliefs and did so in a classic late-Victorian fusion of militarism, christianity, race theory and imperialism. It was a prime example of the ability of the cultural signs of the Siege to bear a variety of meanings at one and the same time, and combine them into a powerful ideological message. Alexander contended that the importance for the empire of the Siege was unequalled because of the 'lesson' it provided:

> Here on the walls of Derry we are reminded that 'Principles are reined in blood' ... the expiation of Calvary is the highest specimen of the universal law whereby shedding of blood is necessary ... The earth is soaked with blood. Many of its fields – those around this very city – have been altars of immolation ... For myself I confess that I hold this. A nation which is committed to the charge of vast masses of the human race cannot abnegate its military position without being guilty of treason against humanity. A race which has been imperial cannot say I will never go to war under any circumstances without contracting a taint which thins its blood and dooms it to permanent deterioration ... Let us observe that a good cause and a good conscience were not wanting to those who were penned behind these Walls. For loyalty in those days as in these was an instinct strong in the natures of the Scotch and English settlers in Ulster.[47]

Even in the organisation of the Apprentice Boys itself a fledgling network of imperial links was beginning to emerge. While non-Irish branches of the Apprentice Boys clubs were a phenomenon of the twentieth rather than the late nineteenth century, leading members of the Orange Order in Canada and the United States (as well as from England) began to attend the Siege parades from this period onward. Their presence was invariably celebrated as an example of the integrity of the Anglo-Saxon imperial family. As early as 1873 representatives of Orangeism in Canada and John J. Bond, the grand master of the Orange Order in America, took part in the Siege parades. During the laying of the foundation stone of the Memorial Hall these transatlantic visitors were presented with a crimson banner and an address that placed the Siege firmly in the context of empire and nation, 'whether under the starry banner of the great

46 Ibid., 20 Dec. 1888.   47 Ibid., 13 Aug. 1889.

Anglo–Saxon Republic, or the blood-red flag of Britain's glorious empire'.[48] Speaking after the bicentenary Relief parade, a Revd John Moore of Boston, USA, addressed an audience gathered in the Memorial Hall that included, among the Apprentice Boys and city dignitaries, several representatives of Orange lodges from England as well as from other parts of Ireland. Proclaiming his admiration for what he called the 'Puritan brains, intelligence and enterprise' that had 'built up' America, he saw in the Siege a struggle of race and religion that had meaning for, 'the United States [which is] the outgrowth and daughter of Great Britain. We are substantially one race, having the same language and literature, with the same open bible, being the two great pillars of Christian civilisation and liberty.'[49] If the Siege stood for anything it was (argued Moore) that Ireland should not 'be severed from the British empire'.

That the imperial link might be 'severed' was, of course, precisely the prospect that Home Rule held out, exemplified in the introduction of the first Home Rule Bill in 1886. The mixture of populist Orange sectarianism and Victorian imperial patriotism was used as the rhetorical answer to the nationalist claims of cultural and ethnic integrity and the demand of national self-determination. The Siege myth could also provide a parable of the imagined threat of Home Rule in far simpler and starker terms. A clerical member of the Dublin branch of the Apprentice Boys of Derry Club published an account of the life of Walker in 1887. He argued that Walker had lived in a period marked by 'anarchy and outrage', confounded by 'weak administrations … a chronic evil' and surrounded by 'unscrupulous agitators' who were the 'perennial curse of Ireland'.[50] A Wicklow cleric speaking at the Relief bicentenary meeting suggested (with a somewhat immoderate degree of poetic and historical licence) that in 1689 there had been a 'Home Rule parliament' that had also sought to pass an act 'for the repeal of the Union'.[51]

However, if the imagery of empire and the crown were an important part of the Siege myth, their celebration was conditioned by two factors that differentiated Ulster unionism from the wider stream of social imperialism. They were, on the one hand, the limitations of the imperial state and, second, the importance of religious difference. The failure of the state to come to the relief of the city was a theme given a fair airing during the 1880s and 1890s, when Home Rule was very much an issue central to Liberal party policy. Significantly, it was also often accompanied by an emerging sense of Ulster as a distinctive entity, though this was (as yet) a relatively tentative proposition and the Siege defenders were still invariably seen racially as 'English' or 'Anglo-Saxon'. In this vein, on the bicentenary of the Relief of the Siege in 1889, the *Belfast Newsletter*

48 *Derry Journal*, 13 Aug. 1873. **49** *Londonderry Sentinel*, 13 Aug. 1889. **50** Revd A. Dawson, *George Walker and the Siege of Derry: a lecture* (Belfast, 1887), p. 3. **51** *Belfast Newsletter*, 13 Aug. 1889.

described Tryconnell as the 'prototype of Mr Gladstone' and that commemorating the Siege was the 'sacred duty of every *Ulsterman*'.[52] It went on to argue that:

> Considering how much the defence of Derry meant to England it is only remarkable that the bicentenary of such an event was not made the subject of universal celebrations throughout the country. But the people of Ulster have long ago made acquaintance with the difficulty of impressing upon England the position which they have occupied toward the country that 'planted' them ... The battle which was fought on Derry's walls ... is one of the most glorious achievements of the *English race* ... Truly no more need be said to the descendants of such men as successfully defended Derry in 1689 – men whose example of heroism has need to be followed in 1889, when once again the *loyal province* is threatened with disaster.

An even more explicit criticism of the state was voiced by Canon Dougherty during the Shutting of the Gates parade in 1888. Dougherty insisted that the Siege showed the importance of Derry for the maintenance of the empire. However, he continued by promoting the example of 'self-reliance' set during the Siege as the only means to achieve this end and argued that, 'ours is a triumph but it is a triumph of the city. It owes nothing to English soldiery defending the Walls – nothing to English Generals directing the defence'.[53] The eminently Victorian concept of 'self reliance' evidenced here was being translated into a potential legitimation of Ulster Protestant opposition to Home Rule. This was a forerunner of what would soon emerge as a key element of what might be called the 'Honest Ulsterman' persona.[54]

On the one hand, then, the story of the Siege involved the problem for a 'loyal province' of an unreliable English authority. However, as Bishop Alexander suggested, this should not cloud the view of what he understood as the true goal of the Siege, 'to preserve civilisation in this land, to maintain order against the Celtic genius for anarchy'. Similarly if the 'Celt' had an apparently ingrained proclivity for 'anarchy', how stark was the contrast to be drawn with that archetype of the imperial race, the 'men of Ulster', possessed of a 'three-fold characteristic ... the spirit of law, of obedience to the law, the spirit of freedom, the very suspicion of slavery ... (and) ... the spirit of commerce'. It was these attributes that would ensure that 'they would never be broken away from the unity of this great empire'.[55] By the early twentieth century the ideas of loyalty to the crown, the necessity of the Union for maintaining the essential character of the empire and the supposed religio-racial difference of the

52 Ibid.   53 *Londonderry Sentinel*, 20 Dec. 1888.   54 David Miller, *Queen's rebels*. 55 Ibid., 13 Aug. 1889, p. 3.

Catholic-Celt and the Anglo-Saxon Protestant were an integral part of the symbolism of the Siege myth. In turn, such characteristics were conceived, in 'Arnoldian' terms, as reflecting moral 'qualities' that were the inherent traits of different nations. The imagination of the Siege myth was very much imbued with this racial imagination of Victorian and Edwardian imperialism. The Apprentice Boys, as self-sacrificing, patriotic, proud defenders of a city, ever ready for action, were cast in the same mould as the models projected in the popular culture of the British music hall or the pages of juvenile adventure fiction, the 'energising myth of empire'.[56]

In fact, the Siege was the subject of one such children's story. Significantly the *'Prentice Boys who saved an empire: a story of the Siege of Londonderry*, published in 1905, was concerned as much with the promotion of evangelical Protestantism as it was with the imperial mission of English civilisation.[57] The publishers of this book, T.C and E.C. Jack, specialised in juvenile literature with an imperial theme, including a number of books on 'the outposts of Empire'.[58] In the *'Prentice Boys* a 'conniving, manipulative Priest' led a 'vile rabble' consisting of the 'scum of Ireland' against the 'civilised' and 'virtuous 'Prentice Lads' within the walls. Not unlike Charlotte Elizabeth's *Siege of Derry* (an evangelical-inspired fictional account first published in 1836) a single Protestant family, the Tomkins, personify the struggle of the besieged.[59] In this instance their spiritual salvation rests upon the victory of the empire, as one of the family proclaims just as she is about to die, 'bury me with my face toward England; there is the gospel, and from the saints there the light shall come to this dark, dark land'.[60] With the ending of the Siege and the defeat of Catholicism the Tomkin males are feted for their endurance and valour and the young Tomkin girl 'rewarded' with the promise of domestic and marital 'bliss', partnering one of the original 'Apprentice Boys'. Thus, with racial, sectarian and gender relations all safely back in place, the 'Empire is saved'. Such a fusion of political discourses and moral imperatives emphasises the way in which the Siege was less the bearer of a single political message than a worldview. Here the 'inter-relation of gender, religious and historic-political themes' was a means to project at one and the same moment the power of men, Protestants and the empire.[61] It could be particularly influential in the education of the young. At this time the headmaster of Foyle College (the leading Protestant

56 M. Green, *Dreams of adventure, deeds of empire* (London, 1980), p. xi; J. MacKenzie, *Imperialism and popular culture* (Manchester, 1986).   57 N. Wiseman, *The 'Prentice Boys who saved an empire: a tale of the Siege of Londonderry*, (London, 1905).   58 J.M. Mackenzie, *Propaganda and empire: the manipulation of British public opinion, 1880–1960* (Manchester, 1984), p. 215.   59 Charlotte Elizabeth, *The Siege of Derry: a tale of the Revolution of 1688* (London, 1836); Mark McGovern, 'We have a strong city'.   60 N. Wiseman, *'Prentice Boys who saved an empire*, p. 111.   61 Jennifer Todd, 'Two traditions in Unionist political culture', *Irish Political Studies*, 2 (1987), 7.

school in Derry) was M.C. Hime. Hime wrote several books, bearing such titles as *Morality*, *On Human nature as an excuse for sin* and the intriguingly named *Schoolboy's special immorality*. Hime's books reflect his affinity with the values propagated in the Edwardian public school system that was so crucial in promoting the ideology of empire. Hime was also governor of the Apprentice Boys in the first decades of the twentieth century.[62]

By the turn of the century the Siege myth had, therefore, come to encapsulate a political struggle that was defined in terms of both racial and religious difference and which promoted a particular moral value system. The combination of imperial- nationalism with the sectarianism of Protestant exclusivity was central. While there were obviously elements specific to the nature of Ulster Protestant political culture and the particular social formation of late nineteenth-century Ireland, such a definition owed a great deal to the prevailing ideological currents of the day. The character of British patriotism in this age of empire was forged by the right from the early 1870s onward and such patriotism was 'firmly identified with conservatism, militarism, royalism and racialism'.[63] Certainly the Siege myth, the Siege defenders and, by implication, the identity of Ulster Protestants in the period after 1880 were, at least in part, defined within this framework of imperial patriotism. The consolidation of a Victorian ideology, that justified the exploitation of subject peoples throughout the world, was represented as a series of values which, when drawn together, constituted the substance of 'Britain's unique imperial mission'.[64] These same moral and social assumptions were etched onto the Siege myth. Similarly, the militarist culture of the Siege parades, which promoted the mobilisation of popular political activity, fitted into the same model. These various dimensions were then symbolised in the elevated status afforded the increasingly ritualistic role of the crown.

THE EMPIRE AND THE SIEGE

By the late nineteenth century unionist ideology was built around the 'structural opposites' that the Siege myth had come to exemplify. The symbol system of the Siege therefore became not just an historical touchstone, but the very language through which unionism expressed itself. The 'Siege mentality' that emerged as the self-definition of Ulster Protestant political culture provided ideological legitimation first for political rebellion and (after partition) of state

---

62 E. Gaskell, *Ulster leaders: social and political* (London, 1913); J.A. Mangan, 'The grit of our forefathers: invented traditions, propaganda and imperialism', J.M. MacKenzie (ed.), *Imperialism and popular culture*, pp 113–39.   63 H. Cunningham, 'The language of patriotism', p. 78.   64 J. Mackenzie, *Propaganda and empire*, p. 2.

power. But through that historical passage from state support to anti-state action and then state authority, unionism, as constituted through the signs of the Siege myth, re-articulated itself to explain changing circumstance. While the use of the same signs of the Siege cycle gave the semblance of ideological continuity, what is striking is the discontinuity for unionism through this period, and particularly in the circumstances of the Home Rule crisis. The rhetoric accompanying the Siege culture encapsulated this discontinuity. Derry as a 'besieged outpost of empire' is a theme throughout but what the empire meant and how the Siege could be withstood, often differed greatly. At times of crisis the need for independent action of the Ulster Protestant community was symbolised within the Siege myth through the icon of the 'Apprentice Boys'. Just as prominent was the motif of an English relief force either unwilling or unable to come to the aid of the 'besieged'. At such moments 'Lundies' were likely to be found everywhere and the fickleness of the English fleet, their only reliable feature.

To understand the depth of the ideological as well as material dilemma unionism was confronted with by the possible reform of the imperial state, it is necessary to understand the extent to which 'imperial patriotism' was a foundation of its beliefs. The projection of a national-imperial identity and of the cultural values of imperialism were evident within the Siege culture from the mid-nineteenth century onward. As well as placing the political struggles of Ulster into an imperial context, this also meant defining the Siege as a struggle between two forces, those of imperial civilisation and colonised barbarity. Unionists could imagine, through the narrative of the Siege, the triumph of the former over the latter.

It was, however, in the period from 1880 to 1910 that the importance of imperial values and imagery came very much to the fore within the Siege myth and this reflected wider trends. This was the period marked by a sustained and fundamental crisis in the character of the British state and British society that was crystallised in the battle over Home Rule for Ireland. The rise of the Home Rule movement thrust the issue of the Union to the fore in British politics, and reaction against Home Rule was crucial in changing the terrain of British political life. The hegemonic crisis that preservation of the Union unleashed helped forge the new and pervasive force of social imperialism (or imperial collectivism) in British society generally and in British conservatism in particular.[65]

To a great extent the unionist campaigns opposing nationalist demands between the 1880s and 1910s were consciously designed to tap into this dimension of British political culture.[66] However, Ulster Protestants did not merely

65 M.F. Forde, M., *Conservatism and collectivism, 1886–1914* (Edinburgh, 1990); Edward Said, *Culture and imperialism* (London, 1993). 66 Patrick Buckland, *Irish unionism 2: Ulster unionism and the origins of Northern Ireland, 1886–1922* (Dublin, 1973); Irish Unionist Alliance, *Irish Unionist Alliance Publications*, vol.1 (Dublin, 1893); Lord Hartington et al.,

appeal to the cultural assumptions and symbolic allegiances that underwrote the consciousness of social imperialism. They also shared them, often in an accentuated form. For an Ulster Protestant collective identity to legitimate the politics of Ulster unionism, they had to see themselves as the guardians of the imperial imagined community. This involved the promotion of a whole set of moral and cultural assumptions. As Edward Said argues, British imperialism in the late nineteenth century was not simply a material process of acquisition, it was also 'supported and perhaps even impelled by impressive ideological formations that include the notions that certain territories and people require and beseech domination ... so that these decent people could think of the imperium as a protracted, almost metaphysical obligation to rule subordinate, inferior or less advanced peoples'.[67] That both English conservatives and Ulster unionists could argue against Home Rule on the basis that Irish Catholics were unable to govern themselves gave voice to a world view that derived its shape from the presumptions of superiority attendant upon imperialism. However, there were also differences in the nature of imperial identity in England and Ulster and these also conditioned the nature of the Siege myth. Such 'ideological formations' were ordered within a sense of the past and of 'tradition'. Thus within British political culture the legitimacy of the imperial order was grounded in a belief that British constitutional development was superior, definitively Anglo-Saxon and symbolised in the office of the constitutional monarchy. For Ulster unionism, too, imperial ideology was grounded in a sense of the past, and in particular, through the imagery of the Siege.

However, Ulster unionism and the Siege myth differed from the main strains of imperial patriotism in two main areas, both dependent on the nature of Irish social and political life. In the first place this imperial-nationalism was combined with an anti-Catholicism born out of the sectarianised social relations of Irish society. Second, because of the particular relationship of unionists to the British state, there also existed an embryonic, though deeply problematic, notion of Ulster Protestant distinctiveness. Yet, the identity of Ulster unionist ideology and of the Siege culture were so enmeshed in the idea of empire and the invented tradition of the planter that a theoretical basis conceived in 'Ulster nationalist' terms was at best nebulous. The resort to the constitutional discourse of the covenanting tradition was the result as much of the failure of the language of nationalism to legitimate the role of unionists as it was the evocation of a deeply ingrained political tradition.

The Siege myth was therefore shaped by two important dimensions of what the Union came to symbolise during the period 1880 to 1910. First, there was the complex interaction of religious difference, the 'nation' and the empire in

The case for the Union (London, 1886); S. Rosenbaum (ed.), *Against Home Rule: the case for the Union* (London, 1912).   **67** Edward Said, *Culture and imperialism*, pp 8–10.

the idea of the Union as the basis for an Ulster Protestant collective identity. The particular mix of these various elements, at any given time, tended to find expression within the Siege myth through the personified symbolism of the Apprentice Boys, acting as the model of the imagined community. While the Apprentice Boys were invariably described as racially homogeneous, as well as denominationally distinct from the besiegers of the city, their supposed racial character was usually linked to an imperial collective, as 'Anglo-Saxons', or 'British'. There was at times, however, a re-emphasis and re-articulation of the Siege myth that concentrated upon the 'Ulsterness', as well as the 'Protestantism' of the Siege defenders. The Apprentice Boys emerged as the epitome of the 'Honest Ulstermen'.

Linked to this, the relationship of Englishness, Britishness and unionism was also deeply problematic.[68] As Tom Paulin has argued, while Englishness was an 'instinctual, ethnic identification', Britishness lacked 'its inspirational power' and, in certain circumstances, what might be called, a hierarchy of belonging was established within the framework of imperial patriotism.[69] Within the imagery of the Siege the mirror of this was, at times, a negative representation of what 'Englishness' meant. This reflected tensions between the imperial centre and the colonial periphery and reinforcing a sense of difference, as well as projecting commonality, with England, expressed in terms of loyalty and betrayal. The notional 'Ulsterness' of the Apprentice Boys was a reaction to this and would come much more to the fore in the period after 1912. In this vein what became known as the 'conditional loyalty' of early twentieth-century Ulster unionism shared the same conceptual framework as the 'colonial nationalisms' of Australia, New Zealand, South Africa and Canada in the same period.[70]

The tension produced between Ulster unionists and the British state by the time of the Home Rule crisis of 1912–14 saw both the 'Ulsterness' of the Apprentice Boys and the unreliability of the English as a force of 'relief' merge with an emphasis on the sacrificial dimension of the Siege. This was an ideological formula to justify rebellion. The 'enemy within', symbolised in the figure of Lundy, was a powerful means of legitimating not only the need for communal solidarity but also of a potential rejection of authority. The British government playing the role of Lundy, or the government cast not as the honest monarch who assure deliverance, but the reticent fleet which awaits catastrophe, became a means to articulate the cause of armed opposition. Similarly,

68 P. Dodd, 'Englishness and the national culture', and R. Colls, 'Englishness and the political culture', in R. Colls and P. Dodd (eds), *Englishness: politics and culture.* 69 Tom Paulin, 'A new look at the Language Question', in Denis O'Dohoghue (ed.), *Ireland's Field Day* (Derry, 1985), p. 7. 70 J. Eddy and D. Schreuder (eds), *The rise of colonial nationalism. Australia, New Zealand, Canada and South Africa first assert their nationalisms* (London, 1988).

during periods of crisis, the act of defiance in 'Shutting the Gates' and the sacrifices that were made as a result, became a more favoured theme than the moment of deliverance and relief. The Siege myth proved, once again, its ability to project a model for social and political action.

As a result the Siege, now defined as a battle for the preservation of Ulster (rather than of Ireland) as an outpost of empire fought by Ulster Protestants themselves, emerged as a mythic legitimation of partition. As unionism became an official ideology rather than an oppositional political bloc, as the nature of the British empire and identity were re-defined and the Union was reformulated, so the way was left open for the Siege parades to become, by the 1920s, part of the cultural apparatus of the state of Northern Ireland and a celebration of Orange hegemony.

A right to march? The conflict at Dolly's Brae

CHRISTINE KINEALY

On 12 July 1849 a violent sectarian conflict took place in the small village of Dolly's Brae in the townland of Magheramayo in Co. Down. More people were killed in this conflict than in the nationalist uprising in the previous year. It was also the most violent clash between Orangemen and Catholics to have occurred since the 1790s. The collision occurred when the Rathfriland Orange lodge re-routed their annual parade to pass through Dolly's Brae, a mountain village inhabited only by Catholics. During the evening, a battle took place between Orangemen and Ribbonmen that resulted in a number of deaths, including four inhabitants of the village. The event was widely publicized and condemned in both the Irish and British press. It was also debated in parliament, following which an official enquiry was established. The government's response to the conflict caused further outrage and controversy. Three 'Orange' magistrates, including the Earl of Roden, were dismissed from the judiciary for their part in the conflict. Moreover, legislation was introduced in 1850 that banned political marches. Consequently, political marches were illegal in Ireland between 1850 and the repeal of the act in 1872. The anger expressed against this ban was an early example of Orangemen defending their 'traditional' right to march. The incident at Dolly's Brae deepened existing divisions between Protestants and Catholics, as both sides felt let down by the government's handling of the event. It also exposed and intensified the tensions that existed between Irish Protestants and the British government; the former feeling betrayed by the government they had helped to maintain as recently as in 1848. Furthermore, it revealed differences within Orangeism as the lower classes maintained their allegiance to the Orange Institute as a necessary defence against their Catholic neighbours whilst the gentry (not for the first time) distanced themselves from the excesses of the Orange Order. In general, the conflict at Dolly's Brae was a microcosm of wider conflicts within Irish society and demonstrated the ambivalence of the British government towards their traditional Protestant allies. However, the debate that ensued did not resolve but, rather, inflamed these tensions.

The importance of the events in Dolly's Brae in 1849 has been acknowl-edged both by historians and in unionist memory, yet it has been the subject of little scholarly research. The unfolding of events has also remained unclear, largely due to the fact that, from the outset, accounts of the incident were tinged with religious bias. Both the coroner's report and the government inquiry even found it difficult to reach a firm conclusion about the origins of the conflict or the death toll that ensued. The confusion surrounding the number of casualties was because both the Orangemen and the Ribbonmen (the generic term for Catholic secret societies) removed injured and dead people from the scene. Consequently, there is considerable variation in the estimates of the number of people, especially Catholics, killed. Contemporary newspapers estimated between 30 and 50 Catholics had been killed, although the government enquiry favoured the lower figure.[1] The Catholic *Freeman's Journal,* for example, contended that 40 were dead but cautioned 'it is impossible to know at present the exact number as each party is concealing their friends'.[2] The Protestant *Warder* stated that 50 'rebels' had been killed or wounded and four Orangemen wounded.[3] Modern historians have shown more variance; for example, Joe Lee estimated 20, Stewart estimated 6, Jarman estimated 8, and both Kevin Haddick-Flynn and Ruth Dudley Edwards estimated that at least 30 Ribbonmen were killed in the conflict. No mention is made of the fact that four of the dead were villagers, thus making Dolly's Brae appear as a fight simply between two opposing factions.[4]

The Protestant death toll has been even more elusive. The conservative *Newry Telegraph,* which provided full coverage of the incident, reported that no Orangemen had been killed on the day.[5] This interpretation has been repeated by Haddick-Flynn who has asserted that there were no Protestant casualties.[6] Protestant folk tradition also claims that no Orangemen were killed at Dolly's Brae.[7] The Orange Order suggests that 80 people were killed, none of whom were Protestants.[8] George Fitzmaurice, a magistrate who was present, notified Dublin Castle that one Orangeman and four Ribbonmen had been killed.[9] A month later, the death of an Orangemen who had been wounded at Dolly's Brae was reported at Ballyroney. As he was to be buried 'as an Orangeman', police and troops were sent to the area to keep the peace.[10] Protestant folk memory has also distorted the view of some of the key protagonists. Although the role of the local priests, Frs Morgan and Mooney, was

1 *Belfast News-letter,* 20 July 1849. 2 *Freeman's Journal,* 17 July 1849. 3 *Warder,* 21 July 1849. 4 J. Lee, *The modernization of Irish society, 1848–1918* (Dublin, 1973); A.T.Q. Stewart, *The narrow ground* (London, 1977), p .8; Neil Jarman, *Material conflicts: parades and visual displays in Northern Ireland* (1997), p. 5; Kevin Haddick-Flynn, *Orangeism: the making of a tradition* (1999) p. 434; Ruth Dudley Edwards, *The faithful tribe: an intimate portrait of the loyal institutions* (London, 1999), p. 200. 5 Reprinted in *Vindicator,* 14 July 1849. 6 Haddick-Flynn, *Orangeism,* p. 278. 7 From song 'Dolly's Brac' (traditional Protestant folk song) 8 *Ulster History,* http://ourworld.compuserve.com. The traditional version of the song 'Dolly's Brae' states: *'The volleys from the rebel guns had no effect at all, For not a man among our ranks fell by a Papish ball.'* 9 G. Fitzmaurice to Redington, PROL, HO45 OS 2603, 13 July 1849. 10 *Times,* 17 Aug. 1849.

widely praised at the time, even in the Protestant press, for trying to disperse
the Ribbonmen, in Protestant songs they are depicted as having incited the
people.[11] One eponymous song claims:

> Priest Mooney and Priest Murphy went through the rebel lines
> Distributing the wafer god among the philistines;
> Priest Mooney cursed the Orangemen with candle, book and bell,
> While the rebel crowd did cry aloud 'we'll drive them all to hell'.[12]

The role of Robert Jocelyn, third earl of Roden, in the affair was most in
dispute. Roden owned an estate near Castlewellan in Co. Down. He was a committed evangelical, holding bible readings twice daily on his estate.[13] Roden
joined the Orange Order in 1831 and immediately was appointed a grand
officer.[14] In 1834, he convened a meeting at Hillsborough in an attempt to unite
all Protestants against popery, the speakers including the Presbyterian minister,
Henry Cooke.[15] Like many Protestant landlords, Roden was alarmed at the revolutionary fervour in the country in 1848 and offered the lord lieutenant advice
and the support of Orangemen if necessary.[16] In July 1849 the Orange lodges in
the Castlewellan area asked Roden if they could hold their meeting on his
estate.[17] According to some reports, Roden rode out to meet the Orangemen on
a white horse and wearing the regalia of the deputy grand master. After refresh-
ments, speeches were made, including one from Roden. Nationalist accounts of
the day accused Roden of using this as an opportunity to incite the Orangemen
to 'do their duty' and to defend Protestantism.[18] He was also reproached for
giving them 'strong whiskey', which meant that they were intoxicated when
they returned home.[19] Instead of proceeding directly homewards, therefore,
they went by the long route through Dolly's Brae 'to triumph still more'.[20]
Roden, however, denied these allegations. Due to his poor state of health he
claimed that he had discouraged the Orangemen from meeting on his estate and
only agreed because 'he felt a pride in thinking that so many of his fellow
country-men in the humbler class of life were anxious, at great inconvenience
to themselves, to manifest such a feeling of attachment to him'.[21] During his
speech on 12 July, although he contended that Protestants had much to complain of about the way they had been treated in the previous twenty years, he

11 The Protestant *Warder,* for example, says they did everything they could to persuade the
'misguided people' although it added that 'Priest Mooney' used 'unbecoming word to
Orangemen', 21 July. 12 'Dolly's Brae'. Traditional Protestant song. 13 Haddick-
Flynn, *Orangeism,* p. 260. 14 Proceedings of Grand Orange Lodge of Ireland, Trinity
College Library Dublin, Ms. 2288a, 21 Jan. 1832. 15 Jonathan Bardon, *A history of Ulster*
(Belfast, 1992) p. 254. 16 Haddock-Flynn, *Orangeism,* p. 274. 17 Speech of Lord Roden,
Hansard, cvii, 31 July 1849. 18 *Freeman's Journal,* 14 July 1849. 19 *Vindicator,* 21 July
1849. 20 *Freeman's Journal,* 17 July 1849. 21 Speech of Lord Roden, *Hansard,* 31 July
1849, p. 1132.

asked the Orangemen to show 'forbearance and love to all'. He also asked them to show 'to those who disapprove of your organisation that you are not a faction driven by party violence to commit unlawful acts; that you do not desire to infringe on the liberty and happiness of others'.[22] Despite his public statement in parliament regarding his innocence, the government dismissed Roden from the judiciary. In Protestant folk song, however, he is remembered as the champion of the day, regardless of the fact that he did not take part in the procession:

> Lord Roden was Grand Master of the Orangemen just then,
> No better chieftain could be found among the sons of men;
> To Romanists he would not yield, nor any Popish foe,
> He stood firmly like Joshua on the plains of Jericho.[23]

THE BACKGROUND

By the 1840s the annual July processions had acquired a reputation for sectarian violence. Since the foundation of the Orange Order in 1795, the anniversary of the battle of the Boyne had been commemorated with a parade each 12 July. From the outset, however, the day generally ended in fighting between Orangemen and Catholics in Ulster. Following the defeat of the 1798 uprising (in which the Orange Order had acted as a counter-revolutionary force), both the executive in Dublin Castle and the British parliament had increasingly distanced themselves from the Boyne commemorations. In 1823 an act was passed to restrict all political societies in Ireland, whether Catholic or Protestant. It had only limited success in preventing parades in parts of Ulster, especially following the introduction of Catholic Emancipation in 1829. Consequently, the more stringent Anti-Procession Act was passed in 1832, and it was renewed annually until 1845. In 1836 a government enquiry on the Orange Order was unfavourable, criticizing the fact that, despite being illegal, the 12 July marches continued and many were routed deliberately through Catholic districts in order to provoke the local residents. It further noted that the yeomanry, the constabulary and the army contained many lodges.[24] Following the publication of this report, several members of the upper classes and gentry left the Order, only rejoining during the Home Rule crisis. During the subsequent decade, the Order was quiet, but the decision not to renew the legislation banning processions in 1845 resulted in an immediate return to Boyne commemorations, which were larger and more numerous that before.

22 Ibid., p.1134. 23 Ibid. 24 *Report* of Select Committee to Enquire into the Nature, Character, Extent and Tendency of Orange Association in Ireland, 1835.

The July parades in 1849 took place in a highly charged political atmosphere, largely due to the Young Ireland uprising of the previous year. Although the immediate threat of a republican uprising had passed and the repeal movement was in disarray, nationalist activity was still a source of concern to some Protestants. For a number of Protestant groups, the 1848 uprising was equated with Catholic disloyalty, regardless of the fact that many of its leaders had been Protestant. In the preceding years, tension between Catholics and Protestants had also been heightened by the proselytizing activities of some Protestant evangelicals, especially during the Famine years. Attempts to prevent Catholics from converting were criticized in some of the Protestant press, the *Banner of Ulster* mockingly referring to 'Popish cruelty' and the activities of 'skull-cracking priests' who attempted to intimidate their flocks into not changing their religion and persecuting those who had converted.[25]

The alleged differentiation between the 'north' (an area not precisely defined) and the rest of the country was publicized in the spring of 1849 during the dispute over the proposed Rate-in Aid tax. The tax had been suggested by the Whig government as a way of Irish – as opposed to British – taxpayers financing the continuing distress and famine in parts of the country. It was to be levied on all ratepayers in Ireland and then reallocated to Poor Law Unions that were insolvent or indebted. Opposition to the tax was most vehement among ratepayers in unions in the north east of the country. The guardians of the Lurgan Union, for example, passed a resolution condemning the intention 'of taxing Ulster and Leinster for the support of idleness and improvidence elsewhere'.[26] At a meeting held in Belfast a motion was passed condemning the Rate-in-Aid on the grounds that its purpose was to force 'the honest and industrious people of Ulster to support the idle and indolent inhabitants of the South and West'.[27] As the debate progressed, increasingly it was expressed in terms of the Protestants of Ulster supporting the Catholics of Connaught.[28]

Throughout 1848 and the early months of 1849 a number of conflicts took place between Protestants and Catholics in Ulster, some of which ended violently.[29] A number of incendiary fires in parts of Co. Down were attributed to Catholic secret societies acting against Protestant landlords.[30] The local Orange lodges resolved that they would find and bring the perpetrators to justice and attributed the arson attacks to 'those enemies of peace and order to tarnish the fair fame of the North, and calculated to bring us to a level with the savage atrocities of the south and west of Ireland'.[31] An early indication of the heightened religious tensions in parts of the north of Ireland occurred during the St Patrick's Day celebrations on 17 March. Although the Dublin authorities had sent additional troops and constabulary to a number of areas in Ulster,

25 *Banner of Ulster*, 23 Jan. 1849. 26 Ibid., 27 Feb. 1849. 27 *Times*, 6 Mar. 1849. 28 *Banner of Ulster*, 9 Mar. 1849. 29 Abstract of Constabulary Reports, PROL, HO45 os 2416A, Aug. 1848. 30 *Banner of Ulster*, 30 Jan. 1849. 31 Ibid., 16 Feb. 1849.

collisions between Ribbonmen and Orangemen took place in Downpatrick, Crossgar, Rathfriland and Derry. The most violent clash took place at Crossgar where, notwithstanding the presence of troops and military, a young woman and policeman were shot dead, and a number of other people were seriously wounded. A local magistrate was also pelted with stones.[32] The Catholic march had been prevented from proceeding down a Protestant street by the police, and it was unclear as to whether the Ribbonmen or Orangemen initiated the fighting, although the magistrate in charge told the inquest that the former had been dispersing peacefully.[33] On the same day, an Orangeman was killed near Rathfriland and his funeral was preceded by a large procession of Orangemen, accompanied by troops in order to keep the peace. In each case, the Protestant press blamed Ribbonmen, although no arrests were made.[34] The *Warder* regarded these incidents as attacks on innocent Orangemen and claimed that even though Ribbonmen were the aggressors, Protestants were always regarded as the guilty party 'in the eyes of the pro-popery conciliator government'.[35] The nationalist *Belfast Weekly Vindicator* was worried by the increase in the number of Orange lodges and the concurrent growth in sectarian violence over the preceding few years, blaming both the tolerance of the government and the partisan attitude of the police.[36] Following these collisions, there were a number of appeals for party processions to be prohibited.[37] The matter was raised in parliament by Viscount Castlereagh, who asked the government to renew the act banning political processions. Although the home secretary, George Grey, agreed that the processions were becoming more overtly anti-Catholic, he believed that the government needed more time to consider the matter.[38] Consequently, the Boyne parades in 1849 took place against a backdrop of increasing concern about the growth of sectarian conflicts in the north of Ireland.

The approach of 12 July was regarded with trepidation, with moderate Protestants alarmed by the sectarian nature of the processions. The *Fermanagh Reporter* was concerned that the Protestant elite had a vested interest in allowing the parades to continue, suggesting that the July processions were a tool for Protestant landlords to maintain the status quo, arguing that 'The power of government in Ireland is, to a great extent, and that of the landlords to a much greater, owing to Orangeism ... Orangeism has kept landlords in their unnatural position, and that position enabled them to crush those on whose shoulders they were raised.'[39] Some members of the Protestant churches were alarmed by the violence being perpetrated in the defence of Protestantism and, on 5 July, the Anglican bishop of Down and Connor issued a pastoral letter warning

32 Ibid., 20 Mar. 1849.   33 *Armagh Guardian*, 26 Mar. 1849.   34 *Warder*, 24 Mar. 1849. 35 Ibid., 14 July 1849.   36 *Weekly Vindicator*, 24 Mar. 1849.   37 *Banner of Ulster*, 27 Mar. 1849; *Armagh Guardian*, 19 Mar. 1849.   38 *Vindicator*, 24 Mar. 1849.   39 Reprinted in *Times*, 2 July 1849.

about the Boyne parade and the fact that its main purpose had become to express 'a triumph of party'. The response of Lord Massereene of Antrim Castle, in which he defended the Orange processions and justified the use of his park as a meeting place by the processionists, was published in various newspapers including *The Times*. He also pointed out that the processions were often led by clergymen and that 'the clergy appear to be the chief promoters of the Orange demonstrations'. However, Massereene admitted that the reason why the Party Processions Act had not been renewed was that British politicians ruled Ireland by keeping alive 'old and bygone feuds'.[40]

Many Orangemen were indignant at the outcome of a number of recent conflicts. At the beginning of July, four Orangemen were sentenced to nine months' hard labour for their part in a sectarian riot in Banbridge in February, during which one Orangemen had been killed. The subsequent inquiry concluded that such assemblages were illegal. The *Freeman's Journal* interpreted this judgement as being applicable to all Orange gatherings opining that 'if there were no walking, there would be no bloodshed'. Orangemen, however, regarded the sentence and the judgement as harsh.[41] Significantly, a meeting of Orange societies took place a few days before the Boyne anniversary at which Orangemen were called on 'to do their duty'.[42]

In anticipation of confrontation, the authorities in Dublin Castle sent additional militia and police support to a number of districts in the north of the country including Belfast, Ballymena and Dolly's Brae.[43] Because of the trouble at Crossgar and Rathfriland in March, the authorities expected some tension in that locality, but early reports suggested that the day had passed peacefully, despite the large turnout of Orangeman.[44] The parades were larger than in previous years, especially in Derry, Lisburn and Antrim. An estimated 60,000 Orangemen from the Belfast and Antrim lodges had convened on Lord Massereene's estate, and 100,000 people had watched the Belfast Orange lodges parade on their return to town in the evening. Many of the speeches were critical of the liberal attitudes of successive governments for pandering to Catholic demands, citing the examples of the national system of education, the new universities, and Catholic Emancipation, each of which had undermined Protestantism in Ireland. The role of the Orangemen in saving the country from revolutionary threat in the previous year was also referred to frequently.[45] The *Armagh Guardian* praised the Orangemen for their display of loyalty 'despite the ingratitude of the government', warning the latter that Orangeism should not be slighted because, as the previous year had proved, it was 'useful as a friend and ally, but ruinous as a foe'.[46]

---

40 *Times*, 12 July 1849. 41 *Freeman's Journal*, 3 July 1849. 42 *Armagh Guardian*, 9 July 1849. 43 Outrage Papers for Co. Antrim, National Archives, Dublin, July 1849. 44 *Warder*, 14 July 1849. 45 Ibid. 46 *Armagh Guardian*, 16 July 1849.

THE CONFLICT

The initial reports of the parades suggested that they had passed peacefully. An exception occurred in Ballymacarrett in Belfast where a Catholic man was killed during a 'party riot'.[47] The general optimism was short-lived, however, as news of a violent collision between Orangemen and Ribbonmen in Dolly's Brae became known. Although early details were sketchy, it appeared that an incident had taken place when a number of Orange lodges from Rathfriland had decided to return home by way of Dolly's Brae, a route that was neither traditional nor direct. Moreover, the village was inhabited only by Catholics. The decision to march through Dolly's Brae had been made some weeks earlier and the authorities in Dublin Castle had responded by sending extra troops and constabulary to the area. Early on the morning of 12 July, lodges from Rathfriland and Dromara amounting to 1200 Orangemen assembled at Ballyward, the estate of Francis Beers, a local JP and brother of William Beers, the grand county master. An equal number of women and children were also present. The day was unusually hot; in the sun it was estimated to be 110 degrees.[48] Many of the Orangemen were armed and wearing Orange insignia. From the morning, the Orangemen were accompanied by a squadron of the 6th Enniskillen dragoons and a 'large party of police' under Mr Fitzmaurice RM, Mr Scott of Rathfriland JP, and Mr Francis Beers of Ballyward JP. William Beers led the procession. The intention was to march through Dolly's Brae to Castlewellan and then to Tollymore Park, the estate of the earl of Roden, which was the rendezvous for all local Orange lodges. As they passed through the village in the morning they stopped at a bridge, ceremoniously broke a bottle of liquor upon it and renamed it 'William's Bridge'. Although Ribbonmen had been gathering on the hillside since the morning, they did not interfere with the procession. The Orangemen arrived at Tollymore Park, 'with bayonets fixed, and each man carrying forty rounds of ammunition'. The Rathfriland lodges 'attracted considerable notice, having crossed a formidable barrier, known as Dolly's Brae, and in the presence of a vast number of rebels'. Consequently, 'they were loudly cheered by all who recognized them'.[49] At Tollymore Park the Rathfriland lodges were joined by others from Kilkeel, Newcastle, Mourne, making about 50 lodges representing 6000 Orangemen, plus their followers.

A squadron of 18th Light Dragoons, two companies of the 9th foot, and a body of police under Mr Tabiteau RM, remained in Dolly's Brae throughout the day. According to some reports the Ribbonmen spent their time drilling, while they waited for the Orangeman to return.[50] When the Orangemen

47 Reprinted from *Belfast Chronicle* in *Freeman's Journal*, 17 July 1849.   **48** *Freeeman's Journal*, 14 July 1849.   **49** This account of events appeared in the *Dublin Herald*, a newspaper that was sympathetic to the Orange Order. It was reprinted in *Freeman's Journal*, 17 July.   **50** Haddick-Flynn, *Orangeism*, p. 277.

returned in the evening either a shot or a squib was fired, which proved to be the trigger for general fighting. Initially, neither the police nor the army joined in, but after a while the constabulary chased the Ribbonmen up the hill. A group of Orangeman used this an opportunity to set fire to a number of houses and the Catholic Church, the priest's home and the National School. Thirty-seven Catholics were taken to the bridewell at Newry and were charged with appearing with arms and firing shots at the constabulary. Following cross-examination, seventeen of them were committed to appear at the assizes in Downpatrick.[51]

THE AFTERMATH

Because of the partisan reporting of the events, especially in the Irish newspapers, it was hard to get a clear understanding of what had happened. As the days passed, it became apparent that a conflict had been fermenting for a number of months in the area. Although Dolly's Brae was not a traditional route for Orangemen, the Rathfriland lodge had considered marching though it in 1848 but had been persuaded not to do so. In 1849, however, they wanted to do something to pay back for their defeat at Crossgar and other conflicts.[52] According to Haddick-Flynn, 'at fairs and markets they were taunted for their cowardice'; therefore, before 12 July 1849 they announced 'that they were unafraid' and were going to take the old road through Dolly's Brae.[53] There were also rumours that they were going to burn Catholic houses on route. The authorities were alarmed and sent extra forces to the area. According to the Catholic *Freeman's Journal*, the Orangemen then resolved to march as they believed that the military and police would be there to protect them.[54]

Initially details of the day were sparse but, as more information became available, it became tinged with sectarian bias. Although the government had anticipated a sectarian conflict in Dolly's Brae, the early accounts had been positive, even in the nationalist press. The original report in the *Freeman's Journal*, for example, stated that the local Orange lodges 'marched in gallant but peaceful procession through the Earl of Annesley's demesne en route to Tollymore Park, the seat of the Earl of Roden. After a day spent in harmony, the loyal Orangemen of Castlewellan retired to their homes without a single infraction of peace and good order.'[55] Two days later, the paper announced a 'Dreadful loss of life at Castlewellan', averring that 'Once more has Ulster been stained with the deep crime of red murder.' The paper criticized Protestant ministers, the government, the constabulary and the magistracy, for allowing the violence to take place. It accused Protestant clergymen of having 'offered at the altar of

51 *Times*, 18 July 1849. 52 *Freeman's Journal*, 16 July 1849. 53 Haddick-Flynn, *Orangeism*, p. 275. 54 *Freeman's Journal*, 17 July 1849. 55 Ibid., 14 July 1849.

bigotry a sacrifice of human blood' as a result of which 'lifeless corpses and wailing women, and orphan children, and distracted mothers, are scattered over the fields around Castlewellan to testify how powerful is the gory god these crimson priests adore'. The newspaper praised the Catholics for their great patience during the day, especially considering 'the galling and insulting manner' in which the Orangemen had renamed the bridge.[56] It suggested that if the Orangemen had not decided to return through the village, there would have been no trouble.

More controversially, the *Freeman's Journal* accused the police and military of siding with the Orangemen; the police had only fired on Catholics and had allowed some Orangemen to enter the village, destroy buildings and kill a number of inhabitants. Moreover, the magistrates had not prevented this, and one of them had even encouraged these atrocities. The paper also raised what was to be a central source of dissension in the ensuing weeks, when it suggested that the procession should have been prohibited and asked 'Why was this ILLEGAL assemblage not dispersed by the magistrates and the police before it reached the place where the fatal collision took place?' The role of the Irish executive was also regarded as reprehensible although the paper claimed that within Dublin Castle 'This will be looked on as a grand affair, and highly pleasing to Her Majesty's government. Lord Clarendon will be highly delighted, as he certainly had it in his power to prevent it.' It added: 'The whole conduct of the authorities in this matter, from the highest to the lowest - from Lord Clarendon to the policeman who dyed his hands in the blood of his fellow Christians - is most culpable.'[57] Landlords and religious ministers were likewise accused of encouraging these parades because they knew that 'this discord, and strife, and tumult, and unchristian ill-will and red murder are necessary to keep up the enormities of rackrents and the crimes of a bloated "establishment". Hence these bloodstained holidays of discord and inequity are perpetuated.'[58]

The treatment of Catholics in the aftermath of the conflict was also regarded as being partial. The fact that no Orangemen were arrested was described as being 'in keeping with the alliance thus formed between the *constituted authorities* of the law and the *illegal* Orange assemblage, that *Catholics alone* were made prisoners on the occasion'. Furthermore, the prisoners had been taken before 'Orange' magistrates, including Francis Beers who 'has been for years a notorious Orange leader' and who had encouraged the Orange demonstration.[59] The Catholic *Vindicator* was equally critical of the role played by the constabulary and the authorities, accusing them, not for the first time, of being partisan and allowing the Orange violence to take place.[60]

---

56 Ibid., 17 July 1849.　**57** Ibid., 16 July 1849.　**58** Ibid.　**59** The 'Orange' magistrates were Captain Fitzmaurice RM; Mr Tabiteau RM: Captain Skinner JP; Thomas Scott, Esq. JP; Francis Beers, Esq., JP; Captain Tighe JP. *Freeman's Journal*, 16 July 1849. **60** *Vindicator*, 14 July 1849.

In contrast, the conservative *Newry Telegraph* blamed the Ribbonmen for provoking the confrontation, asserting that when the 'brave' Orangemen passed through the village they had been 'hooted and groaned and vilified in the most scurrilous manner' by girls and women who did everything, apart from attacking them 'to exasperate them to the commission of an outrage'.[61] It was only when the Orangemen were 'fired on by a dense mob of Ribbonmen who had lined the pass on either side' that they fired in return 'and dislodged their cowardly assailants from behind the stone walls and ditches where they had taken up positions'. The *Telegraph* also praised the police force for having 'bravely' dispersed the Ribbon party and taking prisoners despite the fact they were armed with 'pikes, muskets, scythes mounted on poles, and other deadly weapons'. The attack on the village was excused on the grounds that the Orangemen 'roused beyond endurance, turned upon their assailants, and set fire to six or seven of the houses'.[62] The *Warder*, a paper founded for the defence of Protestantism, was also unequivocal in its justification of the actions of the Orangeman. The paper alleged that the local Ribbonmen had challenged the Orangemen to meet them in Dolly's Brae, and once there, they attacked them. The attack was premeditated because the Ribbonmen had stolen a barrel of gunpowder two nights earlier. The Orangemen had only set fire to houses because they were 'exasperated beyond measure' and 'in response to 'the cowardly attack that was made on them'. Furthermore, shots had been fired from houses in the village. Throughout, the Orangemen had demonstrated 'very considerable skill and the greatest bravery' and had acted to support the police. Mr Corry, sub-inspector of the constabulary, was commended for risking his life by rushing into a burning house and saving two women from the flames. His bravery was, according to the paper, 'the theme of every tongue'. The paper also praised the Orangemen for, regardless of being under attack, planting their flag on the hillside, whilst playing 'The Protestant Boys'.[63]

Even within the Protestant press, there were disputes about which side had triggered the conflict and there was some condemnation of the activities of the Orangemen. The *Downpatrick Recorder* agreed that an Orangemen had fired the first shot, although it did not regard it as being a signal for fighting. The paper concurred that Dolly's Brae 'from time immemorial has been considered the stronghold of the Roman Catholic party, and until the late 12 July the Orangemen did not think it safe to go in procession by that route'. The decision to pass through in 1849 was attributed to 'some miscalculation or other, [the Orangemen] thought they might pass it on this occasion unmolested'. According to the paper, four Ribbonmen, one Orangeman and a girl looking on were killed, although they had heard that many more were lying dead in the

61 From *Newry Telegraph*, reprinted in *Warder*, 21 July 1849.   62 Reprinted in *Vindicator*, 14 July 1849.   63 *Warder*, 21 July 1849

ditches. Following the conflict, the Orangemen had been escorted back to their lodges at Clarkhill, Cloughram, Clough and Newcastle but they had attacked local Catholics after the military left them. The paper concluded that the most brutal act of the Orangemen was that they 'set fire to all the houses and burnt eleven, and nearly burnt an old women and a cripple'.[64] A correspondent in the *Newry Telegraph*, who had viewed the four dead in Dolly's Brae, reported that 'It was heart-rending to see the grief of the poor people'. He also made it clear that the dead, which included a young boy, an old woman and the village idiot, were non-combatants in the conflict.[65]

In addition to conflicting reports about who provoked the collision, there was also disagreement concerning the numbers present at Dolly's Brae on the evening of 12 July. The estimates of Orangemen present ranged from 1200 to 6000; the *Warder* stated that the march consisted of 24 lodges, numbering 1200 persons, whilst Major Wilkinson, who was in charge of the military, estimated 1500 Orangemen were present, followed by a similar number of women and children. However, the Protestant *Armagh Chronicle* calculated there to be 6000 Orangemen present.[66] The number of Ribbonmen present in the evening also varied between 1000 and 2000; the Protestant *Warder*, which favoured the higher figure, also claimed that the Ribbonmen were each 'armed to the teeth'.[67] George Fitzmaurice, a magistrate who had accompanied the military, reported to the government that between 1000 and 1500 Orangemen had been present and that they had outnumbered the Ribbonmen by three to one.[68]

THE CORONER'S INQUEST

In the days following 12 July, the confusion and anger about what had happened increased. The announcement of a coroner's inquest was welcomed by all sides, the *Down Recorder* opining 'the real truth won't be known until the evidence at the inquest'.[69] An inquest was held at Castlewellan on Monday 16 July. Its stated purpose was to take evidence on how Patrick King, John Sweeny, Anne Traynor and another person had met their deaths. Dr George Tryell was appointed the coroner, and the jury was composed of 21 townspeople. Many of the magistrates on the bench had been present at the conflict, including Francis Beers JP, one of the leaders of the Orangemen.[70] The earl of Roden was not present, but sent a letter saying he was confined to his bed through illness,

64 From *Down Recorder* reprinted in *Freeman's Journal*, 17 July 1849. 65 From *Newry Telegraph* reprinted in *Warder*, 21 July 1849. 66 From *Armagh Chronicle* reprinted in *Freeman's Journal*, 17 July; *Warder*, 21 July 1849. 67 *Warder*, 21 July 1849. 68 George Fitzmaurice RM to T. Redington, Dublin Castle, PROL HO45 os 6423, 13 July 1849. 69 From *Down Recorder* reprinted in *Freeman's Journal* 17 July 1849. 70 The magistrates present at the inquest were, Messrs Tabiteau RM, M'Cance RM, Shaw JP, J.H. Quinn JP, Magennis JP, F.W. Beers JP, Captain Hill JP and Captain Skinner JP.

adding 'every sincere wish that your enquiries may tend to demonstrate who are the really guilty parties in this melancholy affair – and that they may be punished'. Messrs Murland and Murphy, solicitors, appeared for the next of kin of the deceased. A high police presence was evident at the proceedings.[71]

Most of the evidence provided was from the commanders of the military and the constabulary, with only one Catholic prisoner and one Catholic woman being examined. Although some details were clarified, a number of issues remained unclear. The additional military and judicial support had arrived in the district on 10 July and had been told to stay in touch with the local authorities. Many of the constabulary had been sent from Kildare. On the morning of 12 July, Major Arthur Wilkinson of 18th Light Infantry, together with two JPs, Messrs Tabiteau and Skinner, accompanied by a troop of the 13th Light, a company of the 9th foot and a body of constabulary had taken up positions in Dolly's Brae. Shortly afterwards, a group of Ribbonmen had approached, who, according to Wilkinson, were 'all armed either with pikes, pitchforks, muskets, or some description of weapons'. Initially about 300 or 400 had been present, but the number increased during the day. Wilkinson asked the two Catholic clergy present, Frs Mooney and Morgan, to use their influence with the Ribbonmen 'as we were confident the Orange party would not commence the attack unless provoked'. The Ribbonmen agreed not to fire unless fired on. Wilkinson also observed that the Orangemen who paraded through the village were 'armed to the teeth', and he commented on the fact that they had chosen a bad road over a good route. After the Orangemen had marched through the village Wilkinson believed the danger had passed, as he thought that they could be persuaded to return by a different route in the evening. The Revd Morgan, however, realised they might not. During the day the Ribbonmen practised drilling and were 'constantly blazing away with their arms', but no breach of the peace occurred.[72] In the evening, the Orangemen did reappear on the mountain. He estimated there to be about 1500 processionists, who were accompanied by a similar number of 'Orange women'. The Orangemen were all armed. The Catholic women called them names and used 'very irritating language' as they walked through Dolly's Brae. Wilkinson followed the Orangemen as they left the village. Although he heard the first shot, he did not know where it came from. Neither the military nor the constabulary returned fire until Tabiteau gave them orders to load. The police, who were under heavy fire, chased the Ribbonmen up the hill. When they arrived at the village they found some of the houses had been burnt by 'Orange stragglers'.

The evidence of Sydney Darling, captain of the 9th foot, and of Henry Dalrymple White, a major of the 6th Inniskilling Dragoon Guards, largely corroborated that of Wilkinson. White, however, estimated that about 1200 to 1400

---

71 *Warder*, 21 July 1849.   72 *Freeman's Journal*, 17 July 1849.

Ribbonmen were on the hill, many of whom were hiding behind banks and ditches. Although he was not sure where the shot came from, he thought it was fired from the head of the Orange party, and the Ribbonmen instantly returned fire. Like a number of other witnesses, he suggested that rather than a shot, it may have been a squib. When the police pursued the Ribbonmen up hill and fired on them, they were supported by a number of Orangemen who tried to 'rout' the Ribbonmen. Sergeant Major William Sutcliffe of the 6th Dragoons, however, maintained that the first shot, or squib, had come from the Ribbonmen on the hill and had been aimed at the Orangemen.[73]

A slightly different version of events was provided by George Fitzmaurice, a stipendiary magistrate. He had arrived in the area on 10 July, 'by order of the government', and on 12 July had accompanied the military and police on the Orange procession to Dolly's Brae. Fitzmaurice made an early confidential report to the authorities in Dublin, which was forwarded to the Home Office in London. In it, he reported that the Orangemen had acted 'in the most barbarous manner'.[74] He heard a noise like a squib, which he thought came from the Orange party, and the people on the hill fired in return. Although he asked the Orangemen to stop firing, they continued. He tried to stop them setting fire to a number of houses, but believed his intervention made them 'more violent'. Although he did not know who had told the police to fire, he stressed that he had not observed the police 'act with any harshness whatsoever'. He corroborated that four Ribbonmen and one Orangeman had been killed, and 35 Ribbonmen had been arrested.[75]

The evidence of James Ponsonby, the commander of the police, confirmed the confusion that had surrounded the actions of the authorities. He had heard a squib, but he did not know which party it came from. He was also unsure who gave the police and the military the order to fire and admitted that the Riot Act had not been read. Ponsonby thought that the command to chase the Ribbonmen up the hill was made by Captain Skinner, Lord Downshire's agent, but again was not sure. Mr Tabiteau RM led the charge on the Ribbonmen up the mountain. The Ribbonmen fled but, even after the police stopped firing, the Orangemen continued to do so. When asked by the coroner, Ponsonby admitted that he thought the procession was an illegal assembly. He was able to identify many of the Orangemen present, who were from the locality.[76] James Hill, a sub-inspector of the constabulary, also cast doubt on the legality of the parade, saying, 'I think 1500 persons walking in procession armed, were likely to create terror on the minds of HM subjects.' He estimated that between the two parties, more than 1000 shots were fired, even though the conflict lasted only an hour in total.[77]

---

73 Ibid. **74** George Fitzmaurice RM to Redington, HO45 os 2603, 13 July 1849.
75 *Times*, 19 July 1849. **76** *Freeman's Journal*, 17 July 1849. **77** *Warder*, 21 July 1849.

The jury at the inquest were also shown the corpses of the four dead villagers. The remains of a young boy, Hugh King, were lying in the Castlewellan
dispensary, but the bodies of the other three were in their homes. The jury was
shown the houses that had been burnt.[78] The inquest recorded that the four
dead were all Catholics who had lived in Dolly's Brae. Some of their personal
details differed from what had appeared in earlier reports. Among the dead was
Patrick (also referred to as John) King, who was killed while looking after his
elderly mother. A neighbour, Bridget King, testified that fifteen Orangemen
had broken down King's door and then stoned and stabbed him in the garden.
They then set the house on fire. Dr Hunter, who had examined the bodies, confirmed that Patrick King's skull had been fractured and that he had been
stabbed in the hip. His mother had also been stabbed, although not fatally. Anne
(or Nancy) Traynor had been bayoneted in her head and other parts of her body
'while saying her prayers'. Dr Hunter confirmed there were contusions on her
arms and face and attributed her death to her skull being fractured by a blunt
instrument. John Sweeny, who was described as a 'simpleton', had been shot
through the head 'and processionists were said to have jumped on his body'. Dr
Hunter verified that 'his skull was broken to pieces' and that there was a
gunshot wound behind his ear. Finally, Dr Hunter reported that Hugh King
had died as a result of a gunshot wound in his stomach. King was estimated to
be between ten and fourteen years old. In addition to the dead, five other people
were in Castlewellan dispensary, four of whom were mortally wounded. The
inquest also recorded that 14 houses and other buildings, including the
National School at Magheramayo, the Catholic church of Gargory, and the
priest's house had been burnt. Many cattle had been destroyed, furniture shat-
tered, and the stock of two shops wrecked.[79]

Mr Murland, the solicitor on behalf of the deceased, believed that the
Orangemen were the guilty party as the law on illegal assemblies was clearly laid
down by a law officer at a recent inquiry at Newtownards. Accordingly, 'every
one who took part in a procession of armed men under such circumstances as
in the present case would be legally answerable for the lives that had been lost'.
The coroner disagreed with this interpretation, arguing that processions were
not illegal in law. But Murland responded that common law made them illegal
and if the Orangemen had wished to have a procession, they should have done
so unarmed. After the witnesses had been called, the police asked if anybody
outside the door could give evidence. Only two people offered to do so.
Margaret Traynor, a resident of Magheramayo, stated that the men 'who
walked in the mob with sashes' fired into her house and burnt it. She observed
them kill an old women and shoot her husband in the cheek and then imprison
him. She also saw Pat King being dragged out of his house and stoned to death,

78 *Newry Telegraph* reprinted in *Warder*, 21 July 1849.   79 *Freeman's Journal*, 17 July
1849.

even though 'he begged for mercy'. Her husband, Arthur Traynor, who had been imprisoned, also gave evidence. A bullet had been fired in his cheek but he could not identify who had shot him. Following these witnesses, the evidence closed.[80]

After the evidence had been taken, the magistrates passed two resolutions: firstly, they praised the constabulary for having performed their duty in a 'most efficient manner' which had ensured 'the saving of life and property'; and secondly, as the current constabulary force in the county was insufficient, they recommended twenty-three new constables be appointed.[81] The summing up of the coroner favoured the view that the Ribbonmen had been the aggressors. He informed the jury that the history of the case was that 'A procession of Orangemen, as was usual in that neighbourhood, had assembled in large numbers to celebrate the 12th July.' The Ribbonmen who had been gathering on the hillside 'appeared to have been reconnoitering, or going through forms of exercise as if preparing themselves for combat or battle. He accepted that a squib had been fired, probably by the Ribbonmen, and that 'a return of the fire was at once made by the Orange party'.[82] More significantly, the coroner believed that the assemblage was legal and that in this opinion 'he carried with him the opinions of many of the magistrates who sat on the bench'. He explained this view on the grounds that 'The government did not issue any address, either to the public at large, or to the magistracy, forbidding that these processions should take place, or directing them to be put down. Another matter was this, that the government so far countenanced these processions that they sent an armed force to protect, not only the processionists, but to guard the peace of the country.' He concluded by recommending a verdict of 'justifiable homicide' and asked the jury also to consider 'whether the police were entitled to their thanks for the manner in which they had acted'.[83] The jury reached a verdict quickly; Hugh King had died on the morning of Friday, 13 July, 'from a gunshot wound inflicted on him by some person unknown in a party procession' and Patrick King, John Sweeny and Anne Traynor had died on Thursday, 12 July 'by certain violent injuries inflicted on the aforesaid day by some persons unknown of a party procession passing by said townland on same day'.[84]

Overall, apart from confirming that four people were dead, the inquest had done little to clarify what had happened. The role of the police, military and magistrates remained unclear, as did the number of people present, who provoked it and whether the Catholics had acted in self-defence or were the aggressors. Little mention was made of the role of the earl of Roden during the day. However, the coroner had confirmed that the Orangemen did have a right to march, even though they had been armed, whilst the deaths of the four

80 Ibid., 18 July 1849. **81** *Warder*, 21 July 1849. **82** Report of Inquest in *Freeman's Journal*, 18 July 1849. **83** Ibid. **84** *Times*, 19 July 1849.

villagers, who were clearly non-combatants, were described by the coroner as 'justifiable homicide'.[85]

REACTIONS TO THE INQUEST

The verdict of the inquest exacerbated rather than calmed public feeling. *The Times* warned that following the verdict 'Intense excitement prevails in the neighbourhood of Castlewellan, both factions being extremely exasperated'.[86] The results of the inquest particularly angered many Catholics as no Orangemen had been arrested on the day and none had been impugned following the inquest. A county meeting was convened in Downpatrick for the purpose of adopting measures to repress party demonstrations. There were also rumours that a master of one of the Orange lodges was to be proceeded against at the forthcoming assizes, in order to test the legality or otherwise of party processions.[87] The uncertainty was also kept alive by suggestions that further action was to be taken against the Orangemen, one report in the *Armagh Guardian* at the end of July warning that all who had been present at Dolly's Brae were to be arrested for taking part in an illegal assemblage.[88]

On the days following the inquest Irish newspapers carried extensive reports, which became increasingly polarized on the question of who was to blame. The *Warder* continued to describe what had happened as an 'Atrocious Ribbon Outrage' referring to it as 'a murderous attack by Ribbonmen on an Orange procession near Castlewellan'. The paper reaffirmed that the attack on the procession was premeditated, publishing a copy of a letter that had allegedly been sent by local Repealers to Protestant landlords a few days before the parade. The determination of the Orangemen to march through Dolly's Brae was also blamed on the outrages committed by Ribbonmen on Orangemen earlier in the year. The Orangemen who took part in the parade through Dolly's Brae, especially the Benraw and Laganany lodges, were praised for their 'cool and determined bravery'.[89]

The Catholic denunciation of the inquest's findings was led by the *Freeman's Journal*. On 17 July, it carried an extended editorial on the events at Dolly's Brae which was unequivocal about where the blame lay. It described the incident as 'the clerico-Orange burning and murders perpetrated under the auspices of the magisterial landlords, government officials, and anti-Catholic clergymen of the County of Down'. It accused 'unchristian Orangemen' of provoking Catholics with their 'insulting airs' such as 'Croppies lie down' and 'Kick the Pope'. Nevertheless, the day could have passed peacefully 'had not Mr Beers, relying on the protection of the military and the police, resolved to

85 Ibid.   86 Ibid.   87 Ibid.   88 *Armagh Guardian*, 30 July 1849.   89 *Warder*, 21 July 1849.

glut his petty revenge with a SECOND triumphal passage over Dolly's Hill in the evening'. But even that would not have goaded the Catholics until the Orangemen decided to fire: 'It is clear from all these circumstances that the Orangemen were in every sense the aggressors.' Again, the paper repeated its belief that the procession was 'an illegal assemblage', which meant that the authorities were guilty of a neglect of duty. The government was also censured for not intervening to ban party processions earlier, the paper asking 'But what, oh what, must the government think of themselves now, after declining to renew the anti-procession act, notwithstanding they were implored to do so by many Christian and philanthropic individuals after the tragedy enacted at Crossgar on 17 March last.' The lord lieutenant, however, was accused of sending troops and police to Dolly's Brae in order to protect the Orangemen, so that they would not oppose the collection of the rate in aid. The paper demanded a public enquiry into the role of the magistrates and military who had stood by whilst the battle had taken place.[90]

The editorial in the *Freeman's Journal* on 18 July was dedicated to the results of the inquest, which it described as 'The Farce after the Tragedy'. It accused the 'Orange police, Orange soldiers, Orange magistrates, Orange landlords, Orange clergymen, and Orange Castle officials' of having 'triumphed in the murderous tragedy and laughed over the farcical investigation that followed it'. Orangemen were described as 'those black, slimy serpents who crawl in and out of Orange lodges, teaching unchristian enmity in the name of God'. The objectivity of the inquest was also questioned as Francis Beers, who was grand master of the county and the organizer and leader of the procession, had been allowed to preside 'as an *impartial* magistrate on the occasion', whilst his fellow Orangeman, Captain Skinner - who had led the police charge after the Ribbonmen - was imputed to have shown 'bitter sectarian feeling'. Furthermore, the inquest had been carried out in 'undue haste' and Catholic witnesses had felt too intimidated to attend it.[91]

The debates on Dolly's Brae did not remain confined to Ireland. The event was widely criticized in the British press, with some papers recommending that Roden should be dismissed from the magistracy.[92] It was also discussed in parliament where, despite some support for the Orange Order in general, and Lord Roden in particular, the march through Dolly's Brae was condemned. The magistrates were singled out for particular criticism and accused of being partisan. It was also suggested that armed parades were unlawful. Castlereagh, who in March had asked for political parades to be banned, demanded a government investigation into the incident.[93] Mr Moore, the member for Mayo, criticized the government for allowing the ban on processions to expire in 1845, despite the calls for its continuation. He did not, however, blame the government for what

90 *Freeman's Journal*, 17 July 1849. 91 Ibid., 18 July 1849. 92 *Liverpool Mercury*, 7 Aug. 1849. 93 *Vindicator*, 21 July 1849.

had happened, on the grounds that they 'know little of the hearts, souls and brains of the Orangemen of the north of Ireland' who, despite the fact that the country had undergone three years of famine, regarded the parade as suitable 'for the Moloch of Protestant ascendancy, which had ground down the energies of the people for three centuries'. He blamed the magistrates and gentry, rather than the rank-and-file Orangemen, for the affair, and the police who during the conflict 'were transformed into furious and fiery partisans'. Moore was particularly critical of the fact that the same magistrates who had supported the procession had been put in charge of the subsequent trials of the Ribbonmen. In relation to Roden, he averred 'Weak men like Lord Roden were more dangerous than vicious.'[94] John Bright, the MP for Manchester, criticized the incident on the grounds that it was an illegal gathering that should have been stopped. Although he singled out Roden for criticism, Bright was disparaging of the actions of the constabulary, averring that when the conflict began 'the police regarded the Catholics alone as their enemies and the Orangemen as friends' adding that 'In that sentiment was conveyed the whole history of Ireland'. He supported the call for a government inquiry but insisted that it be 'searching and impartial'.[95] A bitter attack was also made on the actions of the Orange leaders by an Irish MP, Mr Reynolds, who cited two earlier occasions when prominent Orangemen had been deprived of their commissions for acting in an intemperate way. He emphasized the point that as carrying arms was illegal, the Orangemen should have been arrested. However, the criticisms of Lord Roden and the events of 12 July did not have the support of all members, a number of whom viewed the debate as being a partisan attack on Orangeism.

The Irish executive were robust in defending the government's actions. Sir William Sommerville, the chief secretary for Ireland, justified the decision not to ban the processions on the grounds that they hoped 'that the time had arrived when the common sense of all parties would have rendered such a renewal unnecessary' but added 'in this case the government and the country had been disappointed'. Henry Labouchere, a former member of the Irish executive, also denied that the march had been illegal. Nonetheless, they agreed that there should be an official enquiry following which the government would reconsider the issue of banning party processions. It was also resolved that there should be no further discussion of Dolly's Brae until after the enquiry.[96]

Before the enquiry could sit, the earl of Roden publicly defended his actions, prompted by an article in the *Morning Chronicle* accusing him of being responsible for the deaths at Dolly's Brae. On 31 July he addressed the house of lords and apologized for not having done so earlier. Roden maintained that he had endeavoured to do all he could to prevent a collision. He said that people were

94 *Hansard*, 19 July 1849, vol. cvii, pp. 606–10. 95 *Banner of Ulster*, 24 July 1849.
96 *Hansard*, 19 July 1849, vol. cvii, pp 615–16.

happy when the Processions Act expired as they were 'extremely attached to these processions'. Roden also averred that in 1848, when 'the spirit of rebellion was very widely spread through the southern and western portions of the kingdom', the Orangemen had used the 12th of July to show their opposition to repeal. In 1849 the local lodges wanted to show their affection for him and he reluctantly agreed to let them meet on his estate. The meeting was peaceful and although some of the Orangemen carried arms he did not think it was illegal as they had done so the previous year. Roden denied giving the men strong whiskey, only beer. He also denied telling them to return via Dolly's Brae or to use force against the Catholics. However, Roden admitted criticizing recent governments for the way they had treated Irish Protestants. The members of the Lords also agreed not to discuss the matter because of the forthcoming enquiry.[97] The public concern with Dolly's Brae was overshadowed, temporarily, by the impending visit of Queen Victoria to Ireland at the beginning of August – her first visit since her accession to the throne. Despite his public disgrace, Roden was prominent in the public welcomes to Victoria, being part of the reception parties in both Dublin and Belfast and, in the latter place, being granted a private interview with her.[98]

The announcement of a government enquiry caused concern in Ireland, with both factions fearing that it would be partisan. Following deliberation, Walter Berwick QC was appointed, although he was described by the *Times* as being a 'staunch supporter of Whigs and Whiggery'.[99] The enquiry sat for a week in September at Castlewellan National School and evidence was taken from the military, Lord Roden and William and Francis Beers, but no rank and file Orangemen. Roden and his fellow magistrates refused to give information against any of the Orangemen involved. Berwick was critical of the magistrates, averring that they could have 'adopted a line of conduct which would have prevented the outrages then perpetrated, and which the information they possessed ought to have suggested to their minds ... they appear to have acted with a great misunderstanding of the nature of their duties – some of them to such an extent as actually to give countenance and protection to persons engaged in proceeding at variance with the law'. At the same time, he believed that if the magistrates, troops and police had not been present, the loss of life would have been higher. The fact that no Orange members had been arrested he regarded as 'a matter of both surprise and regret'.[100] Moreover, Berwick suggested that no Orangeman ought to be a magistrate as 'the Orange body is an exclusive body, plainly opposed by the Roman Catholic party, and looked upon by them as an enemy'.[101]

Clarendon publicly accepted Berwick's report and recommended to the lord chancellor that William and Francis Beers and the earl of Roden be dismissed

97 Ibid., pp 1129–36. **98** *Banner of Ulster*, 10 Aug., 14 Aug., 17 Aug. 1849. **99** *Times*, 30 July 1849. **100** Haddick-Flynn, *Orangeism*, p. 278. **101** *Times*, 10 Dec. 1849.

as commissioners of the peace. Clarendon took this action reluctantly, admitting privately that in the circumstances 'I could not adopt any other [measure] consistent with my sense of public duty.'[102] A number of the other magistrates present at Dolly's Brae were also reprimanded privately for failing to disperse the Ribbonmen during the day and for allowing the Orange procession to continue.[103] The report convinced Clarendon of the necessity to reintroduce a Party Processions Act which, unlike previous legislation, was to be permanent. Clarendon was optimistic that his actions would be beneficial, predicting, incorrectly, that one of the consequences of Dolly's Brae would be 'the extinction of Orangeism'.[104] In the wake of Dolly's Brae the attitude of the British government to the Orange Order became more ambivalent. The attempt to distance themselves from Orangeism was demonstrated in 1850 when the government refused to accept an address by the grand lodge.[105] Clarendon's actions had not been sweeping enough to satisfy Catholics, whilst supporters of Orangeism viewed his response as a further example of government attacks on Protestants. Although no Orangemen were convicted following the enquiry, they felt that the report had unfairly damaged them. Both Clarendon and Berwick were accused of hostility to Orangeism, whereas Roden and the Beers brothers received many letters of support, with one address from Co. Down containing 8,000 signatures.[106] The reaction in Ulster led Clarendon to inform the home secretary that 'The North is in a state of rabies because Roden's dismissal is a token that Law and Order are not to be trampled on with impunity.'[107]

The defence of Lord Roden by the Irish gentry and his fellow Orangemen was spirited. Most of the anger was directed at Clarendon, who was felt to have slighted all Protestants by his actions. On 30 October, the Ulster Protestant Association drew up an address to Roden in which the actions of the Irish executive were described as 'an almost unparalleled act of injustice, arbitrary power and ingratitude'. These actions were described as being part of the policy adopted by successive governments to make 'infatuated concessions and encouragements to popery'. Roden responded to the address by alluding to the dangers which threatened Protestantism.[108] On 1 November, a meeting of Irish gentry convened by Viscount Lorton took place in Dublin to protest about Roden's dismissal from the magistracy. Lorton claimed to have received only one letter of dissent, from Lord Massereene.[109] The meeting was attended by many large landowners and MPs, including the earl of Enniskillen, the earl of Mayo and George Hamilton, the Orange MP for Dublin University. The earl

102 Clarendon to Grey, PROL, HO 45 os 2603, 13 Oct. 1849.   103 Redington, Dublin Castle, to Joseph Tabiteau and George Fitzmaurice, PROL. H045 os 2603, 6 Oct. 1849. 104 Ibid., Clarendon to G. Lewis, 28 Apr. 1850.   105 Haddick-Flynn, *Orangeism*, p. 280 106 *Down Recorder*, 1 Dec. 1849.   107 Clarendon to Grey, Clarendon Letterbook, 19 Oct. 1849.   108 From *Belfast Chronicle* reprinted in *Times*, 17 Nov. 1849.   109 *Times*, 17 Nov. 1849.

of Enniskillen asserted the purpose of the gathering was to show 'our confidence in the honour, impartiality and justice of the earl of Roden' who had a 'long, consistent and patriotic life of usefulness' which 'had not been impaired by the stigma cast on him by government'. A committee was formed, which passed a number of resolutions, all of which were couched in strong language. The Earl of Mayo viewed Roden's removal with 'alarm and dissatisfaction' and warned about its implications for the independence of the magistracy. Lord Downes stated that 'considering the high position which Lord Roden has occupied for so many years as one of the most distinguished among the Protestants of Ireland' the attempt to degrade him was 'a design of reverting again to the fatal policy of setting party against party in this country, with a view to political objects' at a time when they should be seeking cooperation. In addition to praising Roden, some of those present also offered opinions on the events of 12 July. Lord Castlemaine and Mr McClintock, MP for Banbury, averred that the Ribbonmen were the aggressors at Dolly's Brae, although they did not support the continuation of party processions. Lord Dunsany and Joseph Napier MP also blamed the Ribbonmen for planning the conflict and suggested that the evidence and proceedings at the recent enquiry had been 'defective and misdirected'. To show their disapprobation of the government in the affair, an address was sent to the lord lieutenant and a petition to be signed by Roden's fellow magistrates to the houses of commons and lords requesting an enquiry into the reasons for Roden's dismissal.[110] The committee met a few days later in order to 'pronounce on the act of tyranny perpetuated by the government on Lord Roden and Messrs Beers and to petition the Queen to recall Lord Clarendon'. The meeting opined that by acting in such a way, Clarendon was threatening the British empire.[111] These actions were supported by William Ormsby-Gore, MP for Shropshire, on the grounds that Clarendon was putting the country in peril by sacking some of the magistracy. Moreover, he believed, the British government had once again proved themselves willing 'to pander to the encroaching passions of an inveterate party', whilst treating those who supported the British connection unjustly.[112]

The anger felt against Clarendon by the Orange Order was intensified by the fact that they believed that they had supported him during the uprising of the previous year. Clarendon's denial of this collaboration further angered Orangemen and resulted in the grand Orange lodge convening a meeting in Dublin in November to make their position public.[113] The earl of Enniskillen, who was the grand master for Ireland, presided and he promised a full and frank disclosure of Clarendon's actions. The Protestant press in Dublin saw the

110 The committee consisted of Lord Lorton, Lord Enniskillen, Lord Mayo, Lord Dunsany, Lord Castlemaine, Lord Downes, Colonel Bruen, Mr Napier, Mr Woods, Mr Barlow, Mr Nugent, Mr G.A. Hamilton, Mr McClintock jr. *Times*, 2 Nov. 1849. 111 *Times*, 8 Nov. 1849. 112 Ibid., 17 Nov. 1849. 113 Ibid., 10 Nov. 1849.

disagreement as a contest between the government and the Orangeman, and urged Enniskillen to tell the truth in justice to the 'poor, deceived procession-ists of Dolly's Brae'.[114] Lodges from all over the country attended and appointed a select committee to draw up details of negotiations made in the previous year with the government and to send messages of support to Roden and Beers.[115] The *Evening Mail* supported the committee on the grounds that Clarendon had made 'scandalous libel on the character of the Earl of Roden'.[116] Yet, despite much discussion about impending revelations, none ever appeared.[117] The *Freeman's Journal* believed that the Orange leaders had duped their followers yet again.[118] *The Times*, however, suggested that Clarendon had reached an understanding with the Orange Order in order to guarantee their silence.[119] The report of the grand Orange lodge, when it finally appeared in December, made little reference to 1848. Instead, it censured the government for making concessions to Catholics which had served 'to betray and crush Protestantism', yet relying on Protestants when they felt menaced. The Berwick Report was also condemned and Berwick was accused of misrepre-senting both the 'Riband conspiracy' and the nature of the Orange Order, 'the one a foul confederacy for the dismemberment of the empire and the extermi-nation of Protestants from Ireland; the other, a strictly defensive association, entered into by loyal men for mutual support and defence'. Unsurprisingly, the enquiry was described as 'eminently unconstitutional' and Berwick was per-sonally characterized as an 'incarnation of evil'.[120]

Whilst this public debate continued, tension between Catholics and Protestants was evident in a number of localities, especially in counties Down and Armagh. In Belfast, there were weekly skirmishes in the centre of the town between the local Ribbonmen and Orangemen, a number of which were violent.[121] There was also a rumour that to celebrate the defeat of the Gunpowder Plot on 5 November, Orangemen were going to parade in various locations in Ulster, including Dolly's Brae. In turn, Ribbonmen from as far away as Co. Louth were reported to be amassing at Dolly's Brae in expectation of a conflict. The government responded to this information by sending rein-forcements of military and constabulary to the village and to other areas regarded as danger spots.[122] The fact that no Orange processions took place was attributed by Protestants to Roden's personal intervention.[123]

The resentment of the Orangemen towards the government continued for months, renewed by their anger at the introduction of the Party Processions Act in February 1850. Unlike previous legislation, this ban on party proces-sions was intended to be permanent. The act proclaimed that:

114 Ibid., 21 Nov. 1849.   115 Ibid., 24 Nov. 1849.   116 Ibid., 26 Nov. 1849.   117 Ibid., 27 Nov. 1849.   118 Ibid., 28 Nov. 1849.   119 Ibid., 1 Dec. 1849.   120 Ibid., 10 Dec. 1849.   121 *Banner of Ulster*, 14 Sept. 1849.   122 *Times*, 2 Nov. 1849.   123 Ibid., 8 Nov. 1849, 10 Nov. 1849.

> From and after the passing of this act all assemblies of persons in proces-
> sion, and who shall bear, wear, or have amongst them any fire-arms or
> other offensive weapons, or any Banner, Emblem, Flag or Symbol, the
> display whereof may be calculated or tend to provoke animosity between
> different classes of Her Majesty's subjects, shall be unlawful assemblies,
> and every person present there shall be guilty of Misdemeanour, and
> upon conviction thereof shall be published accordingly.[124]

To show disapproval of the act, a number of lodges in counties Armagh and
Tyrone destroyed their banners and emblems, which had a been a 'token of
their attachment to the British constitution', as a protest against the government's treatment of the Orangemen.[125] Support for those associated with
Dolly's Brae continued to be expressed in a variety of ways. In April 1850, the
Orange lodges in Dublin organized a soiree to honour Francis and William
Beers and 'mark the esteem in which the noble conduct of these distinguished
gentlemen was regarded with reference to the events of 12 July last'.[126] In the
same month, the Poor Law guardians in Kilkeel, Co. Down, elected Roden as
chairman of the board, a position he had lost when he had been dismissed from
the judiciary.[127] Regardless of the animosity towards the government, the 12
July 1850 was peaceful, with only one incident between the police and
Orangemen in Belfast. Although there were no marches, the day was observed
as a holiday in the north of Ireland by Protestants.[128] In 1860, following a sectarian clash near Lurgan, the Party Emblems Act was passed, which reinforced
the earlier legislation. It forbade the display of party banners, emblems or flags,
the playing of party tunes and the discharging of firearms for ceremonial
purposes.[129]

CONCLUSION

Although the involvement of the gentry in Orangeism declined after 1849, the
Orange Order did not disappear and it proved ready to respond to the challenge
of Home Rule after 1870. Moreover, despite the ban in 1850 some parades continued on 12 July and the day often ended in conflict, notably in 1857, 1864 and
1867. In 1864, the earl of Enniskillen and William Beers, who had been dismissed in 1849, made speeches during the Boyne commemorations saying that
'nothing can induce the Orangemen of Ulster to give up their demonstrations
in memory of the battle of the Boyne'. Marches took place in a number of locations in Ulster and extra troops and constabulary were drafted to the largest

---

124 *An Act to Restrain Party Processions in Ireland*, 10 Victoria Cap 11, 12 Mar. 1850.
125 *Times*, 15 Apr. 1850, 22 Apr. 1850.   126 Ibid., 6 Apr. 1850   127 Ibid., 8 Apr. 1850.
128 *Armagh Guardian*, 15 July 1850.   129 Haddick-Flynn, *Orangeism*, p. 281.

ones. Yet, despite the illegality of the parades, they were usually allowed by the authorities to take place.[130] The repeal of the Party Procession Act in 1872 was largely due to the activities of William Johnson, the MP for South Belfast, who had deliberately flouted it for a number of years.[131] It also demonstrated the fact that the majority of the British government were sympathetic to the revival of Orange marches. The repeal of the act, however, was followed by anti-Catholic riots in parts of Ulster, notably Belfast.[132]

Following Dolly's Brae, Roden had little public involvement with the Orange Order, although he continued his evangelical work, taking part in a proselytizing tour of Connemara in 1851, rewarding those who sang 'God save the Queen' with soup and bread.[133] He was also involved in the religious revival in 1859. Roden died in 1870, two years before the repeal of the Party Processions Act; the repeal being largely due to the actions of another Orange hero, William Johnston. Nevertheless, Roden's role in Dolly's Brae and his place in Orange history was guaranteed as he continued to be commemorated in songs, banners and on Orange memorabilia. Ironically, Roden's public disgrace had made him the hero of Dolly's Brae, despite the fact that he had not been present at the scene of the conflict.

Clearly, the conflict at Dolly's Brae was a microcosm of wider tensions within Irish society and between Ireland and Britain. For many Protestants the battle at Dolly's Brae represented a larger ideological battle for the survival of a way of life which they believed to be under attack, not just from Catholics, but from successive British governments. The *Warder*, one of the most outspoken of the Protestant press, regarded the Protestants of Ireland as being involved in a crusade, not only to defend their position, but also to preserve the United Kingdom and, ultimately, the British Empire from what they saw as the 'Papal project and Roman led Jew plot' to destroy it.[134] Regardless of the Young Irelanders appeal to non-sectarianism in the 1848 uprising, even moderate Protestants had been alarmed by the revolutionary invective and armed insurrection of the previous year, offering their services to the government as a counter-insurrectionary force.[135] The events of 1848 had reminded them of their vulnerability as a minority within the country and the Orange Order had provided a forum to display their unity and opposition.

Despite the public opprobrium that had resulted, Dolly's Brae became a watchword for ordinary Orangemen. It was allegedly shouted, together with 'No Surrender', at the Battle of the Somme and other First World War battles.[136] In Orange folk history also, Dolly's Brae was added to the battles at Derry, the Boyne, Aughrim, and the Diamond, each of which they believed was

130 *Times*, 14 July 1864. 131 Ibid., 12 July 1883. 132 Ibid., 30 Sept. 1872. 133 Haddick-Flynn, *Orangeism*, p.260. 134 *Warder*, 6 Jan. 1849. 135 George Grey, Whitehall to LL, ACR, HO45 OS 2416A, 5 Aug. 1848. 136 Quoted in Dudley Edwards, *Faithful tribe*, p. 248.

fought in defence of Protestantism.[137] The incorporation of the event into a number of songs also ensured it retained a central place in folk memory:

> So now my song I mean to end, my pen I will throw down
> I say success to every man who supports the British Crown,
> And generation yet unborn shall sing this loyal lay,
> And speak of those that beat their foes at famous Dolly's Brae.

137 Dominic Bryan, *Orange parades. The politics of ritual, tradition and control* (London, 2000) p. 107.

Identities in transition: Irish migrant outlooks in mid-Victorian Manchester

MERVYN BUSTEED

Like all national identities, the concept of an Irish nation is a relatively recent, resilient and flexible social construction,[1] and is capable of renewal and re-invention in response to changing social, economic and political circumstances. As with many European counterparts, there are traces of an Irish 'proto-nationalism' in early modern times, but the key period for the formulation of modern nationalism was the nineteenth century.[2] During this process of evolu-tion and construction, some aspects of the Irish historical and contemporary experience were selected for emphasis and embellishment whilst others were elided or re-interpreted in a fashion which suited the nationalist project.[3] The result is that during this formative period one can discern shifts in attitudes towards elements in the Irish experience and changes in the manner in which they were expressed. In this chapter it is proposed to discuss some features of this transition using one medium of expression popular amongst Irish migrants.

One of the distinctive features of the development of Irish nationalism is the role of the diaspora. By the mid-nineteenth century there were large Irish born and Irish-descended populations in the USA, and in Great Britain, Canada, Australia and other parts of the British empire, as well as some parts of South America.[4] As time passed they played an increasingly important role in the political campaigns for Irish Home Rule, land reform and independence. However, relatively little work has focused on the sense of identity within nine-teenth-century Irish migrant communities themselves, caught as they were between memories of and aspirations for Ireland and the need to make their way in the countries where they had settled.

The purpose of this chapter is to discuss some aspects of the shifting nature of identity among Irish migrants in Manchester during the 1850s and 1860s, using a selection of the Irish street ballads which were printed and circulated in the city during that time.

1 Peter Jackson & Susan Smith, 'Introduction: Placing "race" and nation' in P. Jackson & S. Smith (eds), *Constructions of race, place and nation* (London, 1993), pp 1–26. 2 George Boyce, *Nationalism in Ireland* (London, 1995). 3 Thomas E. Hachey & Lawrence McCaffrey (eds), *Perspectives on Irish nationalism* (Lexington, 1989). 4 Andy Bielenberg (ed.), *The Irish diaspora* (London, 2000)

Street ballads were originally an English medium of popular entertainment, which was diffused into Ireland and was carried back to Britain by Irish migrants. Their significance for study purposes lies in the fact that they both reflected and influenced popular sentiment. They provide an insight into popular as opposed to official sentiment and cultural preoccupations[5] because 'the writers, printers and publishers of the trade were socially fairly close to their popular audience, and extraordinarily sensitive to its tastes and expectations.'[6] It has also been argued that they not merely reflected history: 'but also seek to affect it …'[7] Henry Mayhew, one of the few contemporary observers to attempt an analysis of the ballad trade as opposed to merely sentimentalising over its demise, quoted with approval the opinion of an anonymous acquaintance that 'in them the character of the nation displays itself in striking colours'.[8]

To a considerable extent Irish street ballads are derivative of English (and Scottish) ballads, but there are some quite significant differences because of the Irish historical and cultural context. There are indications that they were being imported into Ireland as early as 1593,[9] and the earliest extant Irish ballad dates from 1626.[10] They were a flourishing branch of the printing trade in eighteenth-century Dublin and by the early nineteenth century were also being produced in the smaller towns.[11] As with English compositions, authorship[12] and dating[13] are problematic, and they were sold and often sung in the streets wherever large crowds of people gathered, though the pub seems to have been a

5 Roy Palmer, *The sound of history: songs and social comment* (London, 1996).   6 Patrick Joyce, *Visions of the people: industrial England and the question of class, 1848–1914* (Cambridge, 1991), pp 231–2.   7 Palmer, *The sound of history*, p. 29.   8 Henry Mayhew, *London labour and the London poor*, vol. 1: *The street folk* (1851; reprinted London, 1967), p. 275.   9 Fintan Vallely (ed.), *The companion to Irish traditional music* (Cork, 1999), p. 44.   10 Hugh Shields, 'Ballad', in Vallely, *Companion to Irish traditional music*, p. 19.   11 Niall Ó Ciosáin, *Print and popular culture in Ireland, 1750–1850* (London, 1997), p.57; Georges-Denis Zimmermann, *Songs of Irish rebellion: political street ballads and rebel songs, 1780–1900* (Dublin: Allen Figgis, 1967; reprinted Dublin, 2002), p. 21. Ballads were printed on poor quality sheets of A5 size paper; if printed on one side only they were 'broadside ballads', if on both sides 'broadsheet ballads'. If several ballads were printed on a long sheet they were 'slip ballads' or 'garlands'. A 'chapbook' consisted of a small number of ballads bound into a booklet. Standard works on British street ballads are Leslie Shepard, *The broadside ballad : a study in origins and meaning: the development of the street ballad from traditional songs to popular newspaper* (London, 1966); *The history of street literature* (Newton Abbot, 1973); Claude Simpson, *The British broadside ballad and its music* (New Brunswick, NJ, 1966).   12 James N. Healy (ed.), *The Mercier book of old Irish street ballads*, vol. 1 (Cork, 1967), p. 8.   13 Zimmermann, *Songs*, p. 117; for a more lengthy discussion of origins, authorship, dating and subject matter of street ballads in Great Britain, see Mervyn Busteed, 'Little Islands of Erin: Irish settlement and identity in mid-nineteenth century Manchester', in *Immigrants and Minorities*, 18, 2 & 3 (1999), pp 96–8.

more significant venue in Ireland. The itinerant pedlar, sometimes travelling over quite wide areas,[14] appears as a particularly important vendor.[15] As in Great Britain, music rarely accompanied the ballads and for the majority its provenance is obscure.[16]

There is evidence that as the street ballad form settled down it took on some distinctively Irish features. Given its origins and the fact that it diffused into Ireland via the trading towns of the eastern coast, it is hardly surprising that the great majority are in the English language,[17] often preserving language forms obsolete in England itself.[18] Compositions in Irish were rare.[19] Established Gaelic scholars looked on the new medium with contempt,[20] resented the competition and looked on the printed word as cold and lifeless.[21] In any case there was already a strong tradition of public singing of the traditional heroic lays in Irish.[22] Of the few Irish language compositions which are known, most are from Munster and their subject matter is overwhelmingly political.[23] However, a significant number of the English language ballads composed in Ireland have a word ordering, grammatical structure, internal metre and an extravagance in use of language and idiom strongly reminiscent of Irish Gaelic forms.[24] It seems likely that composers, especially those who were bilingual, were unconsciously reflecting their personal linguistic backgrounds or English as it was currently spoken in Ireland.[25] In some cases English ballads include Irish phrases or words rendered phonetically or as simple Gaelic tags.[26] As in Great Britain, indications of tune or music were rare, but with the passage of time traditional Irish airs were increasingly utilised, with many local variations and the result was that, as with much else in these ballads: 'The repertoire of street ballad melodies in Ireland may therefore be described as mixed in origin, but with strong native elements.'[27]

The subject matter of Irish street ballads closely resembled the sensationalist, topical almost tabloid preoccupations found in Great Britain,[28] but with the significant difference that there is a much greater concern with political affairs –

14 Maura Murphy, 'The ballad singer and the role of the seditious ballad in nineteenth-century Ireland: Dublin Castle's view,' in *Ulster Folklife*, 25 (1979), 90–1. 15 Ó Ciosain, *Print and popular culture*, pp 59–67. 16 Harry White, 'Ballads', in Sean Connolly (ed.), *The Oxford companion to Irish history* (Oxford, 1998), p. 34. 17 Vallely, *The companion to Irish traditional music*, pp 111–12. Irish narrative songs in English are often referred to as 'Come-All-Yes' from the traditional invocation in the opening line. See Hugh Shields, *Narrative singing in Ireland: lays, ballads, come-all-yes and other songs* (Dublin, 1993), p. 85. 18 Zimmermann, *Songs*, p. 100. 19 Shields, *Narrative singing*, pp 110–11. 20 Ibid., p. 43 21 Vallely, *The companion to Irish traditional music*, p. 44. 22 Shields, *Narrative singing*, p. 4. 23 Murphy, *The ballad singer*, p. 95. 24 Shields, *Narrative singing*, pp 88–9. 25 Zimmermann, *Songs*, pp 20, 100 & 105. 26 Mervyn Busteed, 'Songs in a strange land – ambiguities of identity amongst Irish migrants in mid-Victorian Manchester' in *Political Geography*, 17, no. 6, (1998), 656. 27 Zimmermann, *Songs*, pp 20, 100, 105. 28 James N. Healy, *The second book of Irish ballads*, (Cork, 1964), foreword; Colm O'Lochlainn, *Irish street ballads* (Dublin, 1939), p. vii.

Zimmermann's by no means exhaustive survey found that between 20 and 40 per cent of the collections he inspected dealt with politics.[29] Moreover, it has been argued that Irish street ballads are not merely 'a running commentary on Irish political life ...'[30] but an active agent in their own right: 'The popular ballad was both cause and effect of much political and social unrest among the populace, and whether contemporaries approved or disapproved of its influence, all were agreed on its power.'[31] The predominant stance of the composers was nationalist, though there are collections of loyalist and Orange songs.[32] The focus of their attention was the fate of Ireland and the Irish as determined by the Anglo-Irish relationship through the ages and every significant socio-economic, cultural, ecclesiastical and political development which affected the Irish in the nineteenth century was commented upon. The appeal of the ballads was as wide as in Great Britain, but they went down particularly well with the peasantry and the urban lower classes amongst whom they helped to 'confirm national identity in an age before popular newspapers'.[33] However, as in Britain, their performance was a contested issue, with shopkeepers frequently protesting and police anxious about the impact of ballad sellers and singers on the flow of life in the streets.[34] But both national and local authorities were more nervous about the threat of subversion[35] and at times of particularly acute political tension – as during the 'Fenian threat' of the late 1860s and the 'Land War' of the early 1880s – ballad sellers were frequently arrested and their stock confiscated.[36]

Given the sensitivity of the authorities, it is hardly surprising that Irish street ballads on political issues frequently resorted to devices which could easily be penetrated by knowing Irish listeners but would help obscure their meaning in official ears.[37] Consequently, there was frequent use of irony,[38]

29 Zimmermann, *Songs*, pp 111–12.   **30** White, *Ballads*, p. 34.   **31** Murphy, *The ballad singer*, p. 84.   **32** There has been relatively little serious examination of loyalist and Orange ballads; Murphy, *The ballad singer*, pp 94 & 98–9 and Zimmermann, *Songs*, p. 45 mention them and the former discusses the role of 'party' songs at sensitive times and places. Ruth Dudley Edwards, *The faithful tribe: an intimate portrait of the loyal institutions* (London, 2000) quotes liberally from historic and contemporary songs but does not attempt analysis. **33** Murphy, *The ballad singer*, p. 93. Street ballads were a contested medium within Irish nationalism itself. In the 1840s several of the Young Irelanders, repelled by the semi-mystical, frequently maudlin, sectarian and burlesque nature of traditional ballads, determined to replace them with compositions presenting the cause of Ireland in the much more assertive and heroic terms of abstract, secular concepts such as liberty, justice and self-determination. Their compositions were published in the *Nation* newspaper and subsequently in various collected editions as *The spirit of the Nation*. These were immensely popular, but so too were the traditional ballads and both continued to circulate throughout the nineteenth century. See David Lloyd, *Anomalous states: Irish writing and the post-colonial movement* (Dublin, 1993), p. 96. O'Lochlainn, p. x implies that a similar tension emerged in the late nineteenth century when he argues that ballads of 'the rollicking type' were driven out by 'the advent of the Gaelic League and a more virile nationality'.   **34** Murphy, *The ballad singer*, pp 93–4. **35** Lloyd, *Anomalous states*, p. 96. **36** Shields, *Narrative singing*, p. 139. **37** Zimmermann, *Songs*, pp 52–3.   **38** Shields, *Narrative singing*, p. 90.

humour,[39] satire,[40] and double entendre.[41] There was also a fondness for outlaw figures such as highwaymen, because of their defiance of legitimate authority.[42] There was frequent use of biblical references and analogies[43] and a liking for messianic, millenarian, apocalyptic thought forms, notably the Pastorini prophecies and the prophecy of St Columbkille which circulated widely in the early 1820s.[44] There were also frequent references to Ireland's hopes of external assistance, either from divine sources or somewhere 'over the sea'.[45]

It has been claimed that Irish nationalism is particularly rich in symbolism in which the nation, its woes and hopes are presented in quasi-mystical, allegorical form.[46] One of the most common of these devices was a derivative of the aisling, or vision poem, a Gaelic motif in which the narrator/singer falls asleep and encounters a female form, either 'Granuaile', the 'Shan Van Vocht',[47] 'Roisin Dubh',[48] or, most often, a beautiful unnamed maiden.[49] In whatever form she appeared, the dream figure lamented the historic woes and contemporary state of Ireland, exhorted Irish menfolk to avenge them and encouraged them to do so with assurances of divine or foreign aid and eventual victory. Other motifs allegorical for Ireland were a rose,[50] birds – especially the blackbird[51] – and a horse.[52] Whilst the aisling was a Gaelic trope, it was carried over into English language ballads, though in degenerate form.[53] Ironically, Irish street ballads, which owed so much to the English originals, were to be carried back to Britain by Irish migrants,[54] and indeed to North America.[55]

THE IRISH AND STREET BALLADS IN MANCHESTER

There are firm indications of a resident Irish population in Manchester as early as 1745 and by 1861 there were just over 52,000 Irish born residents, 15.4 per cent of the total population.[56] Thereafter numbers declined. Whilst the Irish

39 Healy, *The Mercier book*, vol. I, p. 8.   40 Zimmermann, *Songs*, p. 49.   41 Ibid., p.52. 42 Ibid., p. 25.   43 Ibid., pp 33–4.   44 Ó Ciosain, *Print and popular culture*, pp 192–7. 45 Zimmermann, *Songs*, pp 31–3.   46 Ibid., pp 52–3.   47 Ibid., pp 55–6. 'Granuaile' and its variant spellings was Grace O'Malley, a redoubtable pirate chieftain active off the northwest coast of Ireland in the latter half of the sixteenth century. In folklore she came to personify a resourceful, daring Ireland. The 'Shan Van Vocht' ('poor old woman') represented suffering Ireland.   48 Shields, *Narrative singing*, p. 8; literally 'dark haired rose'. 49 Zimmermann, *Songs*, pp 88–90.   50 Ibid., p. 85.   51 Shields, *Narrative singing*, p. 8. 52 Zimmermann, *Songs*, p. 57.   53 Ibid., p.54. Some of these devices may have been widely appreciated popular conventions rather than subterfuges. It also seems likely that at least some Irish policemen would have been quite capable of penetrating such disguises, though they would doubtless have provided ample scope for obfuscation in magistrates' courts - which may have been the intention.   54 Frank Howes, *Folk music in Britain – and beyond* (London, 1969), pp 95, 242.   55 Shields, *Narrative singing*, p. 84.   56 Mervyn Busteed, 'The Irish in nineteenth century Manchester', in *Irish Studies Review*, 18 (Spring 1997), 8–13.

were quite widely scattered throughout the urban fabric, a combination of culture shock, hostile socio-economic and political environment and limited economic resources meant there was a tendency for residential clusters to develop in some of the poorer parts of the city. The most notable were in 'Little Ireland'[57] and Hulme on the southwestern fringes, and in Irish Town, Angel Meadow[58] and Ancoats[59] on the northern side. It was in these northern districts that the six most prolific ballad-publishing firms were to be found during the nineteenth century.[60] Of these the two most notable were located in Ancoats. Bebington, in Goulden Street, were taken over in the early 1860s by Pearson, in nearby Chadderton Street, who bought out and constantly recycled their ballad stock. Pearsons continued in business until the early 1870s; in 1872 they were offering over 2,000 ballads for sale.[61]

Street ballads are ephemera in several senses. They were opportunistic publications, rapid responses to shifting public tastes, moods and events, hurriedly produced on poor quality A5 paper, occasionally embellished with rarely relevant woodcuts and with frequent printing errors. Their survival is due to pure chance or the whims of collectors. In Manchester there are two collections containing a significant Irish element. The Axon collection, compiled in the late nineteenth century and deposited in Chetham's Library in 1963 numbers 280, of which 53 (19 per cent) deal with Irish matters.[62] The collection in the Language and Literature section of the city's Central Library, sometimes referred to as the Pearson collection, contains 12 volumes totalling 3,080 ballads of which 461 (15 per cent) are Irish.[63] The fact that Irish ballads, imbued with Irish nationalist sentiment and couched in traditional Irish ballad terms were printed in such numbers in Manchester suggests that they resonated strongly with the Irish migrant population and that 'in Irish districts Irish songs were in demand'.[64] Clearly therefore an analysis of these ballads will give some insight

57 Mervyn Busteed, '"The most horrible spot"? – the legend of Manchester's Little Ireland', in *Irish Studies Review*, 13 (Winter, 1995–6), 12–20. **58** Mervyn Busteed & Rob Hodgson, 'Irish migrant responses to urban life in mid-nineteenth century Manchester', *Geographical Journal*, 16, no. 2, (1996), 139–53. **59** Mervyn Busteed, 'Little islands of Erin', pp 110–16. **60** Walter Tomlinson, 'A bunch of street ballads', *Papers of the Manchester Literary Club*, 12 (1886), p. 305. **61** Harold Boardman & Roy Palmer, *Manchester ballads: thirty-five facsimile street ballads* (Manchester, 1983), introduction. **62** The great majority of the collection was printed by Pearsons of Chadderton Street in the Ancoats district. Accompanying it is a note which puts the date of printing as around 1870 or earlier and includes the remark: 'There is a considerable proportion of songs which would appeal to the Irish who lived in that part of Manchester.' I would like to thank Chetham's Librarian, Dr Michael Powell, for drawing my attention to this collection. **63** There is a further volume on microfilm, another in the Library strong room and two dating from the late sixteenth and early seventeenth centuries printed in Gothic type and known as 'black letter ballads'. None of these has been used in this study. **64** Joyce, *Visions of the people*, p. 232.

into the outlooks and opinions of Manchester's Irish migrants in the mid-Victorian period.

IDENTITIES IN TRANSITION

Given that there are over 500 Irish ballads available, it is hardly surprising that a vast range of sentiments and issues is present. One of the striking features is the range of opinions even on a single issue. Here it will be argued that analysis of a selection of ballads on Irish political concerns suggests the fitful emergence of a more focused, confident and assertive sense of Irishness within this migrant community, retaining some traditional features, but modified by the migrant experience. These developments are best brought out within three counterpoised categories.

From aisling to issues

Amongst the Manchester ballads are some in which aspects of the aisling tradition are present. In these the narrator takes an evening walk, sits down by running water and falls asleep. In each case a female appears:

> Silently and sincerely to me did appear
> A tall female form she struck me with fear[65]

The figure is variously described as young and beautiful:

> Her cheeks were like two blooming roses
> Her skin was like ivory white[66]

or she was:

> A virtuous queen that was grave and old[67]

In either case, her clothing made clear her identity:

> She was drest in the richest attire,
> And green was the mantle she wore,
> 'Twas trim'd with the rose and shamrock,
> That blooms upon Erin's green shore[68]

65 *St Patrick's Day*, ballad collection, Language and Literature Department, Manchester Central Library, pressmark Q 398.8.S9, vol.1; henceforth only title and pressmark will be given. 66 *Erin's Green Shore*, Q 398.8.S9, vol.2. 67 *The Rights of Man*, Q 821.04.B2, vol. 2. 68 *Erin's Green Shore*.

The role of the woman was to lament the state of Ireland and to warn its people:

> This fertile country near seven centuries
> Since Strongbow's entry upon our land
> Has been kept under with woes unnumbered
> And always plundered of the rights of man[69]

But there was also encouragement:

> When you do true wisdom possess
> No enemy will come to your door
> For the joys of real freedom shall beam
> On the poor upon Erin's green shore[70]

Occasionally another figure would appear with a message of comfort for the troubled faithful. Like the female figure, he was never explicitly identified, but to those with the least knowledge of Irish legend, this was not necessary:

> His dazzling mitre and cross was brighter,
> Than stars by night or the noonday sun ...
> For their inspection and clear direction
> And grand direction the three leafed plant
> He elevated and consecrated ...[71]

The narrator awoke refreshed and renewed in his nationalistic faith:

> May the sunbeams of freedom illumine
> The natives of Erin's green shore[72]

Such ballads are deeply rooted within venerable Irish popular conventions. They are a mix of history, legend, popular superstition, folk religion, Catholicism, traditional grievances and vague hopes. At one level they simply do not cohere, but this of course is the essence of a dream, and it may help explain why the dream motif survived so long. But at another level it was also an appropriate way of expressing the fact that in Irish history there are some periods of severe disruption and discontinuity, most notably in the sixteenth and seventeenth centuries with the final defeat of the old Gaelic order and its large scale replacement in some areas with a population very different in its historical, religious and cultural traditions. Moreover, for a migrant population who saw themselves as compelled to leave their native land and cope with a very

69 *The Rights of Man.* **70** *Erin's Green Shore.* **71** *The Rights of Man.* **72** *Erin's Green Shore.*

different environment the conglomerate of ideas and pictures may have been both an apt reflection of their mixed and confused emotions and a form of escapism.

But there are also ballads which have a much clearer, sharper focus and engage closely with contemporary affairs and power structures. In some cases these are an intriguing mix of the traditional and contemporary. *Duffy's Advice to His Country* reaches as far back as the twelfth-century high king Rory O'Connor to conjure up an Ireland that was free, united and unplagued by sects, tithe proctors and conquest. Current Irish conditions are blamed on disunity fomented by England. Thus far the analysis is perfectly traditional in content, style, terminology and historical references, but there is a strikingly novel element in the opening verse which specifically addresses Irish migrants living in Britain and, though couched in well worn terms, appeals to them as a possible source of assistance.

> You sons of Granua that wanders through Britannia,
> Despised and exil'd from your dear country ...
> Arise from your slumbers no longer be in bondage,
> From the chains of oppression, tyranny and woe.[73]

Even more sharply focused are the ballads which deal with specific issues. An historic grievance amongst Irish Catholics - and Protestant nonconformists - was the subordinate position of their church in relation to the established Church of Ireland. By the mid-nineteenth century almost all discriminatory legislation had been repealed and tithes were no longer a separate levy, but the anomaly of a state church supported by only 12 per cent of the population persisted until disestablished by Gladstone's Liberal administration in 1869. One ballad specifically addresses the issue. Whilst invoking some historic grievances from the sixteenth century, it couches its demands for redress in the name of the abstract concept of justice and displays a knowledge of the British party politics and personalities involved:

> The Church, and State, and Queen, my boys,
> Are all well in their way:
> But down the Irish Church must come,
> If England means fair play ...
> The men of whom we all should boast
> The Glory of the land –
> Are Gladstone, Bright and many more,
> Who all for Justice stand[74]

73 *Duffy's Advice to His Country*, Q 398.8.S9, vol. 2.   74 *The Men of Sixty-Nine*. This is one of the very few Irish street ballads to carry an indication of music – the tune was 'Auld

In the following year Isaac Butt founded the Home Government Association with the aim of achieving federal home rule for Ireland. Subsequently it evolved into the Home Rule League led by Charles Stewart Parnell. Butt was celebrated in a ballad which asserted the right of self-government within the British state, invoked American and French support and established continuity with the great hero Daniel O'Connell:

> England has no right to rule,
> Or govern Erin's shore,
> Let Irishmen make Irish laws,
> And they'll ask for nothing more ...
> Long life to Butt, he's worthy of,
> All Irishmen's applause,
> Like noble Dan, that is dead and gone,
> His heart lies in our cause.[75]

In many ways this is a remarkably concise statement of the modest political programme of Irish nationalism as it then stood. It is couched in terms of modern concepts of abstract rights, diplomatic pressures from abroad and its chief spokesperson endowed with historical legitimacy by linking him with O'Connell, an important point since Butt was an Anglican. This is a notable contrast with the terminology and content of the aisling tradition. Here there is a strong sense of informed, intelligent engagement with the realities of current Irish and British politics. Moreover, while the historic hope for help from across the sea persists, France as its origin is now joined by America, where so many Irish had settled. Irish hopes were now based increasingly upon Irish realities and Irish resources.

From symbol to participant – Irish women migrants
The female form in the aisling tradition exemplifies the role traditionally assigned to women in Irish literary devices: they could be passive or admonitory, objects of male devotion or sources of rebuke or inspiration but rarely active agents in their own right. This is reflected in many of the ballads dealing with emigration in particular, but there are also indications that, under the economic pressures which provoked migration, gender roles had to be reassessed.

Many ballads portray a man on the verge of emigration or already abroad, mourning his forced departure and separation from his loved one:

Lang Syne'. John Bright (1811–99) was a radical Liberal MP who supported many of the classic reforms of the nineteenth century, including Irish disestablishment.   **75** *Home Rule for Ireland*, Q 821.04.B2, vol. 2.

> Still, still I dream of former bliss,
> And while fond thoughts around me twine,
> I take again the parting pledge,
> And press thy darling hand in mine[76]

The woman in such portrayals is the passive subject of this nostalgia. In some cases there is an alternation of verses in which the narrator first regrets leaving the woman and then at departing from Ireland, and at times it is difficult to disentangle the two.[77] The woman for her part is frequently shown as mourning her man's departure, visiting scenes associated with him, and reliving the wrench of parting:

> Can I ever forget when the big ship was ready,
> The time it had come for my love to depart,
> I cried like a colleen, & said 'Good-bye, Teddy,
> With a tearful eye & a stone at my heart[78]

But there are also indications of a more assertive role for women. Some ballads actually invert the traditional roles of the emigration process and portray situations in which the woman is the migrant and the man is left behind. He is now the one who is worried that the partner will meet someone else or that the relationship will not survive the separation:

> So my Kathleen you're going to leave me,
> All alone by myself in this place,
> But I'm sure you will never deceive me,
> Oh no if there's truth in that face …
> And when you come back to me, Kathleen,
> None the better will I be off then,
> You'll be speaking such beautiful English,
> Sure I won't know my Kathleen again[79]

Another ballad deals with the situation where the woman has departed and it is the man who is unnerved by grief, revisiting favourite places they enjoyed together, recalling the pain of parting and nursing his loneliness:

> Sure when we lent ye to beautiful England,
> Little we thought of the cold winter nights …
> When by the fireside I watch the bright ember,

76 *Norah My Own Mountain Maid*, Q 398.8.S9, vol. 1.   77 Busteed, 'Songs in a strange land', pp 649–50.   78 *Teddy O'Neal*, Q 398.8.S9, vol. 1.   79 *Terence's Farewell*, Q 398.8.S9, vol. 1.

> Then all my heart flies to England and thee,
> Craving to know if my darling remember,
> Or if her thoughts may be crossing to me[80]

The roles have been reassigned, it is the woman who is responding to economic pressures and actively seeking out opportunities abroad and the man who is left to face the personal loss and economic uncertainties of remaining in Ireland. Clearly this is a different type of woman from that shown in the aisling tradition.

From victim to commentator
Similar shifts in thought can be detected in ballads which deal specifically with the migrant situation. The trope of 'exile' has proved immensely useful in describing the fate of the migrant, especially in popular song and newspaper. It presents the migrant as a victim, unwillingly compelled by economic and political forces, often instigated by Britain or its local agents, the landlords, to go into 'exile' abroad.[81] This has been convenient for the exorcism of guilt at leaving and the transfer of blame. The theme of being helpless in the face of uncontrollable forces was taken up in countless ballads:

> Oh, farewell to poor old Erin's isle, I must leave you for a while,
> The rents and taxes are so high, I can no longer stay ...
> If that fruitful land could have her own sons might live and stay at home,
> But since fortune otherwise poor Pat must emigrate ...[82]

The result was a strong aching sense of dislocation, displacement and helplessness. Migrants could reminisce about Ireland, sigh and weep for it, pray for it, but in the end many singers could only offer denial 'all its fond recollections suppressing'.[83] Another coping mechanism was to act out and act up to the traditional 'Paddy' image.[84] This presented 'Pat' as incorrigibly cheerful, optimistic and good natured in the face of every kind of imaginable adversity. But even some of the most cliche ridden ballads could slip in a few lines hinting at a darker side to this almost clownish figure:

> But times have changed the while, in old Erin's isle,
> And many have to wander near and far O

80 *Come Back to Erin*, Q 398.8.S9, vol. 3.   81 Mervyn Busteed, '"Persons who are in a species of exile" – Varieties of Irishness amongst Irish migrants in mid-Victorian Manchester' in Glenda Norquay & Gerry Smyth (eds), *Space & place: the geographies of literature* (Liverpool, 1998), pp 57–76.   82 *Poor Pat Must Emigrate*, Q 398.8.S9, vol. 2. 83 *The Exile of Erin*, Q 821.04 B3.   84 Busteed, 'Songs in a strange land', pp 651–2.

The solution offered was to fall back on eternal sunny optimism:

> … just keep up your heart, you'll find it the better part
> 'Tis the style that always pleases Pat O'Hara[85]

However, there are also ballads which suggest that with time Irish migrants in Britain, whilst never forgetting their Irishness, began to engage more often and more critically with the host society. Moreover, such ballads contain no traces of inferiority, helplessness or victimhood, but rather an increasingly confident, somewhat sardonic tone. In *Picture of England* the singer opens with the declaration that 'Twas myself that was born in Dublin' and goes on to describe how in England the poor are exploited and reduced to slavery by grasping overseers, venal clergy, unjust magistrates and rascally politicians, the chorus ending with:

> Faith but I'm singing the Picture of England,
> The glory and pride of the world[86]

Clearly these are the remarks of an observer who is not cowed by the power structures or achievements of England, real or imagined, but assaults every aspect of them with energy and irony.

There is also evidence that some observers were looking at the Irish migrant population itself with a more detached, self-critical eye. Contemporary analysis and much subsequent academic study of Irish migrants in nineteenth century Britain emphasised their poverty and lack of skills. However, more recent studies have pointed out that there were skilled and professional elements among the migrants[87] and with the passage of time others became prosperous and socially mobile.[88] Reactions within the migrant community itself were doubtless mixed, but one ballad nicely catches the prosperous migrant:

> I am a man of great influence
> And educated to a high degree,
> I came here from Donegal,
> With my cousin Tim I crossed the sea
> At a party or a raffle,
> I always go as an invited guest,
> As conspicuous as the grand Lord Mayor, boys,

85 *Pat O'Hara*, Q 398.8.S9, vol. 4. 86 *Picture of England*, Q 398.8.S9, vol.3. 87 John Belchem, 'Class, creed and country: the Irish middle class in Victorian Liverpool', in Roger Swift & Sheridan Gilley (eds), *The Irish in Victorian Britain: the local dimension* (Dublin, 1999), pp 190–211. 88 Lawrence McBride, *The Reynolds letters: an Irish emigrant family in late Victorian Manchester* (Cork, 1999)

> I wear a rosebud upon my breast ...
> I'm known through England, I'm known through Ireland,
> I'm welcomed heartily by every hand,
> When the band does play, on St Patrick's Day,
> I march away like a solid man[89]

This brilliantly captures the smugness, self-satisfaction and self-importance of the successful migrant who enjoys the public esteem and acclaim he evokes in both countries. The tone is of gentle mockery, a mixture of the pride and begrudgery provoked when a member of a marginalised group becomes materially successful. It is also indicative of a growing maturity and self confidence in a migrant population when it can look not merely at the host society, but at itself in such a critical, gently mocking fashion. The role of the perpetually helpless but cheerful victim has been left far behind.

CONCLUSION

This chapter has analysed a selection of the Irish street ballads on political issues held in Manchester to pick out shifts of opinion amongst the Irish migrant population of the city. Two cautionary points should be borne in mind. First, such survivals are not necessarily a representative sample of the very large number of Irish ballads circulating in the city during the nineteenth century. Second, whilst as has been noted, political concerns loomed larger in Irish than in English ballads, the majority of Irish compositions dealt with the same sensationalist non-political matters which were the mainstay of the street ballad trade in Britain.

The explicitly political ballads discussed here have been categorised and juxtaposed to bring out contrasting outlooks. Clearly there is still a strong sense of Irishness and a concern with the affairs of Ireland and its people. Even when migrant destinations are mentioned, it is within the context of nostalgia for what is still regarded as 'home' and the last two ballads, though set in England, also make it clear the observer hails originally from Ireland. Nevertheless, there are indications of a reorientation of interests. The overwhelming concern with the migrant experience, though replete with regret, guilt and nostalgia, is focused on physically leaving Ireland, coping with the experience of travel, and engaging with the issues and institutions of British political life. There are also signs of a widening of horizons beyond the historic obsession with Anglo-Irish relations and the personal traumas of emigration to take in ironic social comment and criticism, not merely of British society, but of the Irish migrant community itself.

89 *Muldoon the Solid Man*, Q 821.04 B2, vol. 1.

In fact, several of the ballads suggest an increasingly confident Irish migrant population. The aisling device, the traditionally symbolic and passive roles assigned to Irish women and the victim status so often assumed by the Irish in many ballads can be contrasted with situations where they are engaging positively with concrete issues, organising politically, demanding political equality and indulging in astringent social comment. Such actions reveal a population growing increasingly more self assured and in its adoption of British political institutions, methods and assumptions perhaps even integrating to some degree into life in Britain and within the British state.

There is a strong temptation to argue that these trends are evidence for the 'modernisation' of the Irish migrant population in parallel with the restructuring and rationalisation which were taking place in much of the economic, social, ecclesiastical and political life of contemporary Ireland.[90] But while there is a good deal of merit in such analysis, it would be simplistic simply to contrast 'traditional' and 'modern' and assume a smooth linear transition, because aspects of both can co-exist comfortably, as with the incorporation of ancient Irish rural superstitions into late nineteenth century Irish Catholicism.[91] This is particularly true of the world of street ballads, where dating is so difficult and songs could survive simply because the rhythm and tunes were popular, instantly recognisable and easily sung. Consequently, it is highly likely that many of these ballads circulated simultaneously. But there is no doubt that this selection of Irish street ballads, itself an English medium adopted by the Irish, does reveal a process whereby, however fitfully, Irish migrants were adjusting to their new situation, retaining yet modifying aspects of their Irishness and thereby redefining it. The nineteenth century saw the construction and renewal of many European nationalisms, including the Irish variant, and it is clear that these ballads reflect a similar process of redefinition of identity amongst Irish migrants in this part of northwest England. Similar transitions were undoubtedly taking place within the Irish diaspora elsewhere in Great Britain and abroad.

90 Joseph Lee, *The modernisation of Irish society, 1848–1918* (Dublin, 1973)   **91** Ó Ciosain, *Print and popular culture*, pp 201–2.

The English Poor Law, the Irish migrant and the laws of settlement and removal, 1819–1879

FRANK NEAL

Elizabeth Finn was forty-two years of age. She had been born in Monavullen in the parish of Oulart near Enniscorthy, Co. Wexford. When a child the family moved to Liverpool. She later married Owen Finn by whom she had four children. In 1865, work for labourers in Liverpool was hard to find and so Owen left the family to look for a job. While he was away, Elizabeth had to ask for parochial relief and entered the workhouse on 6 December 1865. On 10 January 1866, three parish officers forcibly escorted Elizabeth and her children to the Irish steamer. The children pleaded with her not to struggle as the officers threatened the use of handcuffs. The family were put on the steamer and sent back to Ireland where they became a charge on the Wexford Poor Law Union. Elizabeth had fallen foul of the laws of settlement and removal.[1]

A great deal of academic effort has been expended on studies of the English poor law system, both from the point of view of the legislation which brought it into being and also its administrative structure and financing.[2] Less attention has been given to the laws of settlement and removal. This body of law was an integral part of the whole Poor Law system and is of particular significance to the study of the Irish in Britain. The most useful review article on the laws of settlement and removal following the 1834 Poor Law Amendment Act is that written by Michael Rose in 1976.[3] With regard to the use of these laws to remove Irish persons back to Ireland during the Irish famine crisis, the author of this essay has produced two studies of the applications of the legislation.[4] The objective of this present article is to fill a gap in the study of the laws of settlement and removal by illustrating how the system actually operated at ground level over a period that encompasses the change over from the 'old' Poor Law to the 'new' Poor Law. In essence, this means before and after the 1834

1 British Parliamentary Papers (referred to hereafter as BPP) (HC) 1866 Poor Removal (Ireland). *Copy* of *All Correspondence and Papers in the Office of the Commissioners for Administrating the Laws for the Relief of the Poor in Ireland relating to the Removal of Elizabeth Finn and her Children from Toxteth Park Parish, Liverpool, to the Wexford Union.* 2 For those new to the study of the English Poor Law system, the following works are recommended. G. Taylor, *The problem of poverty, 1660–1834* (London 1969); D. Fraser (ed.), *The new Poor Law in the nineteenth century* (London, 1976); M. Rose (ed.), *The poor and the city: the English Poor Law in its urban context, 1834–1914* (Leicester, 1985). 3 M. Rose, 'Settlement, removal and the new Poor Law', Fraser, *New Poor Law*, pp 25–44.

Poor Law Amendment Act. The choice of the years 1819 to 1879 has been based on a number of considerations. The period witnessed unprecedented urban growth, a phenomenon which exposed the fatuity of a Poor Law policy which, pre-1834, was predicated on the view that rural poverty was essentially the problem to be solved. Also, in 1819, a change in the law made it easier for the Poor Law authorities to remove unwanted paupers out of their parish. In the case of the Irish, this meant removal to an Irish port. Ironically, in 1820, the introduction of steamships on the routes between Irish and English ports made it easier for the Irish to cross to England, thereby undermining the efforts of the authorities to reduce the numbers of Irish paupers in Britain. The Poor Law Amendment Act of 1834 introduced sweeping changes, in particular a much stronger central control over poor relief, so much so, that the period following this act is often referred to as the 'new poor law'. The Irish famine tragedy of 1845–50 witnessed a huge increase in the number of destitute Irish crossing to Britain, causing consternation among poor law officials in British towns and cities.[5] Finally, Irish migration into nineteenth-century Britain peaked in 1861, after which Irish removals decreased. For purposes of clarity of exposition, this essay is divided into four parts. Part one will give a brief survey of the legislation relevant to the issue of settlement and removal enacted before 1819. The second part will examine the legislation and the evidence regarding the actual operation of the system between 1819 and 1833 and the scale of removals. Thirdly, the effects of the 1834 act and subsequent legislation will be analysed and finally, an assessment will be made of the efficacy of the laws of removal as a device for controlling the numbers of Irish in Britain.

I

Any attempt to understand the evolution of the body of legislation dealing with poor relief in England needs to recognise that a corresponding body of law developed to deal with vagrancy. The issue of poverty and vagrancy are linked via the concept of *settlement*.[6] As early as the medieval period, concerns surfaced over the behaviour of large numbers of persons wandering around the country and inculcating fear into the residents of small towns and villages. Essentially, the worries were twofold. First, the charge was made that the arrival of strangers witnessed an increase in begging, robbery, theft, assaults and in many cases, murder. Second, it was a matter of concern that the

4 F. Neal, 'Liverpool, the Irish steamship companies and the Famine Irish', *Immigrants and Minorities*, vol. 5 (Mar. 1986), pp 47–55. F. Neal, *Black '47: Britain and the Famine Irish*, (Basingstoke,1998). 5 For a full account of this see Neal, *Black '47*. 6 A comprehensive survey of the development of the laws regarding vagrancy is to be found in BPP (HC) 1833, *First Report from the Commissioners on the Poor Laws*, Appendix E, Vagrancy.

strangers would become a burden on local charities dispensing money and food for destitute persons. A precursor to the concept of 'settlement' surfaced in the reign of Richard II when, in 1388, an act (12 Ric. c. 7) laid down that if a person became sick, he or she should stay in the place at which they were resident when the act was passed or should move *to the place where they were born and stay there*. Concern over the behaviour of itinerants continued undiminished. An act of Henry VII (2 Henry 7, c. 12) in 1494 laid down that beggars not able to work should be sent to the Hundred (that is, area) where he or she last lived *or was born*, and should stay there. When Henry VIII was on the throne, another act (22 Henry 8 c. 12) stipulated that people caught begging without a licence should be whipped and returned to the place *where they had been born or last lived for three years*. During the whole of this period, the poor and the sick had depended on charities for assistance, usually locally based. In an essentially rural society of small towns and villages, the local elite, landowners, clergy and magistrates, knew the local population and made judgements on the acceptability of claims for help. Unavoidably, such a dispensing of relief was arbitrary and patchy throughout the country. This system, or rather, lack of system, came to an end in the reign of Elizabeth I.

In 1601, the Elizabethan Poor Law was enacted (43 Eliz. c. 2). This comprehensive provision laid down the basis of a state sanctioned poor relief administration which, in its main features, remained unchanged until the sweeping reforms of the 1834 Poor Law Amendment Act. The aims of the 1601 act are simple to state. First was the provision of work for the able-bodied unemployed. Second, pauper children should be educated and apprenticed to a trade. Lastly, help should be given to the sick, the old and the blind. Given the state of economic development at the time, it is not surprising that the underlying assumption behind the new system was that poverty was principally a *rural* problem and that local people should provide for their own neighbours. This manifested itself in the choice of the parish as the unit of administration. A parish was a township, or number of townships, having its own church and a priest. The taxes due to the church were paid to the clergyman who in turn, provided certain services. Within the parish various officials were involved in the administration of parochial affairs. The Overseer was an officer appointed annually by the ratepayers and was mainly concerned with the relief of the poor. Other officials included churchwardens and constables. Money to provide for poor relief was raised from ratepayers. Within the parish, the ratepayers elected members of the select vestry, the body which, in effect, ran the local Poor Law system. This arrangement meant that if the vestry sanctioned too lavish a poor relief provision, causing rates to rise, they would not be re elected. Hence, the desire of many members of select vestries to keep Poor Law expenditure under control. In 1601, there were some 12000 parishes in England, each with a vestry administering the poor relief system. In all parishes there was a concern that strangers could move into an area, become ill, unemployed, or, in the case of women, give birth, and claim relief, thus putting an increased financial burden on the parish. This apprehension was in addition to worries over the lawless behaviour of some itinerants.

The preoccupation with the need to control poor relief expenditure within a parish and the possible ill effects of tramping people, gave rise to the 1662 Act of Settlement and Removal (13 and 14 Charles II c. 12). This act formally introduced the concept of *settlement* in a parish in contrast to the previous vague references to people moving back to their parish of birth. The status of being settled could be achieved in a number of ways. The most obvious example was that of being born in a parish. Others included a derived settlement arising from parents born in the parish, renting a house above a certain value (this simply meant that you were not likely to claim poor relief), marrying a man from the parish or serving as a parish officer. An Irish person could acquire the status of settlement if he or she met some of the criteria. How many Irish did so is not known. Under the 1662 legislation, if a stranger moved into a parish and rented a house of less than an annual value of £10, the Justices of the Peace could order his or her removal to his or her previous parish, if a complaint was made by the parish officers within forty days of the person moving into the parish. Even more threatening, the magistrates had the power to remove someone living in the parish who did not have settlement and who they thought *might* claim poor relief. In effect, a person could be removed without having made claims on the parish. This provision was a constant source of worry to those persons who had lived a long time in a parish but had not acquired settlement. A major criticism of the system was the claim that it inhibited the mobility of labour. The subsequent appearance of a system of certificates seems to have been an acceptance of such criticisms. Under an act passed in 1697 (8 and 9 William 3 c. 3), a certificate could be granted to men who wished to work outside their own parish. This document, signed by his parish officers, meant that if the person became unemployed in a parish where he did not have settlement, his own parish would indemnify the parish where he was claiming relief. The process of tinkering with the system continued. In 1795 a new act (35 Geo. 3, c. 101) admitted that the certificate system for allowing the mobility of labour was inefficient. Importantly, it laid down the principle *that no person could be removed from a parish until he or she actually claimed poor relief and became a charge on the parish*. It is important to note at this juncture that the Elizabethan Poor Law did not apply to Ireland and so no parish in Ireland would accept responsibility for Irish persons removed from England. With regard to the operation of the settlement and removal laws in England, the system became clogged up with litigation. Parishes receiving paupers removed from other parishes challenged the paupers claim to settlement. Often the cost of litigation was such that parishes chose to pay poor relief rather than remove a pauper.

The introduction of the Elizabethan Poor Law did not solve the problems associated with itinerants. In 1744, an Act 'to Amend and make more effectual laws relative to Rogues, Vagabonds and Other Idle and Disorderly Persons ...' was passed (17 Geo, II, c. 5). Under this new law, rogues and vagabonds could be removed to the parish in which they had settlement, or, if settlement could not be established, to the place where they were born. From the point of view of this essay, it is relevant to note that this Act introduced the term *Passing*. The Justices of the Peace were allowed to issue a certificate indicating how the person was to be passed back to his place of settlement, ie., by horse, cart or on foot. For those Irish who had fallen foul of the vagrancy laws and had no parish of settlement, the law laid down they should be passed to a port of departure and there, the ship's master must carry them to Ireland on the basis of a warrant issued by the Justices of the Peace in the port of departure. These justices decided the price of the passage to Ireland. In addition, the Irish vagrants were to be put ashore in Ireland where the vessel normally docked. This meant that, for example, an Irishman convicted under the vagrancy laws and put ashore at Dublin may have come from Galway town. To return to his place of birth, he would had to have walked to Galway. It important to note that this legislation meant that in the case of Irish persons, *only those convicted under the vagrancy laws could be removed (passed) to Ireland.* One of the offences under the vagrancy laws was begging, something which the Irish resorted to easily because of its tolerance in Ireland given the absence of any poor law. Hugh Ruewark was an Irishman from the parish of Kilcullen, Co. Kildare, who came to England to look for work and failing to find any, resorted to begging. He was arrested in Middlewich in Cheshire in 1758, found guilty and declared a rogue and vagabond. As he failed to give proof of settlement, he was transported to Neston on the Wirral and shipped back to Dublin against his will. How many Irish were removed to Ireland before 1800 is not known. What needs to be noted is that those who were removed had committed offences under the vagrancy laws but as the example of Hugh Ruewark shows, many were convicted for offences which were the result of the need to survive rather than criminal intent.[7] An Irish man or woman, innocent of any offence but claiming poor relief in an English parish could be removed to an English parish if they had settlement in that parish. However, if they did not have settlement in an English parish, they could not be removed to Ireland, nor to another parish and so became a charge on the parish in which they made a claim.

---

7 G.W. Place, 'The repatriation of Irish vagrants from Cheshire, 1750–1815', *Journal of the Chester Archaeological Society*, 68 (1985), 125–6.

II

The dawn of the nineteenth century did not witness a falling off in the number
of vagrants. The enclosures of land in the eighteenth century and the
consequent changes to less labour intensive forms of agriculture, increased
rural unemployment. Following the end of the war with France in 1815, large
numbers of ex-servicemen took to tramping and vagrancy. The new century
also saw a large increase in the number of Irish travelling to England, facilitated
by the introduction of steamships on the Irish routes, from 1822 onwards.[8] The
1841 census established that there were 284,128 Irish-born persons resident in
England, concentrated in particular areas. The Irish-born population of
Liverpool was 49639 while the corresponding figure for Manchester and
Salford was 33490, London 73133 and Glasgow 44435. These populations were
to increase over the following twenty years. A large number of the Irish lived on
the borders of poverty and represented a significant proportion of poor relief
expenditure and by 1851, this fact became a target of hostile criticism.

Concern over the rising level of poor relief expenditure resulted in a radical
new policy being introduced in 1819. Under a new act (59 Geo. III, c. 12), the
Justices of the Peace were given the authority to order the removal of any
claimant for poor relief who did not have settlement *and* who had not committed any offence under the vagrancy acts. This meant that the Irish now fell into
three categories. The few that had settlement in an English parish could claim
poor relief without the threat of removal hanging over them. Those Irish who
did not have settlement and claimed relief could be removed to Ireland. The
third group were those Irish who were convicted under the vagrancy acts.
These were removed to Ireland on release from prison. The 1819 act was not an
unmitigated disaster for the Irish in Britain, who were quick to realise the
opportunities it opened up. For example, an Irishman wanting a free trip home
could apply for poor relief and on failing to establish he had settlement in
England, be sent back to Ireland.

The intention behind the Elizabethan Poor Law had been that some central
control would be exercised over the poor relief system. In practice, this did not
happen. central control was minimal. By 1819, the number of parishes was
approaching 15000 and the Poor Law system was firmly under the control of
local aristocrats, gentry and clergy, who provided most of the magistrates. It is
not surprising that the law was interpreted differently among the parishes. The
nature of the system of removing Irish paupers and vagrants, and its inherent
weaknesses, are more easily understood if the mechanics of its operation are
appreciated. What follows is a description of the main features of the system

8 F. Neal, 'Liverpool shipping in the early nineteenth century' in J.R. Harris (ed.), *Liverpool
and Merseyside: essays in the economic and social history of the port and its hinterland* (London,
1969), pp 147–81.

after the passing of the 1819 act. The first thing to be understood is that all the Irish being removed were sent to one of two ports, Bristol or Liverpool. Those from the southern counties of Ireland went to Bristol to be put ashore at Cork. In the case of those from the west of Ireland, the midlands and the north, they were sent to Dublin via Liverpool. This principle was adhered to no matter where in England was the parish removing the Irish person. For example, if a parish in Norfolk was removing a Roscommon man, he would be sent to Liverpool en route for Dublin. In the case of all parishes removing Irish paupers, the most direct routes to Bristol and Liverpool were chosen.

The process of removal started when an Irish person applied for poor relief.[9] The overseer would take the applicant before the magistrates who would question the person to establish whether or not he or she had settlement. If there was no settlement the person could be searched to see if he or she had any money to pay for their removal. If the pauper had no money, the magistrates would make out a pass, ordering a removal to either Cork or Dublin. At this point in the proceedings, the magistrates would state whether the persons being removed should walk to the port or travel by cart. In practice, most travelled by horse and cart. Each parish had a pass master whose job was to arrange the transportation of the pauper or vagrant to the port of embarkation. The pass master would organise a horse and cart which would be accompanied on its journey to the county border by either the pass master or the parish constable. The persons being removed would be transported to the first parish in the next county where they would be handed over to the constable or pass master in that parish. Then they would be transported to the county border and handed over to the constable in the first parish in the next county and so on. At each county handover, the local magistrates should have endorsed the pass for each person.

In examining the cost of removing Irish paupers it is necessary to distinguish between costs incurred by the removing parish and the costs picked up by the counties passed through on the way to Bristol or Liverpool. The magistrates' pass cost 5s. In most cases, the parish constable would accompany the removals to the county border and was paid 5s. a day, irrespective of how many persons were being removed. These costs fell on the parish. In addition, the constable was also paid 3d. per head per mile to cover the incidental expenses such as overnight lodgings for the paupers and vagrants. Each person received 6d. per day subsistence allowance. These costs were borne by the ratepayers of each

9 Information regarding the operation of the removal system, for Irish, English and Scots pre-1834 is to be found in BPP (HC) 1828, *Report from the Select Committee on the Laws relating to Irish and Scots Vagrants*, referred hereafter as *Irish vagrants* (1828), Minutes of Evidence. Also, BPP (HC) 1833, *Report from the Select Committee on Irish Vagrants*, referred to hereafter as *Irish vagrants* (1833). BPP (HC) (1833); *First Report from the Poor Law Commissioners on the Poor Laws*, Appendix E, Irish and Scots Paupers, referred to hereafter as *Irish paupers* (1833).

county the paupers passed through. This system of financing Irish removals was a source of great resentment on the part of county ratepayers. Many counties with small Irish populations were paying for the removal of Irish passed from parishes in other counties. In practice, the majority of removals originated from Lancashire and London.

The system is best illustrated by taking a particular example. An Irishman from Roscommon applying for poor relief in Fareham, Hampshire, would be taken before the magistrates who would establish whether or not he had settlement in England. If not, the magistrates would sign a removal order for passing him to Liverpool, where he would be put onto a vessel for Dublin. All the paupers being passed by Fareham would be assembled and put in a horse and cart and, escorted by the constable, set off to the border between Hampshire and Berkshire. The route went through Winchester and on to Sandleford, near Newbury. At Sandleford they were handed on to the constable in what was the first Berkshire parish. This process was repeated until they reached the poor law office of the City of London. All the Irish being passed from Hampshire, Kent, Surrey and Sussex finished up at the City of London. From here they were passed to St Lukes parish in Middlesex for forwarding to Liverpool. The route to Liverpool and the cost of removing a pauper in 1833 is given in Table 1 below:

Table 1: The average cost and the route travelled by an Irish pauper removed by Metropolitan Poor Law authorities to Dublin via Liverpool

Stages	Distance (miles)	Allowance per mile	Daily pay	Total cost	Paid by
London to South Mimms (Herts.)	15	3*d.*	6*d.*	4*s.* 3*d.*	Middlesex
South Mimms to Market St. (Beds.)	14	2*d.*	6*d.*	2*s.* 10*d.*	Herts.
Market St. to Little Brickhill (Bucks.)	14	2*d.*	6*d.*	2*s.* 10*d.*	Beds.
Little Brickhill to Old Stratford (Northants.)	10	2*d.*	4*d.*	2*s.* 0*d.*	Bucks.
Old Stratford to Willoughby (Warwicks.)	24			6*s.* 6*d.*	Northants.
Willoughby to Drayton Bassett (Staffs.)	35	2¹/₂*d.*	9*d.*	8*s.* ¹/₂*d.*	Warwicks.
Drayton Bassett to Lawton Gate (Ches.)	18	2*d.*	6*d.*	3*s.* 6*d.*	Staffs.
Lawton Gate to Warrington (Lancs.)	28	1¹/₂*d.*	6*d.*	4*s.* 0*d.*	Ches.
Warrington to Liverpool	18	2*d.*	6*d.*	3*s.* 6*d.*	Lancs.
	176			£1 17*s.* 5¹/₂*d.*	

Source: British Parliamentary Papers, *First Report from the Commissioners on the Poor Laws* (1833), Appendix E, pp 21–2.

The journey from St Lukes to South Mimms in Hertfordshire was fifteen miles and cost the ratepayers of Middlesex 4*s.* 3*d.*, even in the case of paupers passed by Fareham in Hampshire. At South Mimms, the removal orders were endorsed by the magistrates and then the paupers were then passed to Market Street in Bedfordshire at a cost per head of two shillings ten pence to the ratepayers of Hertfordshire. The total cost of passing a pauper from Middlesex to Liverpool was £1 17s. 11¹/₂d. The costs involved in passing the Irish to Bristol are given in Table 2.

Table No. 2: The average cost and route travelled by an Irish pauper removed by the Metropolitan authorities, to Cork via Bristol

Stages	Distance (miles)	Allowance per mile	Daily pay	Total cost	Paid by
London to Colnbrook (Bucks.) Middlesex	17	3d.	6d.	4s. 9d.	
Colnbrook to Maidenhead (Berks.)	9¹/₄	2¹/₂d.	6d.	2s. 6d.	Bucks.
Maidenhead to Hungerford (Wilts.)	40	1¹/₄d.	2s. 0d.	7s. 0d.	Berks.
Hungerford to Marshfield (Glos.)	38	2d.	6d.	6s. 10d.	Wilts.
Marshfield to Bristol	12	2d.	8d.	2s. 6d.	Glos.
	116¹/₄			£1 3s. 7d.	

Source: British Parliamentary Papers, *First Report from the Commissioners on the Poor Laws* (1833), Appendix E, p. 22.

The ratepayers of Middlesex, Buckinghamshire, Berkshire, Wiltshire and Gloucestershire bore the cost of removing paupers from outside the county, the total cost to Bristol being £1 3s. 7d. Illustrative of the arbitrary distribution of the cost of removals is the experience of Henry Gill, the pass master of the City of London who, in 1832, received 3071 Irish and Scots paupers from Hampshire, Surrey, Kent and Sussex. They were to be passed to Liverpool, Bristol and Scotland. In the year ending 25 March 1832, St Lukes parish in Middlesex passed 228 paupers of its own plus 460 from southern counties of England. In 1829, the county of Staffordshire passed 2107 Irish paupers, on their way to Liverpool, at a cost of £2000. Yet over a seven-year period, 1827–33, only 68 Irish paupers were removed by Staffordshire parishes. The significance of this is emphasised when it is realised that over the next three years alone, 1827–9, Staffordshire passed 5355 Irish on their way from London to Liverpool.

Such a system was wide open to abuse by both parochial officials and the Irish. A common trick was for Irish persons to claim poor relief on the grounds of destitution when in fact they had money, often after working the harvests. The money could be hidden in their clothing or they would give it to a banker who would travel home separately.[10] The people removed to Ireland would meet

10 Evidence of T.L. Pain, *Irish vagrants* (1828), p. 12. Also evidence of G. Forwood, parochial officer of Liverpool, *Irish vagrants* (1828), pp 15–16; H. Cotteril, overseer, *Irish vagrants* (1833), p. 21.

the banker and retrieve their money. More common was the use of the pass system to indulge a desire to travel round the country. An Irishman could seek poor relief in Middlesex and be subject to a removal order for Liverpool. On reaching Staffordshire say, he could easily abscond and continue his tramping. When fed up with Staffordshire, he could apply for poor relief, claim to be a Cork man and obtain removal to Bristol, absconding again in Gloucestershire and so on. Commenting on this practice, F Clayton, treasurer of Newcastle-upon-Tyne expressed the opinion that:

> a vagrant who is a native of Scotland or Ireland, when it suits him to change his place of residence soon turns himself into a pauper, and is passed towards Scotland or Ireland, from county to county, at great expense, but he proceeds only as far as it may be convenient to himself, when, with the connivance of the Pass Master, who is interested in upholding the system, he is let loose again to become second time, a pauper, when he is passed in the same manner from whatever place he may chance to be in, towards the place of his birth, which perhaps, he never reaches at all ...[11]

This view of the system's weaknesses was widespread among those charged with administering the removal of the Irish. Williamson Etches, pass master of Newark in Nottinghamshire in 1833, describing his experience, stated:

> I do not believe that one fourth of those who obtain magistrates passes intend to go to their alleged places of settlement; and in that part of the country with which I am connected we find they have two modes of imposition; one is by absconding immediately that they get into our county, in which they find the discipline and care of them more precise and severe than it is in the south; another is the going on to the borders of Scotland and if they do not there find the accommodation they require, by declaring themselves natives of the western parts of Ireland, and so getting passed back again through Yorkshire, on their professed route to Bristol ...[12]

Edward Grove, a magistrate in Staffordshire, also had a lot of experience in operating the pass system. He added his views to the growing body of critics:

> with respect to the Irish themselves, their system is decidedly to move about at other people's cost; in many instances, anything but that of returning to their own homes: I am persuaded that it is a sort of trade with a certain class of Irish; that they travel in a circle and that the nearer

11 *Irish paupers* (1833), Appendix E, F. Clayton, p. 64   12 *Irish paupers* (1833), Appendix E, William Etches, p. 60.

they get to their own homes, the greater is their tendency to fly off; we have perpetually instances of their running away. We sometimes carry from 30 to 40 in a wagon, with a man and boy, and under different pretences, they take an opportunity of slipping away and run off. It is not long since we had ten run away ... Many have escaped before they were brought to Stafford ...[13]

The parish constable accompanying the carts was often not bothered by the fact that paupers were disappearing because he received his 5s. a day, irrespective of the number carried. In cases where the journey involved overnight stays, the paupers were often left to fend for themselves. This loose supervision was not illegal but encouraged abscondence. In some cases, on a long journey, the paupers and constable could strike a deal whereby the paupers agreed to walk to the county boundary. In return the constable would split the money he received for carrying them (3d. per head), with the Irish. He then returned home and the paupers disappeared.[14] Henry Gill told of an Irishman, his wife and children being passed from Canterbury. They received 3s. a day subsistence allowance plus walking money. On reaching London they took lodgings and loaned their three children to other Irish persons who then claimed poor relief in order to be passed to Ireland. They received relief for themselves and the children and then returned the children to their parents and fled. The original family then continued on its journey.[15] Yet another fraud occurred when Irish from places such as Antrim, Down, Donegal etc. wanted to avoid removal to Dublin, given that they would have to have walked home. When applying for relief and asking to be passed, they pretended to be Scots, thus being removed to Scotland where they could cross to the north of Ireland from Glasgow. That was a more expensive charge to the English ratepayer.[16] A major fraud arose from the illegal printing of pass certificates. In the case of an Irishman discharged from prison, he was given a certificate of removal, issued by the visiting magistrates. He then went to the nearest parish office, to be removed. Such passes could be bought from persons specialising in fraudulent documents, skilled in forging magistrates' signatures. The forged pass enabled persons who had been refused removal to present themselves to the parish office and obtain a free trip to wherever they wished to go. Henry Gill also told of a woman named Ann McPherson, who he recognised as having used other different names. With a constable, Gill went to her lodgings and found in possession of her husband equipment for forging passes together with orders for poor relief from several different parishes. Gill claimed the woman had been passed fifty

13 *Irish vagrants* (1833), Minutes of Evidence, Edward Grove, q. 628, p. 39.   14 *Irish paupers* (1833), Appendix E, W. Ellcot, p. 62.   15 *Irish Paupers* (1833), Appendix E, Henry Gill, p. 55. Gill was the pass master for the City of London.   16 *Irish paupers* (1833), Appendix E, John Bee, constable of St Lukes and pass master, p. 58.

times.[17] In addition, to outright fraud, officials operating the system were often guilty of sloppiness. For example, a magistrate should have examined each pauper at each stage of the removal process. Often they simply signed the removal orders brought to them without ever seeing the pauper or vagrant. Also, magistrates should have had applicants for passing searched to see if they had money to pay for their journey to Ireland. Often no searches were carried out.

A loosely administered system, riddled with petty fraud, was not the only source of inefficiency and confusion. Despite the large number of acts of parliament dealing with the issues of vagrancy, poor relief and removals, and their subsequent amending acts, the law resulted in unforeseen anomalies which were both expensive and frustrating for the poor law officials. For example, in 1833, Catholic marriages were still not recognised in England. This meant that, legally, the children born of Catholic parents married in a Catholic church, were bastards. Simultaneously, the law regarding settlement also stipulated that an illegitimate child acquired settlement in the parish where it was born. This had consequences the legislators had incredibly, not foreseen. If the law was strictly applied, the family would be split up and the parish inherit the long-term cost of child-rearing. For example, Catherine Harrigan was an Irish Catholic, married to an Irish Catholic. Her husband deserted her in London when she was in advanced state of pregnancy. She applied for relief in Kensington parish and entered the workhouse, where the baby was born. On recovering from childbirth, she left the workhouse to seek work and disappeared, leaving the parish to look after the child, which had settlement. This meant the parish acquired a long-term cost which would have been avoided if both mother and child had been removed. Catherine Harrigan was afraid that if she returned to the workhouse, the authoritics might give her the baby and remove them both, but the child could not be removed as it had acquired settlement in Kensington.[18] Norah Casey was an Irish girl who became pregnant by a married man. She also entered Kensington workhouse where she gave birth to a child. She absconded, leaving the baby to be brought up by the parish. She was subsequently arrested and taken to the workhouse to see the baby but she refused to hold the child out of a misplaced fear that if she did, she would not be able to give it back to the workhouse and they would both be removed to Ireland. This would have been illegal. Also, magistrates were reluctant to split up families.[19] The Brennans were an Irish couple who had been married in a Catholic church in England. They had four children born in different parishes, namely Lewisham, St Martins in the Fields, St Mary Le Bone and St Pauls Covent Garden. The children were legally bastards and the parents were receiving poor relief from four different parishes.[20]

It is appropriate at this stage to examine the evidence concerning the scale of removals to Ireland following the act of 1819. Table 3 below covers the nine years 1823 to 1831 inclusive and shows the number of removals from Bristol to Cork.

17 *Irish paupers* (1833), Appendix E, Henry Gill, p. 55.   18 *Irish paupers* (1833), Appendix E, p. 7. See also *Irish vagrants* (1833), Minutes of Evidence, J. Wall, p. 26.   19 *Irish paupers* (1833), Appendix E, p. 7   20 *Irish paupers* (1833), Appendix A, p. 103.

Table 3: The number of Irish passed by sea from Bristol in each of the financial years 1823–31

Year Ending 25 March	Numbers		
	Under 10 Years	10 Years and over	Total
1823	193	806	999
1824	253	610	863
1825	284	650	934
1826	327	834	1161
1827	482	1161	1643
1828	340	693	1033
1829	409	891	1300
1830	581	1524	2105
1831	920	2628	3548

Source: British Parliamentary Papers HC (1831–32) (710) xliv, *Return of the number of Irish poor shipped under passes from the Port of Bristol to Ireland, in each year since 1823*

The obvious feature of these data is the increase in removals over the nine years. The 3548 removed in 1831 is three and a half times the number removed in 1823. One explanatory factor is that after 1819, the power of the magistrates to remove anyone claiming relief who had not acquired settlement was beginning to make itself felt. Another factor, which can only be speculated on, is that there were more Irish in England, and so we cannot say whether or not the removals expressed a significant proportion of the non-settled Irish. We simply do not know. What we also do not know is how many of the people passed were voluntary as opposed to compulsory removals. In the case of Liverpool, we have more useful data than in the case of Bristol. Table 4 below shows the numbers of Irish passed through Liverpool over the period 1824–31 but breaks down the number on the basis of area of origin

Table 4: The number of Irish paupers shipped from Liverpool to Ireland over the period 1824–31 inclusive, indicating the parish or county in which the passes originated

Year	Liverpool	Rest of Lancs.	Middlesex	Bristol	Yorks.	Rest of country	Total
1824	1455	151	476	140	51	208	2481
1825	1588	279	673	195	43	250	3028
1826	2443	1848	826	264	423	624	6428
1827	2803	962	1379	120	251	540	6055
1828	1956	522	1173	111	234	342	4338
1829	1522	1442	1177	15	385	546	5087
1830	2799	682	1443	2	285	467	5678
1831	2669	649	1576	–	330	639	5893
Totals	17235	6535	8723	847	2002	3616	38958

Source: British Parliamentary Papers (HC) 1833, *An account of the number of Irish poor shipped under passes from the port of Liverpool to Ireland and the charge for passing them, in each year since 1823.*

Again there is a steady increase in the numbers passed to Ireland, the total
for 1831 being nearly two and a half times greater than that in 1824. In 1824, of
the total of 2481 passed, 60 per cent were from the parish of Liverpool. In 1831,
this percentage had fallen to 46 per cent. What is striking are the numbers
passed through Liverpool from Middlesex, reflecting the attraction of London
for Irish migrants. Again, as we do not know the total number of Irish in
England at the time, it is not possible to say if the numbers were significant in
reducing Irish claims on poor relief. What the data for both Bristol and
Liverpool demonstrates is a steady increase in the number of removals. Despite
the misuse of the pass system to facilitate movement around Britain, most Irish
did not want to return to Ireland and the threat of removal was used with some
effect to deter them from claiming poor relief. Concern over the Irish surfaced
in the form of the reports of the Select Committee on Irish and Scottish
Vagrants (1828) and the Select Committee on Irish Vagrants (1833). The 1828
committee report drew the attention of the House of Commons to the increasing numbers of removals to Ireland and the cost involved, and expressed the
view that the problem would increase due to population growth in Ireland combined with a lack of job opportunities. It recommended the abolition of the laws
which resulted in English parishes and counties paying for the removal of the
Irish. It also recommended that they should not be able to claim poor relief in
Britain. The 1833 Committee report, while agreeing with the 1828
Committee's view of the inefficiency and unfairness of the removal system,
declined to support such a drastic measure given the lack of a Poor Law in
Ireland. Instead it recommended that the cost of removing an Irish pauper
should fall entirely on the parish ordering the removal and then the removing
parish should be reimbursed by the county in which the parish was located. In
the event, these reports were not acted upon but the information they gathered
went into the data collection exercise undertaken by the government as it considered the reform of the whole Poor Law system. To this was added the evidence given in 1833 to the Commissioners on the Poor Laws. Appendix E of
their first report had a section on Irish and Scottish paupers. The evidence it
collected supported the thesis of inefficiency, neglect of duty and fraud. In its
final report it recommended that place of birth should be the only criteria for
settlement. If acted on, this would have disbarred the Irish in Britain from
claiming poor relief. In the event, the recommendation was ignored.

III

The reforming zeal of the Whig administration manifested itself in many ways,
including the passing of the Poor Law Amendment Act of 1834. The new Poor
Law laid down that poor relief should not be given outside of the workhouse to

those considered capable of work. To get relief, people would have to enter the workhouse (indoor relief). However, the conditions in the workhouse were to be such that only those desperate for help would agree to enter. In recognition that, in the context of urban development and population growth, the parish was too small an administrative unit, adjacent parishes were organised into Poor Law Unions, and each Union was to have at least one workhouse. All parishes were to contribute to Union costs. Also in recognition that the previous system was a shambles due to what was almost local autonomy, a Poor Law Board was set up and Commissioners appointed to oversee the implementation of the act and exercise a strong central control. Two points are particularly relevant to the theme of this essay. The Irish, in general, intensely disliked the workhouse regime and so were reluctant to apply for relief, where that meant entering the workhouse. Second, the parish remained the administrative unit within which a person had settlement. So that within one Union, a person could move to the next parish and, if claiming relief, be sent back to his or her parish of settlement. After the passing of the 1834 act, the remaining criteria for obtaining settlement were birth in a parish, derived settlement from parents, marriage to a man with settlement, parochial apprenticeship, renting a tenement in a parish, paying rates in a parish and owning property in a parish. With regard to the intention to abolish outdoor relief, for the able bodied, the 1834 act was a failure.

Despite the comprehensive restructuring of the poor relief system, the numbers claiming relief continued to increase. With regard to Irish removals, for the year ending 29 September 1841, 5189 removal orders (10,660 individuals) were made out for Irish and Scots, the overwhelming majority being Irish.[21] In 1845 the potato blight struck in Ireland, the influx of famine refugees stretching the English Poor Law system to breaking point in certain areas and moving the issue of removals up to the political agenda.

Before referring to the effects of the Irish famine in British towns and cities, the removal legislation in being at the time, needs to be noted. In 1845 an act was passed to 'Amend the laws relating to the removal of poor persons born in Scotland, Ireland, the Islands of Man, Scilly, Jersey or Guernsey and chargeable in England, (8 and 9 Vic. c. 117). What turned out later to be the problem part of the law was section 2. In this it was laid down that any Irish person claiming poor relief and who did not have settlement, must be served a summons to appear before two magistrates who would establish whether or not he or she should be removed. The legislation could not have foreseen the problem that this provision was to cause two years later. The act also laid down which ports in Ireland the paupers were to be removed to ie. Dublin, Wexford, Waterford, Cork, Limerick, Derry, Belfast and Dundalk. In 1846, another act

---

21 Unfortunately there are no data on removals to Ireland for the years 1841–6.

(9 and 10 Vic. c. 66) introduced another important amendment to the removal
legislation. Anyone proving five years uninterrupted residence in a parish
acquired the status of *irremoveability* and could not be removed. This new legal
status was not the same as settlement but it conferred the same protection on
individuals who acquired it. In towns such as Liverpool, Glasgow, Manchester
and London, the immediate effect was to increase the number of Irish who
could claim poor relief without fear of removal. Table 5 shows the immediate
effect in Liverpool of the Five Year Residency Act.

Table 5: The numbers of persons in Liverpool obtaining the status of irremoveability under 9 &
10 Vic. c. 56 (1846), distinguishing between Irish and English persons

	English	Irish	Total
Widows	317	367	684
Widows with children	478	747	1225
Males residents	216	431	647
Females residents	332	551	883
Residents' children	406	1509	1915
Total	1749	3605	5354

Source: British Parliamentary Papers, *Sixth Report of the Select Committee on Settlement and Poor
Removal* 1847 (409) xi, Minutes of Evidence, E. Rushton, q. 4340, p. 55

Of the 5354 persons acquiring the status of irremoveability by the end of 1846,
67 per cent were Irish. Edward Rushton, stipendiary magistrate of Liverpool,
estimated that this act cost the Liverpool ratepayers over £10,000 per annum.
A major problem which the legislators did not seem to have considered was the
difficulty of disproving claims to five-year residency in a parish. In working
class areas there was constant movement among the population, particularly in
a port such as Liverpool. Whole streets could change their population in a year,
landlords rarely kept records of the tenants, particularly in the case of lodging
houses. The system was guaranteed to generate endless appeals against the
decisions of the Poor Law officials.

The impact of the Irish famine refugees in British towns and cities has been
dealt with in detail elsewhere.[22] Here selected aspects of the experience of
Liverpool will be used to illustrate problems of applying the removal laws at a
time of exceptional crisis. During 1847 296,000 Irish landed in Liverpool and
of this number 116,000 were described as paupers. Most of these immediately
applied for poor relief. None of them had settlement or irremovability status
and so should have been removed. Edward Rushton, in his capacity as magistrate was in the front line of the crisis. He told the 1847 Select Committee on
Settlement and Removal that the law was inoperable. It was, in his opinion,

22 Neal, *Black '47.*

simply impossible to remove all those new arrivals, the parish did not have the manpower. Also, the 1845 law requiring a summons to be served on paupers simply could not be implemented, it was too difficult to hunt down a pauper and serve the summons. Similarly, under the vagrancy laws, begging was an offence. Rushton took the view that the law could not be enforced. First, the local prison would not be big enough. Second, arresting the women with children would mean the parish would have to take the children into care.[23] In 1847 the law was changed regarding the serving of summons. A pauper asking the parochial officers for poor relief could be taken directly before a magistrate, with a request for a removal order. The removals from Liverpool and Manchester during the years of the famine crisis are shown below:

Table 6: Numbers of Irish paupers removed from Liverpool and Manchester over the period 1846 to 1853 inclusive.

Year	Liverpool	Manchester	Total
1846	5313	286	5599
1847	15008	553	15561
1848	7606	1902	9508
1849	9409	617	10026
1850	7627	275	7902
1851	7808	400	8208
1852	5506	337	5843
1853	4503	362	4865
Total	62780	4732	67512

Source: British Parliamentary Papers. *Select Committee on Poor Removal*, 1854 (396) xvii. The figures were provided to Campbell by the Liverpool select vestry, the body responsible for the administration of poor relief, q. 5026. The Manchester statistics were given by J. Harrop, qq. 6230–4

The obvious feature of the data is the larger number of removals from Liverpool compared with Manchester. There are a number of plausible explanations for this disparity. First, there were more Irish in Liverpool than in Manchester. However, Liverpool removed thirteen times the number removed by Manchester and so size of Irish-born population is not the only factor. A second explanation is that many Irish travelled to Liverpool with the intention of claiming poor relief in order to be removed. A third factor was the fact that the cost of removing an Irishman from Liverpool was cheaper than it was for the Manchester authorities. To remove the Irish, the latter had to pay for the train fare and the labour of the escorting parochial officers. Therefore it was cheaper for the Manchester parish to pay poor relief and hope the paupers

---

23 BPP (HC), *Fifth Report of the Select Committee on Settlement and Poor Removal*, 1847 (226) xi, Minutes of Evidence, referred to hereafter as SC 1847, E. Rushton, q. 4270, p. 56.

would go away. However, more significantly, to encourage the casual Irish to stop claiming relief, the Manchester parish used the threat of removal with some force and undoubtedly frightened off many potential Irish claimants. This, rather than a humane policy of not removing the Irish, is the most probable explanation of the low number of Manchester removals.[24]

By 1853, the overwhelming proportion of the removal orders to Ireland were made out in Lancashire. For example, in the year ending 25 March 1853, of 4823 orders made out in England, 80 per cent originated in Lancashire.[25] Of these, the majority would be Liverpool orders. However, the 1851 census revealed that 520,000 Irish lived in England and Wales. This raises the question of how enthusiastically the authorities used their power of removal. The table below shows the ports in Ireland to which the paupers were removed from Liverpool over the period 1849–53.

Table 7: The number of Irish poor removed from the parish of Liverpool to ports in Ireland and the total cost involved, for each of the years, 1849–53

Port	Year					Total Number
	1849	1850	1851	1852	1853	
Dublin	6749	5335	5809	4110	3225	25228
Drogheda	999	274	286	219	234	2012
Newry	454	264	214	121	129	1182
Belfast	399	523	404	360	286	1972
Dundalk	324	193	198	106	135	956
Sligo	109	158	176	116	77	636
Cork	126	369	314	188	170	1167
Waterford	128	392	243	165	165	1093
Londonderry	77	81	72	51	73	354
Wexford	37	37	21	49	28	172
Portrush	2	–	1	5	1	9
Youghal	5	–	–	–	–	5
Limerick	–	–	–	–	2	2
Total	9409	7626	7738	5490	4525	3478
Total cost	£2519	£1488	£1951	£1456	£1130	

Source: British Parliamentary Papers (1854), 374, *A Return of the number of Irish poor removed from the parish of Liverpool to Ireland, distinguishing the ports to which such paupers were removed*

Over the five years, 34,787 individuals were removed to Ireland and of these, 78 per cent went to Dublin or Drogheda. By 1853, the number of removals had

24 For a critical view of the policy of the Manchester parochial authorities see BPP(HC), *Report of the Select Committee on Poor Removal*, 1854 (396), xvii referred hereafter as SC (1854), Appendix 17, R Pashley, p. 665. 25 Op. cit., p. 666. Note that the number of orders is not the same as the number of individuals.

almost halved and costs had fallen by 55 per cent. This does not reflect a less-
ening of the Irish pauper problem in Lancashire, rather it is the result of many
Irish not seeking relief out of fear of removal. Seven years later, the number of
persons removed from Liverpool to Ireland had fallen to 1788.

Table 8: The number of persons removed from Liverpool to Ireland during the year 1860, distinguishing between the different periods of time each has been in Liverpool prior to removal

Period of residence in Liverpool	Number of Persons
Under 1 year	1420
1 year but under 3years	163
3 years but under 5 years	82
5 years but under 10 years	66
10 years but under 15 years	34
15 years but under 20 years	17
20 years but under 30 years	4
30 years but under 40 years	2
Total	1788

Source: *British Parliamentary Papers* HC (1878–79) (282) xii, *Report of the Select Committee on Poor
Removal*, Minutes of Evidence, J.H. Hagger, q. 1775, p. 97

Of the total number of persons removed, 89 per cent had been resident in
Liverpool for less than five years, significantly, 79 per cent less than one year. Of
those who had been resident longer than five years, the reason that they had
been removed may have been that they had moved parish, so losing the status
of irremoveability or they asked to be passed to Ireland. Of the latter, many
were old people returning to die in Ireland.[26]

The great volume of evidence collected by the various select committees
contained a recurrent theme, that of the injustice of removing people who were
attempting to establish a life for themselves and their families. The Five Year
Residency Act had been a concession to such criticism and in 1861, another act
(24 and 25 Vic. c. 66) reduced the period for gaining irremoveable status from
five to three years. Another act passed in 1861 (24 and 25 Vic. c. 26) placed the
cost of removing an Irish pauper to his home parish on to the removing parish
in England Not surprisingly, the number of removals to Ireland (and elsewhere)
fell even more.

26 BPP, HC, *Report of the Select Committee on Settlement and Irremoveability of Paupers*,
1878–79 (282) xii referred to hereafter as SC 1879, minutes of evidence, J.H. Hagger, q.
1757, p. 96.

Table No. 9: Pauper removals from the parish of Liverpool in each of the years 1869 to 1878, inclusive, distinguishing between Irish, Scots and English

Year	Irish	English	Scots	Total
1869	204	15	20	239
1870	120	15	9	144
1871	67	19	13	99
1872	82	15	–	97
1873	53	5	–	58
1874	95	26	2	123
1875	118	27	4	149
1876	112	18	3	133
1877	102	34	4	140
1876	88	29	6	123
Total	1041	203	61	1305

Source: *British Parliamentary Papers* (HC) 1878–79 (282) xii, *Report of the Select Committee on Poor Removal*, Minutes of Evidence, J.H. Hagger, p. 91

The Irish still accounted for 80 per cent of all Liverpool removals but by 1878, the absolute number of Irish persons removed had fallen to 88, in dramatic contrast to the 15,000 removed during 1847. Following on quickly, an act of 1865, the Union Chargeability Act (28 and 29 Vic. c. 79) took all responsibility for rating and settlement away from parishes and on to the Union. Importantly, one year's continuous *residence in a Union* secured the status of irremoveability. In 1876, the Divided Parishes Act (39 and 40 Vic. c. 61) stipulated that three years continuous residence in a Union gave a person the status of settled. These further reduced the Irish migrants' fear of being sent back to Ireland. They also reflected the growing concern over the need for a mobile labour force. In 1879, yet another select committee was set up to inquire into the laws of settlement and removal, with 'special reference to the case of removals to Ireland'. Again, large amounts of evidence were collected and the general views given reflected those of earlier investigations. By 1878, settlement could be obtained by birth or by three years' residence in a parish. The status of irremoveability was acquired by one year's residence in a Union. In Ireland, there was still no law of settlement or removal.

IV

The recurring criticisms of the system came under the following headings. First, the laws were an infringement of the basic right of freedom of movement. This criticism was not new. Adam Smith, the father of the discipline of economics, wrote 'to remove a man, who has committed no misdemeanour, from the parish where he chooses to reside, is an evident violation of natural liberty and justice'.[27] Granville Pigott, giving evidence to the 1847 Select Committee, was a savage critic of the whole system of removal and settlement. He commented:

> If, instead of patching and tampering, instead of timidly following in the steps of the single and well timed measure of Elizabeth, a measure, however, the avowed insufficiency of which caused the necessity for further legislation, instead of adhering to the narrow system of parochial relief and liability, and riveting on the back of the poor the enslaving bond of settlement, the legislative had taken a more comprehensive view, and, following a bolder course, had set labour altogether free, what an amount of sorrow, what a waste of substance, would have been spared during these two centuries of litigation and wrong ...[28]

In retrospect, Pigott's view seems correct; the whole history of the laws of settlement and removal is one of tampering and short term thinking. The 1878 Select Committee hearings revealed essentially the same concerns as earlier investigations. The laws of settlement were an infringement of the freedom to offer one's labour wherever one wished and this was harmful to the economy. Every man had a right to offer his labour wherever he thought he could get the best bargain and there was widespread recognition of the value of Irish labour to the economy. Second, there was much, and consistent, criticism of the cost of inter-parochial law suits, both in time and money. Third, the laws were often applied with much cruelty. There are many such instances. For example, in 1847, the case of Michael Duignan caused an uproar. The twelve-year-old boy, crippled and ill, was removed from Rochdale, with his brother and sister. On the voyage from Liverpool to Dublin, he was crushed to death.[29] Terence McNally was an Irish man living in Birkenhead. He was a French polisher by trade but had been sick for a while. On 22 July 1854, Terence, his wife Bridget and their five children were removed to Dublin via Liverpool. They arrived in Dublin at 3 a.m. and had nowhere to go. They used what money they had been given by Birkenhead parish to buy tickets back to Liverpool that same evening, illustrating the inability of removal to stop the movement of Irish into Britain. They travelled on the deck with the cattle and it rained most of the trip. In Birkenhead they had nothing to eat but were frightened of applying for poor relief in case they were removed again. The family were willing to risk starvation rather than be sent back to Ireland.[30] Parish officials often harassed paupers in an attempt to get them to move to another parish.

Against those hostile to the laws were ranged those who feared that the abolition of the laws of removal would result in a large increase in Irish migration into

---

27 Quoted in SC (1847), Appendix No. 3, G. Pigott, p. 41   28 G. Pigott, op. cit., p. 44
29 Neal, *Black '47*, pp 29–236. This case is dealt with in great detail as it reveals the inefficient running of the system.   30 SC 1854, Minutes of evidences, A. Doyle, q. 2386.

Britain. In the case of officials from Liverpool and Glasgow, the horrors of the
famine years thirty years earlier, still haunted them but the fact was that immigration continued, despite the laws of removal. In none of the evidence presented was
there any in-depth economic analysis of the labour markets though it was recognised that the Irish moved to Britain principally because of the lack of job opportunities at home. Another objection to the abandonment of the laws of settlement
and removal was the fact that they were used as a workhouse test. An Irish pauper
asking for poor relief could be given the choice of removal or going in the workhouse. If he or she refused the workhouse, it was assumed they were not desperate and so were liable to removal. Knowing of this policy, many Irish stopped
applying for relief. It was also feared that the abandonment of the laws would lead
to an increase in vagrancy. Despite these opinions the Select Committee of 1879
recommended that the laws of settlement be abolished. Its views were ignored.

Though there was continued support in some quarters for the maintenance
of the laws of settlement and removal, as has been observed, the numbers
removed declined rapidly after 1860. The number of Irish-born in Britain in
1881 was 562,374 yet in the year ending 25 March 1882, only 248 Irish were
removed.[31] After this year, Irish removals ceased to be a matter of concern. This
did not mean the problem of Irish poverty in England had been resolved. Fear
of removal undoubtedly reduced the numbers of Irish claiming relief but it
drove many into abject poverty, begging and petty crime. It is impossible to
quantify this deterrent effect of the removal laws, but all the available evidence
suggests that it was significant. Despite this deterrent effect, it is interesting to
note that in June 1879, of the 2413 paupers receiving outdoor relief in Liverpool,
1185 were Irish.[32] It must be assumed the majority had settlement or the status
of irremovcability. However, the laws did not affect the numbers of Irish coming
to England. Poverty in England was considered better than poverty in Ireland.
People removed could get another ship back to Britain and the system of administering the settlement and removal laws was too inefficient to stop such practices. The truth of the proposition that people follow jobs was reinforced in the
1930s and post Second World War, when Irish migration into Britain ran at high
levels as the labour market, particularly during and after the war, offered jobs
galore.[33] Between 1921 and the early 1970s, approximately one and a half million
Irish emigrated, most going to Britain. In the same vein, the booming Irish
economy since 1990, has stopped the flow of emigration for the first time in 170
years. After 1879, the matter of poverty continued to generate government
reports but removal was not an issue. The laws of settlement and removal, which
applied to both English and Irish, remained on the statute book until 1948.

31 M Rose, 'Settlement, removal and the new Poor Law' in D. Fraser, *The new Poor Law*, p.
44.   32 BPP, SC 1879, Hagger, q. 1693, p. 92.   33 For a full discussion of Irish migration
to Britain following the creation of the Irish Free State, see E. Delaney, *Demography, state
and society: Irish migration to Britain, 1921–1971* (London, 2000).

Thomas Carlyle and Ireland

ROGER SWIFT

'Crowds of miserable Irish darken all our towns.'[1]

Thus wrote Thomas Carlyle in his famous long pamphlet *Chartism*, published in December 1839. But what moved Carlyle, the intellectual hero of the age, to direct attention in *Chartism* to England's relationship with Ireland and to the Irish presence in the early Victorian city? Why did he present the Irish in England in such negative terms? Was his analysis correct? How far was his interest in Irish issues sustained and developed in later years? And what was the wider significance of his critique? These, as Carlyle might have said, are measurable questions and they form the essential framework of this essay. Yet it is impossible to respond to these questions without first examining the contemporary social, economic, and political contexts within which *Chartism* was written, Carlyle's development as an historian in the early 1830s, and the purpose of *Chartism*, including the chapter on the Irish entitled 'The finest peasantry in the world'.

Chartism was written at the end of a decade when the social and economic consequences of industrialisation and urbanisation were not only becoming all too visible but were increasingly the subject of parliamentary and extra-parliamentary scrutiny and inquiry. The rapid growth of industry and the increasing concentration of an expanding population in industrial and manufacturing centres served to both exacerbate and magnify the depressed social condition of the working classes and to highlight the growing gulf between the rich and the poor. In particular, the social issues of poverty, crime, ignorance, low standards of public health and housing, and harsh working conditions provided the focus for an intellectual and political debate between those who argued that industrialisation, supported by the political economy of laissez-faire, was a progressive development, the genesis of unbounded wealth and the mark of an advancing civilisation, and those who held that it was essentially regressive, the harbinger of social disharmony and environmental decay, and the potential source for political conflict between the propertied and privileged sectors of society – bolstered by the political settlement enshrined in the Great Reform Act of 1832 –

---

1 Thomas Carlyle, *Chartism* (London, 1839; reprinted, with an introduction by Ian Cambell, in Thomas Carlyle, *Selected essays* (London 1972), p. 182.

117

and the disenfranchised masses. The decade had commenced with rural unrest in the shape of the 'Swing' riots of 1830 in the southern counties of England; yet by the late-1830s working-class discontent in the manufacturing districts, compounded by the exclusion of the working classes from the 1832 settlement and the Benthamite-inspired class legislation (most notably the New Poor Law of 1834) of successive Whig governments, had found political expression in Chartism against the immediate backcloth of the worst economic depression of the nineteenth century. The Chartist movement, with its six-point manifesto for democratic reform, published in 1838 as 'The People's Charter', represented a radical political response by working people to their condition, and it was the very nature of that condition, placed in its wider historical context, that Carlyle sought to address in his pamphlet of 1839.[2]

Carlyle held a lifelong interest in history, which he regarded as the most profitable of all studies. This interest reflected Carlyle's awareness of the mysteriousness of Time as the medium in which all human action occurs, hence his concern to recover the lost past and to make it live again, which he saw as a major responsibility of the historian and which owed much to Germanic influences, and particularly to Hegel. It also derived from Carlyle's perception of history as Bible, as the revelation of a just providence working in human affairs; thus, by studying the chastisements visited upon erring societies in the past, existing societies can mend their ways in the present, and this providential view of history informed much of Carlyle's historical writing in the 1830s.[3] Moreover, as Peter Keating has observed, Carlyle's preoccupation as an historian with the inter-connectedness of the past, the present, and the future within a continuum reflected one of the distinguishing characteristics of modern

---

2 For social and economic conditions in England during the 1830s, see especially J.L. & B. Hammond, *The town labourer* (London, 1917); E.P. Thompson, *The making of the English working class* (London, 1963); G.B.A.M. Finlayson, *England in the eighteen thirties: decade of reform* (London, 1969); B. Inglis, *Poverty and the Industrial Revolution* (London, 1971); E.J. Hobsbawm and G. Rude, *Captain Swing* (London 1973); A.J. Taylor (ed.), *The standard of living in Britain in the Industrial Revolution* (London 1975); D. Roberts, *Paternalism in early Victorian England* (London, 1979); U.R. Henriques, *Before the Welfare State: social administration in early industrial Britain* (London, 1979).   3 A.L. Le Quesne, 'Carlyle', in A.L. Le Quesne, G.P. Landow, S. Collini and P. Stansky, *Victorian thinkers* (Oxford, 1982), pp 39–41. For Carlyle's life and work, see also J. Holloway, *The Victorian sage* (London, 1953); J.P. Seigel (ed.), *Thomas Carlyle: the critical heritage* (London, 1971); J. Clubbe (ed.), *Carlyle and his contemporaries* (Durham, North Carolina, 1976); F. Kaplan, *Thomas Carlyle: a biography* (Cambridge, 1983); B.V. Qualls, *The secular pilgrims of Victorian fiction* (Cambridge, 1983); J.D. Rosenberg, *Carlyle and the burden of history* (Oxford, 1985); Clyde de L. Ryals, Kenneth J. Fielding, Ian Campbell, Aileen Christianson, Hilary J. Smith, and Bill Bell (eds), *The collected letters of Thomas and Jane Welsh Carlyle*, vols. 22–4 (Durham and London 1995). For Carlyle as historian, see also Richard W. Schoch, '"We do nothing but enact history": Thomas Carlyle stages the past', *Nineteenth-Century Literature*, 54, no. 1 (June 1999), 27–52.

prophetic literature.[4] In 1829 Carlyle published an important essay, 'Signs of the times', in the *Edinburgh Review*.[5] This essay, which was perhaps his first major contribution to the social thought of the day, had articulated a direct and critical response to the England of his times, to Industrialism, which he was the first to name, and to the quality of men's reactions to what he defined as 'the Age of Machinery, in every outward and inward sense of that word'. In damning 'faith in mechanism', Carlyle had also pointed to the socially-destructive and disorienting impact of Industrialism by altering old social relationships and increasing the distance between rich and poor.[6]

Indeed, by the late 1830s, the social condition of England had become his chief preoccupation. As Peter Keating observes, this was the period when his influence was at its strongest, for his gospel of work and fierce demands that the new industrial society should be studied and understood were important features of the early Victorian mood.[7] In 1837 Carlyle published *The French Revolution* and the ideas it expressed contributed to his growing reputation as a social prophet. For Carlyle, the French Revolution was the central fact of modern history and represented a sentence of divine justice on a corrupt society; as such, it was a cause for hope rather than fear at a time when the Revolution and the ideas associated with it were anathema to the governing classes of Europe, including Britain, after 1815. Carlyle argued that the horrors and violence of the Revolution, which he described graphically, were no more than the result of all that had gone before; judgements wreaked on a corrupt society in which rulers had abrogated their divinely-ordained responsibilities to the ruled. Yet *The French Revolution* was also of obvious and ominous relevance to the social condition of England in the early 1830s, for the parallels between his description of the plight of the French poor in the years before 1789 in *The French Revolution* and the condition of the English working classes in the 1830s were self-evident. In short, Carlyle intended *The French Revolution* to serve in part as a great history lesson that the world was ruled in the last resort by a just providence, a lesson that his fellow-countymen might learn and learn from before it was too late.[8]

A similar theme emerged in *Chartism*, which has generally been acknowledged as one of Carlyle's supreme works: for Raymond Williams the pamphlet was a fine example of Carlyle's developed method and convictions;[9] A. Le Quesne has suggested that *Chartism* could be considered the best piece of social

4 Peter Keating, *The Victorian prophets: a reader from Carlyle to Wells* (London, 1981), p. 18; See also Robin Gilmour, *The Victorian period: the intellectual and cultural context of English literature, 1830–1890* (London, 1993), pp 31–7. 5 See especially Lawrence Poston, 'Millites and millenarians: the context of Carlyle's "Signs of the Times",' *Victorian Studies*, 26, no. 4 (1983), 381–406. 6 Raymond Williams, *Culture and society, 1780–1950* (London, 1958), pp 72–5. 7 Keating, *The Victorian prophets*, p. 43. 8 Le Quesne, *Victorian thinkers*, pp 49–50. 9 Williams, *Culture and society*, p. 71.

criticism that Carlyle ever wrote;[10] whilst Simon Heffer has described *Chartism* as 'the essence of Carlyle's political thought, the clearest statement of his beliefs'.[11] Carlyle began writing *Chartism* in August 1839, and completed it on 8 November, noting in his Journal 'I have just finished a long review article, thick pamphlet, or little volume, entitled "Chartism".'[12] The actual theme of the pamphlet is not Chartism itself, but the depth of human misery and suffering – the product of an increasingly Godless and materialistic society – that had given rise to the movement. It begins by articulating contemporary anxieties in regard to the social condition of the masses:

> A feeling very generally exists that the condition and disposition of the Working Classes is a rather ominous matter at present; that something ought to be said, something ought to be done, in regard to it.[13]

It then proceeds, with characteristic insight, to recognise Chartism as:

> the bitter discontent grown fierce and mad, the wrong condition therefore or the wrong disposition, of the Working Classes of England. It is a new name for a thing which has had many names, which will yet have many. The matter of Chartism is weighty, deep-rooted, far-extending.[14]

Then Carlyle poses the famous 'Condition-of-England question:

> What means this bitter discontent of the Working Classes? Whence comes it, whither it goes? Above all, at what price, on what terms, will it probably consent to depart from us and die into rest? These are measurable questions ... The condition of the great body of people in a country is the condition of the country itself ... Surely Honorable Members ought to speak of the Condition- of-England question too?[15]

Hence for Carlyle, Chartism was the latest and most alarming manifestation of the 'deep-lying struggle in the whole fabric of society', the product of Industrialism, that he had identified previously in 'Signs of the times'. Indeed, in describing the discontent and disorder manifest in Chartism as 'our French Revolution', Carlyle not only articulated a sense that the material degradation of large masses of the population was morally offensive, but also presented an apocalyptical vision of the future – that if the economic and social consequences of industrialization were allowed to proceed without amelioration, catastrophic social unrest and communal violence would result.[16]

10 Le Quesne, *Victorian thinkers*, p. 54.   11 Simon Heffer, *Moral desperado: a life of Thomas Carlyle* (London, 1995), p. 193.   12 J.A. Froude, *Carlyle's life in London*, 2 vols (London, 1902), vol. 1, p. 183.   13 Carlyle, *Chartism*, p. 182.   14 Ibid.   15 Ibid. 16 Barry Supple, 'Material development: the condition of England, 1830–1860', in Laurence Lerner (ed.), *The context of English literature: the Victorians* (New York, 1978), p. 50.

Thus *Chartism* presented both a radical and incisive critique of the impact of industrial capitalism on contemporary society and a savage indictment of the ruling class for allowing such human suffering to materialise. For Carlyle, the moral and physical well-being – the cultural health – of society was the responsibility of the ruling class (in England, aristocratic government), and their prime duty was to provide sufficient work for the masses to do; in turn, the ruling class was responsible to the divine justice that presided over the social order. In *Chartism* Carlyle held that the English ruling classes had abrogated such responsibilities and that their dereliction of duty had contributed to the emergence of the Chartist movement; here, Carlyle's belief in providential justice working itself out is history is evident – it was mis-government that lay at the root of social distress and discontent. Moreover, he argued that this failure of government was the product of the domination of the public conscience by Benthamite Utilitarianism, a philosophy that he abhorred. In November 1839 Carlyle had observed that 'no sect in our day has made a wretcheder figure than the Bentham Radical sect'.[17] Indeed, he held that the practical application of Benthamism had reduced human emotions and relationships to measurable quantities and mechanical interactions based on calculations of profit and loss – 'the cash-nexus' – and had replaced spiritual and social obligations by economic and financial ones.[18]

Chartism thus presented a moral indictment of industrialisation and its social consequences. Heffer describes it as 'a belated, and hopeless, cry against the industrial revolution',[19] yet it was a cry that not only subsequently informed, via Charles Kingsley, the theoretical foundations of Christian Socialism,[20] but also provided a significant critique of capitalist society that was acknowledged by Karl Marx.[21] As such, the pamphlet not only focused attention on the problems of the poor but also contributed to an intellectual and political debate during the 1840s among the educated and/or propertied classes within which the phrases 'Condition-of-England Question' and 'cash-nexus' became commonplace. Carlyle's demand was for rational enquiry, for these were 'measurable questions' to which the proliferation of Statistical Societies had failed to respond effectively, and he saw the failure of the legislature to seek such evidence as a symptom of the spirit of laissez-faire. Hence Carlyle's call was for more government, not less; more order, not less. Later he was to call to the classes with power – the middle classes, 'the Captains of Industry' – to purge themselves of what he termed 'Donothingism' and make themselves an active and responsible governing class who would transform the social and human relationships hitherto dictated by the 'laws' of political economy.[22]

17 Froude, *Carlyle's life in London*, vol. 1, p.183.   18 Heffer, *Moral desperado*, p.194.
19 Ibid.   20 David Amigoni, *Victorian biography: intellectuals and the ordering of discourse* (London, 1993), pp 72–3.   21 Le Quesne, *Victorian thinkers*, pp 72–3.   22 Williams, *Culture and society*, pp 71–83.

This said, while Carlyle shared the Chartists' concern over the 'Condition of England Question', he vehemently opposed their prescription, for he had little sympathy with the struggle for democracy inherent in the movement.[23] Prior to the publication of *Chartism* he had been widely regarded as an extreme radical and many of his earlier writings had appeared in Whig or Radical journals. But the contents of *Chartism* reflected his rejection of the democratic forms of radicalism; indeed, as a realist, Carlyle saw democracy as an unpractical system, a Utopian creed which had already (as in the French Revolution) failed the test of history.[24] Moreover, the record of the reformed parliament since 1832 provided him with little evidence for believing that a further extension of the franchise (universal male suffrage being the pre-eminent Chartist demand) would provide the solution to contemporary social problems. Indeed, Carlyle held that it had been the failure of the reformed Parliament and its elected representatives to both address and discover the root causes of distress that had given rise to Chartism. In his later writings, in his search for stability in a sea of change, Carlyle increasingly moved to an alternative solution based on heroic leadership and reverent obedience, as reflected in *Heroes and hero-worship* (1841), *Past and present* (1843), *Oliver Cromwell's letters and speeches* (1845), *Latter day pamphlets* (1850), and *Frederick the Great* (1865). By the time of *Shooting Niagara: And after?* (1867) Carlyle had become utterly contemptuous of the masses, whom he described as a 'Swarmery' who were characterised chiefly by 'blockheadism, gullibility, bribeability, amenability to beer and balderdash'.[25]

Chartism was stronger on destructive than constructive criticism and Carlyle's prescriptions were uncertain. In particular, Carlyle believed that the solution to the nation's ills could be achieved by programmes of state-promoted popular education and the planned emigration of surplus working people. The emphasis on the former, to promote culture (which he defined as the first duty of government), reflects Carlyle's belief that society was composed of much more than economic relationships with cash payment as the sole nexus (which was the root of his attack on industrialism), whilst the latter owed much to Malthusianism. His apocalyptic vision also proved unjustified, for the 1850s gave way to relative social calm. Nevertheless, *Chartism* changed public perceptions of Carlyle: 850 copies of the pamphlet were quickly sold and a second edition prepared and, as Carlyle had forecast, 'such an article, equally astonishing to Girondins, Radicals, do-nothing Aristocrats, Conservatives, and unbelieving dilettante Whigs, can hope for no harbour in any Review'.[26]

The chapter entitled 'The finest peasantry in the world' deals exclusively with England's relationship with Ireland and the socio-economic consequences

23 Gertrude Himmelfarb, *The idea of poverty: England in the early industrial age* (London, 1984), p. 199.   24 Le Quesne, *Victorian thinkers*, p. 58.   25 Williams, *Culture and society*, p. 84.   26 Froude, *Carlyle's life in London*, vol. 1, p. 183.

of Irish immigration on English society. For Carlyle, Ireland offered an historical case-study, an exemplar, of the consequences of English misgovernance.
Carlyle begins by referring to the scale of poverty in Ireland:

> There is one fact which Statistic Science has communicated, and a most
> astonishing one; the inference from which is pregnant to this matter.
> Ireland has near seven millions of working people, the third unit of
> whom, it appears by Statistic Science, has not for thirty weeks as many
> third-rate potatoes as will suffice him.[27]

He then goes on to blame British misgovernment for creating starvation in
Ireland:

> We English pay, even now, the bitter smart of long centuries of injustice
> to our neighbour Island. Injustice, doubt it not, abounds; or Ireland
> would not be miserable.[28]

But he goes further:

> England is guilty towards Ireland; and reaps at last, in full measure, the
> fruit of fifteen generations of wrong doing.[29]

Here again we have an illustration of Carlyle's belief in providential justice
working itself out in history, for the consequence of British misgovernment in
Ireland had been the arrival in England during the 1830s of an increasing
number of Irish poor who, unable to survive in their own country, sought work
in England, undercutting wages and contributing to unemployment which, in
turn, contributed to popular discontent in the form of Chartism. Thus, for
Carlyle, the growing presence of the Irish poor in Early Victorian England was
England's punishment for her mistreatment of Ireland.

Then, in perhaps the most famous and much-quoted passage from the
chapter, Carlyle describes the moral and physical condition of the Irish in
England:

> Crowds of miserable Irish darken all our towns. The wild Milesian fea-
> tures, looking false ingenuity, restlessness, unreason, misery and mockery,
> salute you on all highways and byways. The English coachman, as he
> whirls past, lashes the Milesian with his whip, curses him with his tongue;
> the Milesian is holding out his hat to beg. He is the sorest evil this country
> has to strive with. In his rags and laughing savagery, he is there to under-

27 Carlyle, *Chartism*, p. 180.   28 Ibid., p. 182.   29 Ibid.

take all work that can be done by mere strength of hand and back; for
wages that will purchase him potatoes. He needs only salt for condiment;
he lodges to his mind in any pighutch or doghutch, roosts in outhouses;
and wears a suit of tatters, the getting off and on of which is said to be a
difficult operation, transacted only in festivals and the hightides of the
calendar. The Saxon man if he cannot work on these terms, finds no
work. He too may be ignorant; but he has not sunk from decent manhood
to squalid apehood; he cannot continue there … There abides he, in his
squalor and unreason, in his falsity and drunken violence, as the ready-
made nucleus of degradation and disorder.[30]

Here the poverty-stricken Irish are clearly presented as a blight on contemporary urban society, swarming into towns and cities with their uncivilised ways
and exacerbating the 'Condition of England Question'. The Irish character is
impugned in the most vitriolic terms and the Irish are presented, as inferior
beings within a wholly negative stereotype, as a threat not only to social order
and stability but also to the very fabric of society. All this 'is lamentable to look
upon', says Carlyle, but he acknowledges that it is not the fault of 'these poor
Celtiberian Irish brothers' who 'cannot stay at home, and starve'; it is natural
that they migrate. But their arrival in England represents 'a curse', a punishment for English mistreatment of Ireland in the past, which Carlyle then seeks
to explain by placing the impact of Irish immigration into a wider social and
economic context:

> That the condition of the lower multitude of English labourers approxi-
> mates more and more to that of the Irish competing with them in all
> markets; that whatsoever labour, to which mere strength with little skill
> will suffice, is to be done, will be done, not at the English price, but at an
> approximation to the Irish price; at a price superior as yet to the Irish, that
> is, superior to scarcity of third-rate potatoes for thirty weeks yearly; supe-
> rior, yet hourly, with the arrival of every new steamboat, sinking nearer to
> an equality with that.[31]

So here we have Irish competition in the labour market undercutting English
wages, with its inevitable impact on the scale of English unemployment,
poverty, living standards, and discontent.

It should be noted from the outset that Carlyle's explanation for Irish emigration, the negative stereotype of the Irish character that he presented, and
the deteriorationist consequences of Irish immigration on the English
economy and the standard of living of English workers were neither original
nor unique. Similar observations had already been made by Dr James Phillips

30 Ibid., pp 182–3.   31 Ibid., p. 184.

Kay in his pamphlet of 1832, *The moral and physical condition of the working classes employed in the cotton manufacture in Manchester*, which argued that the Irish, with their debased peasant ways and their ability to survive on the bare minimum required for existence, taught the English working class a 'pernicious lesson', bringing down living standards wherever they settled.[32] Four years later, echoes of Kay's views emerged in *The Report of the Royal Commission on the state of the Irish poor in Great Britain* (1836), which sought in part to examine the extent to which Irish immigrants exercised a negative influence on the English and Scotch working classes by lowering their wages and debasing their moral character. The architect of the report, Sir George Cornewall Lewis, ultimately endorsed the views of many employers by emphasising the economic value of Irish immigrant labour:

> We ought not, however, to overlook the advantage of the demand for labour in England and Scotland being amply and adequately supplied, and at a cheap rate and at very short notice, by Irish; it is to be remembered that these Irish have been, and are, most efficient workmen; and they came in the hour of need, and that they afforded the chief part of the animal strength by which the great works of our manufacturing districts have been executed.[33]

Yet much of the evidence presented by middle-class observers to the *Report on the state of the Irish poor in Great Britain* also presented the Irish as uniformly poverty-stricken, dirty, unthrifty, dissolute, and criminal, and Cornewall Lewis acknowledged that in consequence of their social condition the Irish were not only extremely unpopular in those towns where they settled but also served to provide 'an example of a less civilized population spreading themselves, as a kind of substratum, beneath a more civilized community'.[34]

The work of Kay and Cornewall Lewis illustrates that anti-Irish stereotypes were well-entrenched prior to the publication of *Chartism* and, indeed, informed Carlyle's analysis of the Irish in England. Moreover, Kay and Cornewall Lewis not only provided a forum for deep-rooted anti-Irish antagonisms to surface during the 1830s but also helped to initiate an historiographical tradition which presented an overtly negative image of Irish immigrants as the outcasts of contemporary society.[35] That Carlyle made a powerful and influential contribution to the development of this genre is without question, for his

---

32 James Phillips Kay, *The moral and physical condition of the working classes employed in the cotton manufacture in Manchester* (Manchester, 1832), p. 20.   33 *Report on the State of the Irish Poor in Great Britain, Parliamentary Papers*, (1836), 34, xxxiv, pp 456–7.   34 Ibid. 35 Donald M. MacRaild, 'Irish immigration and the "Condition of England" Question: the roots of an historiographical tradition', *Immigrants and Minorities*, 14, no. 1 (Mar. 1995), 67–85.

analysis of the Irish in *Chartism* clearly informed subsequent and equally negative portrayals of the Irish by Frederick Engels, in *The condition of the working
class in England*,[36] and by Angus Reach, in his reports on the Irish in the north
of England for the *Morning Chronicle* in 1849.[37]

Professor Perry Curtis, Jr, an American historian, has argued that these
examples of anti-Irish prejudice, articulated as they were by representatives of
the Victorian intelligensia, including Carlyle, were essentially racist because
they were based on the assumption that the native Irish were inferior in culture
and alien in race to the Anglo-Saxons, an assumption that also underpinned
simianized representations of the Irish in Victorian cartoons, most notably in
Punch.[38] This thesis has been challenged by several historians, most notably
Sheridan Gilley, who has argued that the British stereotype of 'Paddy' had a
benign as well as a menacing face and was as much an Irish creation as a British
one. Hence, whilst the Irish were held, on the one hand, to be feckless, stupid,
violent, unreliable and drunken, they were also perceived, on the other, as
chaste, hospitable, witty, kindly and generous. Gilley has also suggested that
there were understandable contemporary social and economic reasons for much
of the hostility shown towards the Irish, reasons which do not in themselves
justify the term 'racial prejudice'.[39]

Clearly, the anti-Celtic stereotype was a complex one. Victorian racial theory
was in the form of the claim that the English were superior as a 'mixed race',
not as a pure one, to the Celts; hence the best mongrel English had the good
Celtic qualities as well as the good Anglo-Saxon ones. In this context, the extent
to which Anglo-Saxonism, a product of the Victorian intelligentsia, informed
popular perceptions of the Irish and influenced the activities of anti-Irish disorders in English cities remains obscure. Moreover, anti-Celtism does not
appear to have impeded the advancement of the small Irish Catholic middle
class in Victorian Britain, and it is possible that the prejudice which undoubtedly manifested itself was one essentially focused on Irish paupers, as a parallel with the more negative attitudes towards the English poor. Yet, as Roy Foster
has observed, Celticism was an ambiguous concept during the Victorian period

36 F. Engels, *The condition of the working class in England* (1844: ed., London, 1987), pp
123–6. For Engels and Carlyle on Ireland see especially J. Lea and G. Pilling (eds), *The condition of Britain: essays on Frederick Engels* (London 1996), pp 120–3, 144–6; M. Levin, *The
condition of England Question: Carlyle, Mill, Engels* (London, 1998), pp 42–59, 138–42. 37
MacRaild, *Immigrants and minorities*, pp 78–81. 38 L.P. Curtis, *Apes and angels: the
Irishman in Victorian caricature* (Newton Abbot, 1971). See also Curtis' recent defence of his
thesis in 'Historical revisionism and constructions of Paddy and Pat' in the revised edition
of *Apes and angels* (Washington and London, 1997), pp 109–147; Catherine M. Eagan,
'Simianization meets postcolonial theory' (a review of the 1997 edition of *Apes and angels*),
Irish Literary Supplement (Fall, 1997), pp 27–8. 39 Sheridan Gilley, 'English attitudes to
the Irish in England, 1780–1900', in Colin Holmes (ed.), *Immigrants and minorities in British
society* (London, 1978), pp 81–110.

and many who might, at first sight, have seemed anti-Celtic also valued the Celtic contribution to what was perceived to be the British identity.[40] On the other hand, there was an almost universal tendency from the 1840s onwards to describe the immigrant Irish in distinctly racial terms, terms which have retained their use into more recent times.

Yet there were other deep-seated reasons for anti-Irish prejudice in English society. In matters of religion, Irish immigrants were largely Roman Catholic whereas the English, Scots and Welsh were overwhelmingly Protestant by tradition. After 1790 the strength of popular Protestantism was greatly reinforced by the Evangelical Revival, whilst Protestant 'No Popery' also gained an increasing ascendency over the established Church of Ireland and Ulster immigrants of the Orange Order introduced their fratricidal strife with Irish Catholics into a number of British cities, notably Liverpool, where sectarian competition for jobs in a weakly-unionised economy polarised local politics between the Orange and the Green. Religion proved subsequently to be a vital ingredient in determining Anglo-Irish relations on a local level, particularly during the mid-Victorian period. The terms 'Irish' and 'Catholic' were virtually synonymous in British eyes and although anti-Irish sentiment was more diffuse than anti-Catholicism, it is evident that the resurgence of popular Protestantism in the wake of the Tractarian controversy of the 1840s and the re-establishment of the Roman Catholic hierarchy in 1850 provided an additional cutting-edge to Anglo-Irish tensions and contributed to the serious clashes between the English and the Irish during the period.[41] Yet whilst the Catholicism of the Irish may well have contributed to their isolation, they were not more 'outcast' as Catholics than English or foreign Catholics on the ground of their Catholicism alone. Catholicism was unpopular as a living ideological force and Victorian 'No Popery' was much more than anti-Irishness: Catholicism was regarded by Victorian liberals as foreign, exotic and dangerous, the religion of Britain's traditional enemies, France and Spain, the ally of reactionary governments and the creed of superstitious peasants everywhere.[42]

40 Roy Foster, *Paddy and Mr Punch: connections in English and Irish history* (London, 1993), p. 193.   41 For further details of these disturbances, see especially Pauline Millward, 'The Stockport Riots of 1852: a study of anti-Catholic and anti-Irish sentiment', in Roger Swift and Sheridan Gilley (eds), *The Irish in the Victorian city* (London, 1985), pp 207–24; J. Foster, *Class struggle and the Industrial Revolution* (London, 1974), pp 243–6; Frank Neal, 'The Birkenhead Garibaldi riots of 1862', *Transactions of the Historic Society of Lancashire and Cheshire*, 131 (1982), pp 87–111; Sheridan Gilley, 'The Garibaldi riots of 1862', *Historical Journal*, 16, no. 4 (1973), pp 697–732; W.J. Arnstein, 'The Murphy riots: a Victorian dilemma', *Victorian Studies*, 19 (1975), 51–71; Roger Swift, 'Anti-Catholicism and Irish disturbances: public order in mid-Victorian Wolverhampton', *Midland History*, 9 (1984), 87–108; Frank Neal, *Sectarian violence: the Liverpool experience, 1819–1914* (Manchester, 1987).   42 For further details, see especially D.W. Miller, 'Irish Catholicism and the Great Famine', *Journal of Social History*, 9 (1975), pp 81–98; Gerard Connolly, 'Irish and Catholic:

Irish nationalism offered further grounds for British prejudice, in the tradition of Irish agrarian outrage, and of the 'physical force' resort to street violence and armed rebellion, or more impressively, the recourse to mass defiance. Yet the whole conception of the Irish as offering the 'outcast' alternative in English radical politics requires the most sensitive statement. Certainly, the Irish nationalist members of parliament after 1829 formed an often discordant element in English political life; different aspects of the Irish question helped to defeat the Tory party in 1846; there was a significant Irish dimension to Chartism, particularly during its later phases; and Irish agitation for the repeal of the Act of Union of 1800, spearheaded by Daniel O'Connell – 'The Irish Liberator' – during the 1830s and early-1840s, did seem to many Englishmen to threaten the destruction of the empire at its very heart. Moreover, the disorders in Ireland associated with the activities of the repeal movement, coupled with O'Connell's support in parliament for the Whigs during the 1830s, provided an additional political sub-text for *Chartism*, for Carlyle supported the Union as vehemently as he opposed the Whigs. Yet there is also evidence to suggest that the actual Irish threat to the empire was greatly exaggerated and that the vast majority of Irish Catholic immigrants and their children were loyal if not always enthusiastic subjects of the Crown in England, Scotland and Wales.[43]

That anti-Irish prejudice was an odd compound of religious, social and political elements, both rational and irrational, is indisputable, but during the early-Victorian period it served to increase the isolation of the Irish poor in particular, who were variously perceived in Carlylean terms as a nuisance, a threat, or a contagion. Outcast from British capitalism as the poorest of the poor, from mainstream British politics as separatist nationalists and republicans, from the 'Anglo-Saxon' race as 'Celts', and as Catholics from the dominant forms of British Protestantism, the Irish were presented as the outsiders of contemporary society on the basis of class, nationality, race and religion, a people set apart, rejected and despised. In this context, Carlyle's references to the Irish in *Chartism* merely served to confirm what was already widely held to be the case – that Irish immigration was a social evil that highlighted basic differences between the English and the Irish – although they also represented a powerful, even infamous, contribution to an historiographical tradition that subsequently exercised an enormous influence on the historical study of the Irish in Britain.

myth or reality', in Swift and Gilley, *The Irish in the Victorian city*, pp 225–54; Sheridan Gilley, 'The Catholic faith of the Irish slums: London, 1840–70', in H.J. Dyos and M. Wolff (eds), *The Victorian city: images and realities*, 2 vols. (London, 1973), vol. 2, pp 837–53; see also Dr Gilley's 'Vulgar piety and the Brompton Oratory, 1850–60', in Swift and Gilley, *The Irish in the Victorian city*, pp 255–66; Raphael Samuel, 'The Roman Catholic church and the Irish poor', in Swift and Gilley, *The Irish in the Victorian city*, pp 267–300.   **43** For further details, see especially Dorothy Thompson, 'Ireland and the Irish in English radicalism before 1850', in James Epstein and Dorothy Thompson (eds), *The Chartist experience* (London, 1982), pp 120–51.

Yet it is also important to acknowledge that recent research has shed doubt on many of the assumptions inherent in the Carlylean analysis. First, the causes of Irish migration to England during the period have been the subject of considerable historical debate. The classic explanation, voiced by Carlyle and others, held that Irish emigration was largely the consequence of a mounting Irish economic crisis of Malthusian dimensions, whereby a backward agrarian economy was increasingly unable to support a population that had virtually doubled between 1760 and 1840. Central to this argument was the belief that Ireland's agrarian problems were the product of feudal tenurial arrangements and an abundance of discontented labourers and petty farmers, who kept wages low and prevented Irish landlords and British investors from modernising agriculture and making it profitable. Similarly, over-population was regarded as the product of Catholic improvidence. Hence poverty, dearth and distress, which reached their peak during the Great Famine of 1845–52, were regarded as the inevitable outcome of Ireland's backwardness and mass emigration as the only escape from famine and destitution. However, this explanation appears increasingly inadequate in the light of recent research which has shed doubt on the whole concept of a mounting Irish economic crisis[44] and has sought to explain the complex causes of pre-Famine Irish emigration in terms of the interaction of a combination of social and economic factors, some 'pushing' the Irish out of Ireland, others 'pulling' them from Ireland.[45] Moreover, emigration was becoming an increasingly feasible proposition, due largely to the improvement in communications between Ireland and Britain, hence for those who could afford it, emigration was becoming relatively easy and inexpensive. Of course, in the last resort, people had to want to leave Ireland, and during the pre-Famine period it was essentially those with the resources, the will, the information and the aspiration to move who sought a new life abroad.[46]

Second, the Irish were not 'crowding' British cities during the 1830s to the degree that Carlyle implied. Certainly Irish immigration was increasing: in 1831 the number of Irish-born in Britain totalled about 290,000; by 1841 this had increased to 415,725, with 289,404 in England and Wales and 126,321 in Scotland. But the scale of Irish immigration was much greater during the 1840s – the Famine decade – than the 1830s. During this period the Irish-born population of Britain virtually doubled, with 727,326 Irish-born in Britain by 1851, comprising 519,959 in England and Wales and 207,367 in Scotland. Moreover,

44 J. Mokyr, *Why Ireland starved: a quantitative and analytical history of the Irish economy, 1800–1850* (London, 1983); C. O'Grada, 'Some aspects of nineteenth century Irish emigration', in L.M. Cullen and T.C. Smout (eds), *Comparative aspects of Scottish and Irish economic and social history, 1600–1900* (Edinburgh, 1977). 45 David Fitzpatrick, *Irish emigration, 1801–1921* (Dublin, 1984), pp 26–9; see also Kerby A. Miller, *Emigrants and exiles: Ireland and the Irish exodus to North America* (Oxford, 1985), pp 267–80. 46 Colin Holmes, *John Bull's Island: immigration and British society, 1871–1971* (London, 1988), p. 22.

even during the 1830s, the Irish-born population of English towns was not evenly distributed: while there were large concentrations in Liverpool, Manchester, and other Lancashire towns, and in London, there were smaller and relatively insignificant numbers in other towns and cities. And even in 1841, two years after *Chartism* had been published, the Irish-born comprised only 1.8 per cent of the total population of England and Wales.[47]

Third, the Irish people who migrated to England during this period were by no means an homogeneous group of 'miserable Irish', for their ranks contained both rich and poor, skilled and unskilled, Catholics and Protestants (and unbelievers), Nationalists and Loyalists, and men and women from a variety of distinctive provincial cultures in Ireland. Neither were they all uniformly poor, although poor Irish Catholics were the largest and most visible group of emigrants, and their experience bulked large in the story of Irish migration and, as David Fitzpatrick has suggested, 'to alien eyes and ears it often mattered little whether an Irish emigrant was from Dublin or Mayo, a Protestant or a Catholic, a labourer or an artisan, a parent or on the loose. To their great indignation, the Irish overseas tended to be lumped together as ignorant, dirty and primitive Paddies or Biddies.'[48] Yet by mid-century the ranks of the Irish in England also included a small middle-class world of professional men, doctors, lawyers, soldiers, shopkeepers, merchants and journalists.[49]

Fourth, in addressing Carlyle's claim that Irish immigrants 'darken all our towns', there is further cause for debate, although it is difficult to strike a proper mean between the lighter and darker sides of the Irish urban experience, which differed from one settlement to another. Much contemporary qualitative evidence, including *Chartism*, suggested that the newcomers were located in socially-immobile and unintegrated ghettos, popularly described as 'Little Irelands', which were isolated in particular streets and courts from the surrounding populations. However, historians have increasingly rejected the concept of Irish 'ghettoisation' as little more than a myth, suggesting that the Irish did not congregate in 'ghettos' to the exclusion of other ethnic groups.[50] Indeed, the quantitative analysis of contemporary census data by social geographers and historical demographers has recently engendered a lively argument on the subject. For example, studies of Irish settlement in London, York, Liverpool, Blackburn and Bolton suggests that while there were areas of concentrated Irish settlement they were not wholly isolated from the host

47 For further details, see J.A. Jackson, *The Irish in Britain* (London, 1963), p. 11.
48 Fitzpatrick, *Irish emigration*, p.13.   49 See, for example, Owen Dudley Edwards and Patricia Storey, 'The Irish press in Victorian Britain', in Swift and Gilley, *The Irish in the Victorian city*, pp 158–78. 50 Thompson, *The making of the English working class*, pp 469–81; Graham Davis, *The Irish in Britain, 1815–1914* (Dublin, 1991); Mervyn A. Busteed, Robert I. Hodgson and Thomas F. Kennedy, 'The myth and reality of Irish migrants in Manchester: a preliminary study', in Patrick O'Sullivan (ed.), *The Irish world wide*, vol. 2, *The Irish in the new communities* (Leicester, 1994).

community, and even where Irish immigrants dominated particular streets, courts and squares they were seldom shut off from the native population and that the Irish lived cheek by jowl besides natives of the same social class.[51] In short, the poor Irish lived among the English poor, and the upwardly-mobile among the English upper-working or middle class.

Admittedly, poverty, the most obvious of the immigrant's disadvantages, was a driving force of Irish emigration and in many respects the Irish experience in England was unique, for in their flight from poverty and misery in Ireland they found themselves in the towns and cities of the very country many blamed for their misfortune. Their living conditions were generally the very worst which the Victorian slum could offer and displayed the full spectrum of social evils: appalling overcrowding, little or no sanitation, open sewers and cesspools, unhealthy diet, inadequate clothing, vagrancy, disease, alcoholism and general squalor, a high quota of unemployed paupers or of underemployed casual labourers, and a high incidence of casual violence.[52] These were the conditions which attracted the attention of early-Victorian social investigators and, for some, including Carlyle, the influx of poverty-stricken Irish men, women and children was regarded as little short of a social disaster which, it was held, exacerbated urban squalor, constituted a health hazard, and increased the burden on the poor rates, whilst Irish fertility rates aroused fears of racial deterioration.[53]

Yet such fears need also to be understood in the context of the many contemporary issues – urban squalor, disease, disorder, vagrancy and unemployment – with which they became entangled and, in a sense, it was a tragic coincidence that the growing awareness of acute urban problems during the 1830s and 1840s, reflected in the 'Condition of England Question' which Carlyle defined, occurred at the same time as the rising tide of Irish immigration. Against this background, the Irish became an easy target and the poor Irish, who were the only visible Irish, became convenient scapegoats for environmental deterioration. Yet the plethora of urban social problems was clearly not the product of Irish immigration: these conditions had existed long before

51 See, for example, J.D. Papworth, 'The Irish in Liverpool 1835–71: family structure and residential mobility'. (unpublished PhD thesis, University of Liverpool, 1982); Lynn Lees, *Exiles of Erin: Irish migrants in Victorian London* (Manchester, 1979), pp 55–87; Frances Finnegan, *Poverty and prejudice: Irish immigrants in York, 1840–75* (Cork, 1982), pp 16–68. 52 M.A.G. O'Tuathaigh, 'The Irish in nineteenth-century Britain: problems of integration', *Transactions of the Royal Historical Society*, 31 (1981), 149–74. 53 For a useful local study of the perceived link between the Irish presence and low standards of public health, see Audrey Coney, 'Mid Nineteenth-Century Ormskirk: disease, overcrowding and the Irish in a Lancashire market town', *Transactions of the Historic Society of Lancashire and Cheshire*, 139 (1990), 83–111. The extent to which Irish living conditions influenced the both the contemporary social policy debate and contemporary social reforms are discussed by Catherine Jones, *Immigration and social policy in Britain* (London, 1977), pp 43–65.

the pronounced influx of the late 1840s, which in practice served only to magnify and exacerbate them. Furthermore, although the Irish were widely perceived to be a burden on the poor rates, even in 1847, the worst year of the Great Famine, when tens of thousands of destitute Irish men, women, and children fled to English towns, only 2 per cent of gross expenditure on poor relief in England and Wales was expended on Irish paupers.[54] Similarly, recent studies of Irish employment patterns in Bristol and York have suggested that, at least before 1860 and the relaxation of the settlement provisions of the 1834 Poor Law, the Irish made a much smaller demand on public and private charity than their poverty and English prejudice might lead one to suppose.[55]

And were the 'Wild Milesians' really 'the ready-made nucleus of degradation and disorder'? True, it was widely held that Irish immigrants were the harbingers of crime and disorder, the ancilliaries of urban poverty and environmental deterioration. Indeed, whilst crime and disorder had long been regarded as Irish traits, it was also held that the Irish were more criminal than other sections of British society and, as such, represented a challenge on the part of 'the dangerous classes', in which the Irish bulked large, to authority and order in nineteenth-century Britain. Statistical evidence suggests that the Irish-born were almost three times as likely to face prosecution than their English neighbours and more than five times as likely to be convicted and imprisoned. Yet even here some important qualifications should be made. First, there is a wealth of evidence to suggest that Irish criminality was overwhelmingly concentrated in less-serious or petty categories. In general, the Irish were not noted for crimes of great violence. Second, the evidence suggests that the Irish were not over-represented in all categories of petty crime but that Irish criminality was highly concentrated in the often inter-related categories of drunkenness, disorderly behaviour and assault (including assaults on the police) and, to a lesser extent, petty theft and vagrancy. Moreover, many of the so-called 'Irish disorders' which so concerned contemporary opinion were in practice 'anti-Irish disorders', where Irish involvement was clearly defensive rather than offensive. It is also important to recognise that the stereotype of the brutalized 'Paddy' was well-entrenched in the public mind, hence so-called 'Irish districts' were expected to be hotbeds of crime and disorder and anti-social behaviour by the Irish merely confirmed preconceived notions regarding the irresponsibility and criminality of the Celt. It also, of course, influenced the attitudes of police and magistrates in their attempts to combat urban crime and disorder.[56]

54 Frank Neal, *Black '47: Britain and the Famine Irish* (London, 1997).   55 David Large, 'The Irish in Bristol in 1851: a census enumeration', in Swift and Gilley, *The Irish in the Victorian city*, pp 37–58; Finnegan, *Poverty and prejudice*, pp 110–18.   56 For a full discussion of the relationship between Irish immigration and crime, see Roger Swift, 'Crime and the Irish in nineteenth-century Britain', in Roger Swift and Sheridan Gilley (eds), *The Irish in Britain, 1815–1939* (London 1989), pp 217–33. For a local dimension, see especially Frank

This said, there is much in *Chartism* to endorse David Newsome's assertion that the pamphlet showed Carlyle to be 'not only an angry but a frightened man'.[57] Indeed, Carlyle's fear of disorder and of mob violence, whether fomented by the Irish or the non-Irish, echoed a more generally held fear of the educated middle classes which formed an underlying theme in Early Victorian fiction. Consider, for example, the initiation of Dandy Mick into a trade union in Disraeli's *Sybil* (1845); the fortunes of John Barton in Elizabeth Gaskell's *Mary Barton* (1848); the experiences of Alton Locke in Kingsley's *Alton Locke, tailor and poet* (1850); the representation of Slackbridge in Dickens' *Hard times* (1854); or the circumstances surrounding the arrest and imprisonment of the central character of George Eliot's *Felix Holt: the Radical* (1866).[58]

This leaves us with the question of the extent to which the Irish threatened English living standards. The great majority of Irish immigrants, largely illiterate and unskilled, most certainly entered the lowliest and least healthy of urban occupations, unless they enlisted in the army, which was 30 per cent Irish in the mid-Victorian period. Overall, among the country immigrants to British towns and cities, the Irish were generally the least prepared to succeed in their new environment, as the *Report on the state of the Irish poor in Great Britain* illustrated. Yet the 'classic view', endorsed by Carlyle, that Irish immigrants provided a large pool of cheap labour at a time of rapid industrial expansion and therefore played a crucial role in retarding workers' living standards, in contributing to rising inequality, and in fostering industrialization has been challenged by historians. For example, E.H. Hunt has observed that the 'classic view' presumed a labour shortage in industrial Britain, yet increasing Irish immigration occurred against the background of fears of the Malthusian 'trap', increased emigration from Britain, and native hostility to the importation of Irish labour which, it was feared, would reduce workers' living standards by taking work, reducing wages and weakening trade unions. Moreover, Hunt argues that much of the heavy work on turnpikes, canals, docks, harbours and, to a lesser extent, railways, was achieved by native labour before Irish immigration was of much consequence, concluding that 'the effect of Irish immigration upon the pace of British industrialization was therefore not great'.[59] This thesis has been confirmed by a rigorous quantitative study by Jeffrey G. Williamson, who concludes that Irish labour did not play a significant role in accounting for rising inequality, lagging real wages, or rapid industrialization. Indeed, Williamson suggests that Irish labour was, in general, 'simply not crucial to the

Neal, 'A criminal profile of the Liverpool Irish', *Transactions of the Historic Society of Lancashire and Cheshire*, 140 (1991), 161–99.   **57** David Newsome, *The Victorian world picture: perceptions and introspections in an age of change* (London, 1997), p. 41.   **58** Williams, *Culture and society*, pp 87–109; See also Rebecca Stott, 'Thomas Carlyle and the crowd: revolution, geology and the convulsive "nature" of time', *Journal of Victorian Culture*, 4, no. 1 (Spring, 1999), 1–24.   **59** E.H. Hunt, *British labour history, 1815–1914* (London, 1981), pp 158–79.

British Standard-of-Living Debate', and that, although the Irish-born comprised 8.8 per cent of the British labour force by 1861, their impact as a predominantly unskilled minority of workers on the British economy was a very
small one.[60] So here too, Carlyle's analysis is again open to question.

Yet it is also worth noting Carlyle's general ambivalence towards the Irish.
For example, in *Past and present*, published in 1843, Ireland is barely mentioned
and, when one explicit reference to the Irish in Britain is made the tone is sympathetic rather than harsh. Here, in contrasting the health of the rich with the
relative ill-health of the poor (which he saw as further proof of the denial of the
brotherhood of man), Carlyle drew on the case of an Irish widow with three
children living in Edinburgh in 1840 who, denied charitable relief,

> sank down in typhus-fever; died, and infected her Lane with fever, so that
> seventeen other persons died of fever there in consequence. The humane
> Physician asks thereupon, as with a heart too full for speaking, Would it
> not have been economy to help this poor Widow? She took typhus-fever,
> and killed seventeen of you! – Very curious. The forlorn Irish Widow
> applies to her fellow-creatures, as if saying, 'Behold I am sinking, bare of
> help: ye must help me!' I am your sister, bone of your bone; one God
> made us: ye must help me!' They answer, 'No, impossible; thou art no
> sister of ours.' But she proves her sisterhood; her typus-fever kills them:
> they actually were her brothers, though denying it! Had human creature
> ever to go lower for a proof.[61]

Thus, with this tragic case, Carlyle sought to show that society was one, united
beyond the cash-nexus, and that laissez-faire was disproved.[62]

Another illustration of Carlyle's ambivalence lies in the fact that the writer
who spoke of English injustice towards Ireland in *Chartism* subsequently published, in 1845, *Letters and speeches of Oliver Cromwell*, which was a eulogy to its
subject, who emerged as a Protestant hero, visionary leader and man of destiny.
It included an approval of the massacres of Irish Catholics at Drogheda and
Wexford during Cromwell's suppression of the Irish rebellion, events which
were presented as examples of the providential chastisement of a wilfully rebel-
lious people.[63]

A further illustration, which is somewhat ironic, given Carlyle's dislike of
O'Connell and all that he represented, is provided by Carlyle's friendship with
Charles Gavan Duffy and other leaders of the 'Young Ireland' movement. Of

60 Jeffrey G. Williamson, 'The impact of the Irish on British labour markets during the
Industrial Revolution', *Journal of Economic History*, 46 (1986), pp 693–720.   61 Thomas
Carlyle, *Past and present* (1843), Book I, 'Midas', pp 2–3.   62 See Levin, *The condition of
England Question*, p. 59; Rosenberg, *Carlyle and the burden of history*, pp 118–23.
63 Gilmour, *The Victorian period*, p. 51.

course, unlike the 'Irish savages' chastised by Carlyle in *Chartism*, these were middle-class intellectuals, and Carlyle warmed to their sincerity and idealism even though he supported the Union and disapproved of the militant methods they advocated for its overthrow.[64] In April 1845, Duffy, Pigot and O'Hagan, then young law students, had requested an introduction to Carlyle, which was facilitated by Frederick Lucas, the editor of the *Tablet*. According to Duffy, the purpose of the meeting, which was held at Carlyle's Chelsea home, was to ascertain if 'he [Carlyle] was not in his heart so unjust towards Ireland as his writings led one to suppose'.[65] The three Young Irelanders were impressed by Carlyle, and Duffy, the future prime minister of Victoria (knighted in 1873 for his services to the colony) recalled, 'We had a long talk about Ireland, of which he has wrong notions, but not unkindly feelings.'[66] In the aftermath of this meeting, on 12 May 1845, Carlyle wrote to Duffy expressing his wish for 'Justice to Ireland – Justice to all lands, and to Ireland first as the land that needs it most – the whole English nation ... does honestly wish you that.'[67] Later, in the Autumn of 1846, Duffy helped to arrange Carlyle's first visit to Ireland, meeting him in Dublin and introducing him to many of the Young Irelanders. They also attended a meeting in Conciliation Hall addressed by O'Connell, whom Carlyle subsequently described as 'perhaps the most disgusting sight to me in that side of the water'; 'the chief quack of the then world'; 'a lying scoundrel'; and 'this Demosthenes of blarney'.[68] Carlyle's friendship with Duffy, marked by meetings and correspondence, lasted until Carlyle's death in 1881. Indeed, in *Conversations with Carlyle*, published in 1892, Duffy referred to only one dispute with 'The Titan', which occurred sometime in the late-1860s:

> In all our intercourse for more than a generation I had only one quarrel with Carlyle ... Commenting on some transaction of the day, I spoke with indignation of the treatment of Ireland by her stronger sister. Carlyle replied that if he must say the whole truth, it was his opinion that Ireland had brought all her misfortunes on herself. She had committed a great sin in refusing and resisting the Reformation ... Ireland refused to believe and must take the consequences, one of which, he would venture to point out, was a population preternaturally ignorant and lazy. I was very angry, as he knew my opinions on these points and had no justification for a homily.[69]

Yet this was a temporary disagreement, soon forgotten, and Duffy joined Carlyle the same evening for dinner, which, according to Duffy, showed that

64 Froude, *Carlyle's life in London*, vol. 1, pp 426–30; see also Ryals, Fielding et al., *Collected letters*, vol. 23, p. 144. 65 Charles Gavan Duffy, *Conversations with Carlyle* (London, 1892), p. 2. 66 Ibid., p. 5. 67 Ibid., pp 7–8. 68 Heffer, *Moral desperado*, p. 257. 69 Duffy, *Conversations*, p. 223.

Carlyle was not 'a man of impatient temper and arrogant overbearing self-will' (as many believed him to be).[70]

In the spring of 1848, at the height of the Irish Famine and the Repeal Agitation, and against the backcloth of revolution in Europe, Carlyle turned his attention more specifically to Irish issues in four articles, published in the *Examiner* and the *Spectator*, which sought to provide a critical analysis of the condition of Ireland and to examine possible solutions. These essays, little known even to Carlyle scholars (although reprinted in 1892, with an introduction by Percy Newberry, as *Rescued essays of Thomas Carlyle*),[71] comprised 'The repeal of the Union' (*Examiner*, 29 April, 1848); 'Legislation for Ireland' (*Examiner*, 13 May 1848); 'Ireland and the British chief governor' (*Spectator*, 13 May 1848); and 'Irish regiments of the new era' (*Spectator*, 13 May 1848).

The tone of these essays – combining bitter satire and caustic sarcasm with a harsh and offensive rhetoric – and their contents – reflecting a scorn for democracy, a denunciation of 'Irish savagery', aristocratic complacency, officialdom and parliamentary cant, and a belief in providentialism and arbitrary authority – is in some respects reminiscent of *Chartism*. Indeed, Carlyle again identifies British misgovernment as a prime cause of Ireland's problems, arguing that the presence of the poor Irish in England – 'the Irish lackall' – was both a consequence and constant reminder of this:

> Not a wandering Irish lackall that comes over to us, to parade his rags and hunger, and sin and misery, but comes in all senses as an irreepressible missionary of the like to our own people; an inarticulate prophet of God's justice to Nations; heralding to us also a doom like his own. Of our miseries and fearful entanglement, here in Britain, he, the Irish lackall, is by far the heaviest; and we cannot shake him off. No, we have deserved him: by our incompetence and unveracity – by our cowardly, false, and altogether criminal neglect of Ireland.[72]

Yet he is also at pains to point out that, although 'the wretched Irish populations have enough to complain of', these problems were not unique: 'We too in this island have our woes; governing classes that do not in the least govern, and working classes that cannot longer do without governing.'[73] Elaborating on the fomer observation, Carlyle then proceeds to blame the Irish aristocracy for Ireland's difficulties by their inaction and irresponsibility in failing to govern effectively:

70 Ibid., p. 228 71 Percy Newberry (ed.), *Rescued essays of Thomas Carlyle* (London, 1892). 72 'Ireland and the British chief governor', *Spectator*, 13 May 1848; Newberry, *Essays*, p. 76. 73 'The repeal of the Union', *Examiner*, 29 Apr., 1848; Newberry, *Essays*, p. 46.

a governing class glittering in foreign capitals, or at home sitting idly in its drawing-rooms, its hunting-saddles, like a class quite unconcerned with governing, concerned only to get the rents and wages of governing, and the governable ungovernable millions sunk meanwhile in dark cabins, in ignorance, sloth, confusion, superstition, and putrid ignominy, dying the hunger-death, or, what is worse, living the hunger-life, in degradation below that of dogs. A human dog-kennel five millions strong, is that a thing to be quiet over?[74]

Moreover, the failings of the Irish peasantry, embodied in 'Irish savagery', and, in particular, their unwillingness to reconcile themselves with the laws of Nature, are also held responsible for Ireland's crisis:

The Celt of Connemara, and other repealing finest peasantry, are white and not black; but it is not the colour of the skin that determines the sav- agery of a man. He is a savage who in his sullen stupidity, in his chronic rage and misery, cannot know the facts of this world when he sees them; whom suffering does not teach but only madden; who blames all men and all things except the one only that can be blamed with advantage, namely himself ; who believes, on the hill of Tara or elsewhere, what is palpably untrue, being himself unluckily a liar, and the truth, or any sense of the truth, not in him; who curses instead of thinks and considers; brandishes his tomahawk against the laws of Nature, and prevails therein as we can fancy and can see![75]

Where did the answer to Ireland's problems lie? Not, Carlyle, argued, in the repeal of the Union. Indeed, his essay on 'The repeal of the Union' not only endorsed Lord Morpeth's recent speech defending the Union,[76] but went further, arguing that Ireland's self-image, as 'an immense element in the sum of British Power', was baseless – 'much the reverse of the fact' – and in words rem- iniscent of his critique in *Chartism*, Carlyle argued that the benefits to Britain if Repeal were granted would be slight:

Our share in the said happiness would sell at a light figure in any market. To have our lands overrun with hordes of hungry white savages, covered with dirt and rags, full of noise, falsity, and turbulence, deranging every relation between rich and poor, feeding the gibbets all along our western coats, submerging our population into the depths of dirt, savagery and degradation: here is no great share of blessedness that we should covet it and go forth in arms to vindicate it.[77]

74 Ibid.; Newberry, *Essays*, p. 22. **75** Ibid.; Newberry, *Essays*, pp 50–1. **76** *Hansard*, 3S, 98, p. 215. **77** 'The repeal of the Union', *Examiner*, 29 Apr., 1848; Newberry, *Essays*, p. 25.

Carlyle held that Ireland could never be divorced from Britain on the grounds of language and ethnicity: 'Ireland is inhabited by seven or eight millions, who unfortunately speak a partially intelligible dialect of the English language, and having a white skin and European features, cannot be prevented from circulating among us at discretion, and to all manner of lengths and breadths.'[78] Ireland's geographical proximity to Britain also precluded divorce, 'with an Irish Channel everywhere bridged over by ships, steamers, herring-busses, boats, bomb-ketches, length of said bridge varying from six hours to one hour'.[79] Finally, he argued that Britain's destiny as a world power, governing, regulating and conquering anarchy by force of arms, precluded separation: 'the stern Destinies have laid upon England a terrible job of labour in these centuries and will inexorably (as their wont is) have it done … A law higher than that of Parliament, as we have said, an Eternal Law proclaims the Union unrepealable in these centuries.'[80] Under such circumstances, England could not afford to have 'a foreign nation lodged in her back-parlour'.

Neither did the answer lie in Irish insurrection: 'Fruitless, futile insurrection, continual sanguinary broils and riot that make his dwelling-place a horror to mankind, mark his progress generation after generation.'[81] The Irish, Carlyle argued, should learn from the English that progress could only be attained by the articulation of feasible proposals:

> We have decided by an immense majority to endure our woes, and wait for feasible proposals; to reserve barricades, insurrections, revolutionary pikes to the very last extremity. Considerable constitutional and social improvements have been made in this island; really very considerable; – but what is remarkable, by pikes and insurrection not one of them hitherto.[82]

Indeed, Carlyle argued that Irish violence was counter-productive, resulting in the presence of 50,000 soldiers in Ireland, which merely tackled the symptom rather than the cause of Irish misery: 'here is prohibition of Repeal treason, but here is no cure of the disease which produces Repeal treason, and other madness and treasons among us'.[83]

Carlyle was also extremely sceptical of the value of constitutional reform in addressing Ireland's problems, dismissing, in words which reflected both his distaste for democracy and his increasing sympathy for authoritarianism, the two measures thus far intended for Ireland – a bill for improved Registration of Irish County Voters and a bill for the Irish Municipalities – as irrelevant:

78 Ibid.; Newberry, Essays, pp 32–3. 79 Ibid.; Newberry, *Essays*, p. 33. 80 Ibid.; Newberry, *Essays*, p. 44. 81 Ibid.; Newberry, *Essays*, pp 50–1. 82 Ibid.; Newberry, *Essays*, pp 46–7. 83 'Ireland and the British chief governor', *Spectator*, 13 May 1848; Newberry, *Essays*, p. 74.

Extension of the electoral suffrage, – good Heavens, what will that do for a country which labours under the frightfullest immediate want of potatoes? … Not by extending the electoral or other suffrage, but by immensely curtailing it (were the good method once found), could a constitutional benefit be done, there or here! Not who votes, but who or what is voted for, what is decided on: that is the important question!.[84]

How, he asks, can England, with Chartism 'under deck', Ireland 'indissolubly chained to her', and subjected to the influences of 'an anarchic Europe', cope? Not, he suggests by 'the old constitutional methods'.[85] By what means, then, are Irish wrongs to be addressed? His essential plea is for 'feasible proposals, and determination silently made up, wrought out in long dark struggles into conformity with the laws of fact, and unalterable by the same … in which nobler methods we invite all Irish reformers to join us',[86] and for remedial measures, 'for Ireland's sake, and indeed for Britain's, which is indissolubly chained to her, and is drifting along with her and by reason of her, close in the rear of her, towards unspeakable destinies otherwise'.[87] So what did Carlyle propose?

Carlyle regarded the destruction of the Irish potato crop as a symptom of Divine intervention which would, in the long run, prove beneficial: 'And all of us thank God for the merciful destruction of the potato … and perceive that with the potato rotten, Irish existence can no longer, by any human cunning, be maintained in the hideous quiet chronic state.'[88] In this sense, he saw the Famine as a watershed, because 'the Irish potato has, practically speaking, fallen extinct; that the hideous form of Irish so-called ''social existence'' sustained thereby, has henceforth become impossible?' Thus, 'some new existence, deserving a little more to be called ''social'', will have to introduce itself there', and it followed that it was the duty of government to effect this 'new existence': 'a real government, come from where it can, is indispensible for the human beings that inhabit Ireland'.[89] In the short-term, Carlyle believed that Irish landlords had an important role to play in facilitating change, and he urged Lord John Russell to press ahead with the Sale of Encumbered Estates Bill for Ireland – 'the preliminary and foundation-stone of all other Irish arrangements whatsoever' – in the belief that this would bring Irish landlords face to face with the reality of their situation and force them to act responsibly:

The Irish landlord should instantly be brought into free contact and unlimited power of manipulation, and action and reaction with his land;

84 Ibid.; Newberry, *Essays*, pp 80–2. 85 Ibid.; Newberry, *Essays*, pp 87–8. 86 'The repeal of the Union', *Examiner*, 29 Apr., 1848; Newberry, *Essays*, p. 48. 87 'Ireland and the British chief governor', *Spectator*, 13 May 1848. Newberry, *Essays*, pp 74–5. 88 'Legislation for Ireland', *Examiner*, 13 May 1848; Newberry, *Essays*, p. 61. 89 'Ireland and the British chief governor', *Spectator*, 13 May 1848; Newberry, *Essays*, pp 84–5.

that he should enter on his stern crucial experiment, with at least the possibility of trying to get through it! ... Swiftly, instantly, should this bill, all manner of needful bills to facilitate the sale of encumbered estates, – to bring a man into contact with the chaotic problem he has got, or at once absolve him from it, – be passed through Parliament.[90]

Yet for Carlyle, the prime solution to Ireland's problems lay in the provision of work and the organisation of Irish labour. In 'The repeal of the Union', he observed 'if no beneficient hand will chain him into wholesome slavery, and, with whip on back or otherwise, try to tame him and get some work out of him, – Nature herself, intent to have her work tilled, has no resource but to exterminate him',[91] whilst in 'Ireland and the British chief governor' he called for the 'possibility of work that will procure potatoes, or a substitute for that sad root' in order to 'enable the electors to sustain themselves alive'.[92] This argument is taken further in 'Irish regiments of the new era', where Carlyle makes a plea, on one level, for the organisation of Irish labour; on another, for Order. Carlyle notes the legendary reputation of efficiency of the Irish when organised within the army:

> The unemployed vagrant miscellaneous Irish, once dressed in proper red coats, and put under proper drill-sergeants, with strict military law above them, can be trained into soldiers; and will march to any quarter of the globe and fight fiercely, and will keep step and pas-de-charge, and subdue the enemy for you, like real soldiers, – none better, I understand, or few, in this world.[93]

Thus in the army the Irish fighting talent – 'several thousand years of faction-fights, pike-skirmishes, combustions, private duels by shillelagh, by dirk and fist, and still feller methods' – was effectively utilised and carried with it 'inestimable advantages' – the maintenance of public order and government authority, no less. Carlyle then poses the question: 'Is organization to fight, the only organization achievable by Irishmen under proper sergeants?' His answer is that the Irish had another talent, and one which should be exploited in the immediate interests of Ireland:

> The Irish have in all times shown, and do now show, an indisputable talent for spade-work, which, under slight modifications, means all kinds of husbandry work. Men skilled in the business testify that, with the spade,

90 'Legislation for Ireland', *Examiner*, 13 May 1848; Newberry, *Essays*, pp 63–4.   91 'The repeal of the Union', *Examiner*, 29 Apr., 1848; Newberry, *Essays*, pp 50–1.   92 'Ireland and the British chief governor', *Spectator*, 13 May 1848; Newberry, *Essays*, p. 80.   93 'Irish regiments of the new era', *Spectator*, 13 May 1848; Newberry, *Essays*, p. 93.

there is no defter or tougher workers than the common Irishman at present ... And, I think, one regiment, ten regiments, of diggers on the Bog of Allen, would look as well almost as ten regiments of shooters on the field of Waterloo'.[94]

Thus Carlyle argued that the effective organisation of Irish labour was fundamental to the creation of a 'loyal peace' in Ireland and the curtailing of 'the mad cry of Repeal', and that the responsibility for achieving this lay in the hands of the British government. Only thus could anarchy be averted: 'Some regimenting of spade-work can, by honest life-and-death effort long continued on the part of governing men, be done, and even must be done. All Nations, and I think our own foremost, will either get a beginning made towards doing it, or die in nameless anarchies before long!'[95]

By any standards, Carlyle's prescriptions for Ireland's ills were at best limited and the content of his Irish essays was overlain with a sense of foreboding, of some impending political apocalypse, symptomatic of the conflict between democracy and the laws of nature, which threatened to engulf not only Ireland and England, but also the rest of Europe:

> Ireland, which was never yet organic with other than make-believe arrangement, now writhes in bitter agony, plainly disorganic from shore to shore; its perennial hunger grown too sharp even for Irish nerves. England has her Chartisms, her justly discontented workpeople countable by the million; repressed for the moment, not at all either remedied or extinguished by the glorious 10th of April, for which a monument is to be built. No; and Europe, we say, from Cadiz to Copenhagen, has crashed together suddenly into the bottomless deeps, the thin earth rind, wholly artificial, giving way beneath it; and welters now one huge Democracy, one huge Anarchy or Kinglessness; its 'kings' all flying like a set of mere play-actor kings, and none now even pretending to rule, and heroically, at his life's peril, command and constrain.[96]

The Irish essays, which might well suggest that the Irish crisis of 1848 precipitated Carlyle's swing toward the extremer authoritarianism of his later years, were not generally well-received. David J. DeLaura has argued that they were immediately recognised by Fonblanque and Ritoul, the sympathetic editors of the *Examiner* and the *Spectator*, as far more radical and inflammatory than Carlyle's previous recommendations of repressive force.[97] Some reviewers

94 Ibid.; Newberry, *Essays*, pp 95–101. **95** Ibid.; Newberry, *Essays*, pp.102–3. **96** 'Ireland and the British chief governor', *Spectator*, 13 May 1848; Newberry, *Essays*, pp 86–7.   **97** David J. DeLaura, 'Carlyle and Arnold: the religious issue', in K.J. Fielding and Rodger L. Tarr (eds), *Carlyle past and present: a collection of new essays* (London, 1976), pp 127–54.

recited the familiar view that Caryle offered nothing new and lacked practical wisdom; these included Carlyle's friend Edward Fitzgerald, who observed that 'he raves and foams, but has nothing to propose'.[98] Carlyle's messianism also annoyed John Stuart Mill, whose response to 'The repeal of the Union' article was published in the *Examiner* on 13 May 1848, and Jules Paul Seigel has argued that the Irish essays marked the beginning of the slow erosion of feeling among young liberal intellectuals such as Mill, Arnold and Clough towards Carlyle,[99] while DeLaura has suggested that these essays alone would have provided plenty of basis for Arnold's judgment of September 1849 that Carlyle was a 'moral desperado'.[100]

Nevertheless, in the summer of 1849, in the aftermath of the failed revolution of the Young Irelanders and with Ireland still in the grip of the Famine, Carlyle revisited Ireland in order to see 'the problem lying visible'. The visit, which commenced on 30 June, was again facilitated by Duffy, who not only arranged to meet Carlyle in Dublin (where Carlyle declined dinner with Lord Clarendon) in order to arrange introductions and a route, but also accompanied him on the journey. Carlyle took notes along the way and these were written up in the form of a diary in October, on his return to Scotland. Yet Carlyle never developed the notes of the Irish tour, and the responsibility for the publication of *Reminiscences of my Irish journey in 1849* in 1882, the year after Carlyle's death, lay with J.A. Froude, who saw it as an opportunity to boost support for Gladstone's 1881 Irish Coercion Bill.[101] Later, in the frontespiece of his personal copy of the book, Gladstone wrote:

> This book, in the first half of it especially was egotistical and comes nearer to being trashy than any other of Carlyle's work. It has everywhere the art of succinct portraiture in few and telling words. He did not think the Irish worthy of study. Yet in everything he could not fail to see.[102]

Michael Cotsell has described *Reminiscences of my Irish journey in 1849* as 'a work of hopelessness and anger, envisioning not the promise of society but its complete and desperate failure'.[103] Among the things that Carlyle saw was Irish poverty, which clearly moved him, and Irish workhouses (at Kildare, Kilkenny, Killarney and Westport) which he described as 'swineries' filled with 'human swine', remarking in a letter to his wife, 'Blacklead those two millions idle

98 Ibid., p.129.   99 Seigel, *The critical heritage*, pp 304–9.   100 DeLaura, 'Carlyle and Arnold' in Fielding and Tarr, *Carlyle past and present*, p.129.   101 Malcolm Brown, *The politics of Irish literature: from Thomas Davis to W.B. Yeats* (London, 1972), p. 119.   102 I wish to thank the Revd Peter Francis, warden of St Deiniol's Library, Hawarden, and his staff for allowing me to peruse this volume.   103 Michael Cotsell, 'Carlyle, travel and the enlargements of history', in M. Cotsell (ed.), *Creditable warriors: English literature and the wider world*, vol. 3, *1830–1876* (London 1990), pp 83–96.

beggars ... and sell them in Brazil as Niggers'.[104] Yet the *Reminiscences* also contain other telling phrases which reinforce some of the themes addressed in *Chartism* and the Irish essays. For example, Carlyle noted on Tuesday 3 July:

> Thought of the 'Battle of Vinegar Hill', but not with interest, with sorrow rather and contempt; one of the ten times ten thousand futile fruitless 'battles' this brawling, unreasonable people has fought, – the saddest of distinctions to them among peoples! In Heaven's name learn that 'revolting' is not the trade that will profit you. The unprofitablest of all trades, if you exceed in it.[105]

On Tuesday 10 July, at Kildare railway station, he observed:

> A big blockhead, sitting with his dirty feet on the seat opposite, not stirring them for me, who wanted to sit there: 'One thing we're all agreed on,' said he 'we're very ill governed; Whig, Tory, Radical, Repealer, all admit we're very ill-governed!' – I thought to myself, 'Yes indeed: you govern yourself. He that would govern you well would probably surprise you much my friend, – laying a hearty horsewhip over that back of yours.'[106]

On Sunday 22 July, near Limerick, he recalled:

> All 'religions' that I fell in with in Ireland seemed to me too irreligious; really, in sad truth, doing mischief to the people in place of good.[107]

By Wednesday 1 August, at Sligo, however, his thoughts had returned once more to

> Beggars, beggars; only industry really followed by the Irish people. 'For the love of God, yer hanar'! etc. etc. 'Wouldn't it be worth your consideration, whether you hadn't better drown or hang yourselves, than live a dog's life in this way?' They withdrew from me in horror; did at least withdraw![108]

By Monday 6 August, on the boat from Derry to Glasgow, Carlyle had concluded

> Remedy for Ireland? To cease generally from following the devil: no other remedy that I know of; one general life-element of humbug these two centuries; and now it has fallen bankrupt.[109]

104 Ryals, Fielding et al., *Collected letters*, vol. 24, p. 192. 105 Thomas Carlyle, *Reminiscences of my Irish journey in 1849* (London, 1882), p. 34. 106 Ibid., pp 79–80. 107 Ibid., p. 161. 108 Ibid., p. 223. 109 Ibid., pp 258–9.

On his return to Scotland he commented, 'Thank heaven for the sight of real human industry, with human fruits from it, once more. The sight of fenced fields, weeded crops, and human creatures with whole clothes on their back – it was as if one had got into spring water out of dunghill puddles.'[110]

With the exception of *Reminiscences of my Irish journey*, Irish issues all but disappeared from Carlyle's writing after 1848. Within months of his return from Ireland, Carlyle launched into his infamous 'Occasional discourse on the Negro Question', published in *Fraser's Magazine* in December 1849 and reprinted as a separate pamphlet in 1853, which denigrated black people in the most appalling language (exacerbating, in the process, Carlyle's increasingly acrimonious relationship with Mill, who published an impassioned response in the following edition of *Fraser's Magazine*).[111] Yet, as in some of his earlier writings, Carlyle juxtaposed negroes in the West Indies with the Irish poor – 'beautiful Blacks sitting there up to the ears in pumpkins, and doleful Whites sitting here without potatoes to eat; never till now, I think, did the sun look-down on such a jumble of human nonsenses.'[112] Similarly, Irish issues were barely touched in *Latter-day pamphlets*, published in 1850 at the height of the Famine exodus, although in one specific reference Carlyle returned to the theme outlined in *Chartism* of the threat posed by the Irish to English cities. 'The Irish Giant', he wrote, 'named of Despair, is advancing upon London itself, laying waste all English cities, towns and villages: I notice him in Piccadilly, blue-visaged, thatched in rags, a blue child on each arm; hunger-driven, wide mouthed, seeking whom he may devour; he, missioned by the Just Heavens, too truly and too sadly their "divine missionary" come at last to this authoritative manner, will throw us all into Doubting Castle, I perceive,'[113] which has led Michael Levin to argue that Carlyle assumed that England must set Ireland aright both for Ireland's sake and for its own.[114]

Although historical research has shed considerable doubt on the accuracy of Carlyle's analysis of the Irish in early-Victorian England, 'The finest Peasantry in the world', still constitutes a seminal source for the study of the subject. By providing a micro-study, an exemplar, of the themes explored in *Chartism*, Carlyle places the Irish in early-Victorian England firmly in their broader historical and contemporary contexts. Thus the plight of the Irish in England is presented as symptomatic both of England's misgovernment of

---

110 Froude, *Carlyle's life in London*, vol. 2, p. 8.   111 See David Theo Goldberg, 'Liberalism's limits: Carlyle and Mill on "The Negro Question"', *Nineteenth-Century Contexts*, 22, no. 2 (2000), 203–16. See also Catherine Hall's recent appraisal of Carlyle on the Negro Question in her essay 'The nation within and without' in Catherine Hall, Keith McLelland and Jane Rendall, *Defining the Victorian nation: class, race, gender and the Reform Act of 1867* (Cambridge, 2000), pp 179–233.   112 Thomas Carlyle, 'Occasional discourse on the Negro Question', *Fraser's Magazine*, Dec., 1849, reprinted in *Selected essays*, p. 306. 113 Thomas Carlyle, *Latter-day pamphlets* (1850), p. 94.   114 Levin, *The condition of England Question*, p. 59.

Ireland in the past and of the socio-economic consequences of Industrialism, Mechanism, and laissez-faire Utilitarianism. Moreover, although Carlyle's analysis predated the Great Irish Famine of 1845–52 and its catastrophic consequences (when the condition of the Irish in England was undoubtedly far worse than it had been perceived to be during the 1830s), it also portended that Famine crisis, adding weight to Carlyle's status as the prophet of the age. And of course in 1848, at the height of Famine, and in the year of European Revolutions, the Irish made a major contribution to the final phase of Chartism by providing a revolutionary cutting-edge to a movement that, in essence, believed in securing political concessions from the state by constitutional rather than revolutionary means.[115] Yet the relative failure of Chartism in 1848, coupled with the subsequent improvement in the British economy and the success of the Great Exhibition of 1851, heralded the onset of a period of relative progress and stability in Victorian society, when the fires of discontent appeared burnt out and the threat of revolution checked. In this relatively tranquil and prosperous mid-Victorian context much of what Carlyle had both feared and prophesied in *Chartism* had clearly not come to pass.[116] Yet in the last analysis, whilst accepting that Carlyle's representations of the Irish in *Chartism* subsequently exercised a baneful influence on the historiography of the Irish in Britain, whether Carlyle was right or wrong is immaterial; of greater importance, in regard to both the Condition of England Question in general and the condition of the Irish in England in particular, is the fact that many contemporaries believed this to have been the case rather than the fact that it was not.

This said, while Carlyle might well have articulated effectively the nature and scale of the crisis which faced British social, cultural and political life during the 1830s and 1840s,[117] his critique of Ireland's crisis was problematic and his prescriptions were shallow and impractical. In a sense, perhaps, this illustrates the fundamental paradox of Carlyle, which makes it difficult to place him politically.[118] As Andrew Lang observed when reviewing 'Mr Carlyle's

---

115 John Belchem, 'English working-class radicalism and the Irish, 1815–50', in Swift and Gilley, *The Irish in the Victorian city*, pp 85–97; see also Professor Belchem's analysis, 'Liverpool in the Year of Revolution: the political and associational culture of the Irish immigrant community in 1848', in J. Belchem (ed.), *Popular politics, riot and labour: essays in Liverpool history, 1790–1940* (Liverpool 1992), pp 68–97.   116 For the mid-Victorian years, see especially W.L. Burn, *The age of equipoise* (London, 1964); G. Best, *Mid-Victorian Britain, 1851–75* (London, 1971); K.T. Hoppen, *The mid-Victorian generation, 1846–1886* (London 1998).   117 David Eastwood, 'The age of uncertainty: Britain in the early-nineteenth century', *Transactions of the Royal Historical Society*, Sixth Series, 8 (1998), 105.   118 Levin, *The condition of England Question*, p. 60, has noted that Carlyle's contempt for the powerful and sympathy for the weak and oppressed places him on the political left, while his fear of disorder and increasing authoritarianism places him more firmly on the political right.

Reminiscences' in *Fraser's Magazine* in April 1881, 'his [Carlyle's] politics were as remote as possible from practice … He might be of the party of the poor and the oppressed (as long as the poor and oppressed were not black or Irish), or he might be on the side of Cromwell, or not opposed to the first Bonaparte.'[119]

119 Andrew Lang, 'Mr Carlyle's reminiscences', *Fraser's Magazine*, Apr. 1881, pp 515–28, in Seigel, *The critical heritage*, p. 505.

Isaac Butt, British Liberalism and an alternative nationalist tradition

PHILIP BULL

There is a danger of the originator of the Irish Home Rule movement, Isaac Butt, slipping into being little more than a footnote in the history of a movement which came to be associated with the much more dramatic figure of Charles Stewart Parnell. Moreover, this neglect covers a serious failure to understand crucial aspects of the historical context within which Butt was placed, and the unique and pivotal events with which the height of his career coincided. His relationship – or rather empathy – with the Fenians is often dismissed as merely the respect or affection which arises from a barrister's defence of his clients, while his innate conservatism is used as further evidence of the essentially modest nature of his proposals for Ireland. The declared 'federalist' form and 'imperial' context of his vision is similarly used to locate him as the scene-setter for the full-blooded nationalism of Parnell's movement. His respect for the procedures and forms of the house of commons is likewise used to characterise him as too much of a 'gentleman' in the hurly burly of Irish politics, unable to rise to the challenge of the parliamentary obstruction introduced by his younger and more radical colleagues. As so often happens with historical figures, the shadow cast backwards by the end of the career can misshape perceptions of the nature and context of the earlier contribution. In the case of a Churchill it may add a retrospective lustre and sense of prescience to a melancholy earlier record; in Butt's case the indebtedness, demoralisation and failure of later years serves to obscure the real context and contribution of his formative period.

The neglect of Butt has been noticed before, and was the subject of the opening sentence of David Thornley's admirable study published in 1964.[1] The lack of importance attached to him can be demonstrated by the treatment given him in the *Dictionary of national biography*. While his successor, Parnell, is given 40 columns, and the later nationalist leader, John Redmond, 9 columns, Butt was thought to merit only two and one quarter columns (a mere quarter of a column more than given to William Shaw, who was leader of the Home Rule party for only a year between Butt and Parnell); of this limited space only 13 lines were devoted to his political career as distinct from his work as a lawyer and scholar. Perhaps this was what was to be expected from the person chosen

1 David Thornley, *Isaac Butt and Home Rule* (London, 1964), p. 9.

147

to write the entry, G.C. Boase, a bibliographer and antiquarian, with special interests in Cornish biographies. But despite Thornley's book, and his advocacy of the importance of Butt, two excellent articles by Lawrence J. McCaffrey,[2] and a reassessment by Alan O'Day,[3] the role of the founder of Irish Home Rule has still not significantly informed the historiography of the period in which he made his contribution, nor of the retrospective accounts of the development of Irish politics since his time. Butt was the last of the mainstream Irish nationalist leaders to construct and to articulate his political ideas in the context of a belief that Irish aspirations could be met within the broad structures of the Union with Britain, and it was the failure of British policy makers to respond to his initiatives which doomed his strategy and paved the way for a political ideology which, whether expressed in constitutional or revolutionary forms, ultimately spelt the death both of the Union itself and of a viable basis for Irish national unity.

As excellent and sympathetic a work as Thornley's study of Butt is, there is one defect in its treatment of Butt. Ultimately Thornley's analysis of Butt's achievement suffers from a neglect of the British responses to it. Thus the conclusion to his book, in which he summarises the reasons for Butt's eventual failure, discusses only those factors which arose out of the Irish context or were specific to the functioning of the Irish party. The one exception to this is a single sentence in which Thornley alludes to the implications of Butt having to face at Westminster after 1874 'not the pliant and rational Gladstone, but the … immovable Disraeli'.[4] In fact, it could well be argued that different governmental responses would have undermined the viability of the obstruction policy which ultimately did so much to destroy Butt's strategy and leadership. By far the best and most balanced assessment of Butt's career is that given in R.V. Comerford's chapter, 'Isaac Butt and the home rule party, 1870–77', in volume six of the *New history of Ireland*, an analysis which includes the British context of Butt's failure.[5] This paper does not challenge in substance the account given by Comerford, but argues for a stronger focus on the relationship of Butt's movement, both in its genesis and in its ultimate failure, to British responses, relating his initiatives to the longer term development of Irish nationalist aspirations.

2 Lawrence J. McCaffrey, 'Home rule and the general election of 1874 in Ireland', *Irish Historical Studies*, ix, no. 34 (Sept. 1954), 190–212; and 'Isaac Butt and the home rule movement: A study in conservative nationalism', *Review of Politics*, xxii, no. 1 (Jan. 1960), 72–95. 3 Alan O'Day, 'Isaac Butt and Irish nationality', *The Historian*, 58 (Summer 1998), 18–21; see also O'Day, 'Defining Ireland's place in parliamentary institutions: Isaac Butt and Parnell in the 1870s' in O'Day (ed.), *Government and institutions in the post-1832 United Kingdom* (London, 1995), pp 155–90. 4 Thornley, p. 384. 5 W.E. Vaughan (ed.), *A new history of Ireland*, vol. 6 *Ireland under the Union, II, 1870–1921* (Oxford, 1996), pp 1–25.

Isaac Butt was born in 1813, the son and grandson of Church of Ireland parsons in county Donegal. From the Royal School at Raphoe he went in 1832 to Trinity College, Dublin, where he distinguished himself as a scholar and helped to found in 1833 the *Dublin University Magazine*, of which he was the editor from 1833 to 1838. Between 1836 and 1841 he held the Whateley Chair of Political Economy at Trinity, and in November 1838 he was called to the Irish bar, in 1844 to the inner bar and in 1859 to the English bar. His life was dominated by financial insecurity, and although his career at the bar was a very distinguished one he sacrificed more lucrative cases to defence of those with whom he felt personal sympathy. There was an eclecticism in his character which contributed to the esteem in which he was held by an extraordinarily diverse cross section of Irish people, and it is this which helps to explain the nexus which seems to have arisen between his political commitments and the cases which he defended as a barrister. Thus in 1840 his defence of the old unreformed Dublin Corporation against the Municipal Reform Bill was followed by his election as an alderman of the new corporation, where he served as a champion of the conservative cause; in 1848 he defended Smith O'Brien and the other prisoners in the state trials of that year, and thereafter there emerge signs of a new sympathy with the Young Ireland cause; and, most famously, his defence of the Fenian prisoners between 1865 and 1869 immediately preceded his adoption of home rule and the formation of a Home Government Association.

Traditional views of the nature of Butt's enterprise in the early 1870s can be largely stated in the following terms. Influenced initially by the Young Irelanders whom he had defended, shocked by the Famine, and now greatly impressed by the character, convictions and sincerity of the fenian prisoners Butt sought to establish political structures which could at least in part gratify some of those aspirations. In doing this he saw the opportunity of exploiting the disenchantment of conservative Protestants, their own valued institutions, especially the church and the land, put under threat by the encroachments of supposedly radical Gladstonian liberalism. This combination of nationalists and protestant elite was cemented by a social conservatism based on an ethos predominantly rural or Catholic (or both) and increasingly alienated from the contemporary concerns of urban, liberal England. The failure of his objectives are then, in the traditional perspective, related to his electoral dependency on the tenant farmer and denominational education issues, both of which were bound to alienate protestant supporters of his movement. Once the conservative protestant element had drifted from the party, the power of other elements, especially the Fenian and radical tenant farmer interest, was able to become more dominant, thus creating the situation where Butt's conservative and

conciliatory philosophy and methods were discredited within his own movement. The eclipse of Butt by the obstructionists in the late seventies was thus
the logical outcome of the inherently unstable balance of forces which had been
put together in the early years of the decade.

The benefit of hindsight has long enabled Butt's failures to be juxtaposed
against what has been seen as his achievement. J.G. Swift MacNeill, writing in
1913 on the centenary of Butt's birth, evaluated him principally in terms of the
foundations he laid for the later nationalist leaders, Parnell and Redmond, and
in establishing the lines of the policy which was subsequently to be adopted by
the British Liberal party. MacNeill backed his claim with a quotation from his
own leader, John Redmond, who saw Butt as 'a great link in the chain of
success' from O'Connell to Parnell.[6] Such a nationalist 'whig' view of history
does not adequately place Butt and his party in their immediate context. In
adopting the home rule policy in 1870 and building up first the Home
Government Association and then the Home Rule League, Butt and his colleagues were attempting not only something very distinctive and prescient but
also responding to powerful contemporary forces in both Irish and British politics. The developments associated with him must be lifted out of the succes-
sion of developments to which Redmond alluded if their real intent and import
is to be understood.

III

A direct and simple connection has invariably been drawn between the commitment made by Gladstone in 1868 'to pacify Ireland' and the preceding
episodes of Fenian violence. This misses, however, the depth of the developments in British liberal thought which Gladstone's remark characterised.
Shaped in part by new attitudes towards Ireland, evident for example in the
work of John Stuart Mill, by the early 1860s Liberal politicians were already
showing a disposition towards significant reform in Ireland. The arrival in
Dublin in November 1864 of a new Liberal viceroy, Lord Wodehouse (later the
earl of Kimberley), marked the first significant appearance of this new attitude
in Ireland; it was reinforced in 1866 when an Irish Liberal, Chichester
Fortescue, took over from Sir Robert Peel as chief secretary at Dublin Castle.
Both men were committed to significant reform on what were the three great
issues of the time: disestablishment of the minority protestant church; reform
of the laws governing the relationship of landlord and tenant; and measures to
remove the acute grievance of Roman Catholics at the lack of facilities for a

---

6 J.G. Swift McNeill, 'Isaac Butt, the father of home rule', *Fortnightly Review*, xciv (new
series, Sept. 1913), 448–59.

university education with an ethos acceptable to their church. But in attempting to carry out their reforms Wodehouse was inhibited initially by the reluc-
tance of Palmerston, still prime minister, to countenance significant reform in
Ireland. Then, both before and after Palmerston's death and Lord John
Russell's accession to the premiership in October 1865, both Wodehouse and
Fortescue were constrained in their reform objectives by the priority which
they gave to suppressing the threat posed by the Fenian movement, now at the
height of its strength and not yet weakened by the abortive rebellion of 1867.
Consequently, by the time the Liberals left office in June 1866 nothing had been
achieved of their reform agenda, save the introduction – too late to be enacted
– of Chichester Fortescue's very modest Land Bill.

   This delay meant, first of all, that when Gladstone began in earnest after
1868 his programme of Irish reform it was already compromised by the fact
that it was seen as a response to violence. This need not have been the case. The
influences at work on Liberals in the early sixties had been predominantly that
of leading Irish Liberals – men like Sir John Gray, John Francis Maguire, C.
McCarthy Downing, John Blake Dillon, all members of parliament – all of
whom understood very well what needed to be done by way of Irish reform, not
just to avert violence but in order to undertake the most basic measures of
justice necessary to begin to put Ireland on an equal footing with its partners in
the Union. As early as December 1864 Gladstone, then chancellor of the
exchequer, had already got a grasp of what was needed, pointing out to the
newly appointed viceroy that any discussion of how to apply rules to Ireland
consistent with the rest of the United Kingdom would 'lead us into matters
which are far removed from the regions of finance, and which are at present of
hopeless difficulty'.[7]

   It was not only that reform after 1868 had been made more difficult because
it could be attributed to violence, but also the whole experience of the rebellion
and suppression of the Fenians had upped the ante so far as Irish opinion was
concerned. While in the early 1860s Irish Liberal MPs had been prepared to
settle for modest measures, especially on the land issue, this had been because
they were anxious to achieve as quickly as possible enough reform to be able to
hold their own politically against the rising tide of serious unrest. After the
suppression of the Fenians, however, the mood had changed. Not only was
there a new anger at the fact that rebellion appeared to have been necessary to
impel change, but there seemed little reason to inhibit demands now widely
acknowledged to be long overdue and which a more accommodating approach
had done nothing to advance. Understanding this, Gladstone recognised the
need to show that the reform programme was systemic in its purpose, designed
not merely as a response to discrete grievances, but intended to rectify a deep

7 Gladstone to Wodehouse, 17 Dec. 1864 (copy), Gladstone Papers, British Library. Add.
MS. 44,224, fs. pp 27–30.

underlying disorder of the body politic in Ireland. Thus the concept of the Upas tree, as a metaphor for the pervasive reach of the old, decaying, pre-modern Irish protestant ascendancy, poisoning all it touched.[8] Gladstone set for his first government the task of removing successively three of its great branches: the established Protestant church; the power of the landlords over their tenants; and the denial to Irish Catholics of a university education of a kind amenable to them. 'They are all', he declared, 'so many branches from one trunk and that trunk is the tree of what is called Protestant ascendancy'.[9]

In delivering so effectively what he had promised on church disestablishment Gladstone had created for himself as an English politician a position of unparalleled esteem in Ireland; to sustain this he needed to succeed similarly on other issues. Disestablishment and the university question were issues of special importance to the Roman Catholic constituency in Ireland *per se*. There was, however, a very wide constituency for which the other branch of the Upas tree was of much more immediate importance. The greatest test of Gladstone would be what he could achieve by way of a Land Act. Tenant farmers were the majority of the Irish population, and this issue had great political potency in countering sources of unrest and disorder. In the event the immense imagination and understanding displayed by Gladstone on this issue was not reflected in the legislation. Gladstone had come in his own thinking to accommodate the Irish tenant perspective to a remarkable extent. In particular, to the alarm of many of his cabinet colleagues, he had seized upon the 'idea of restitution', recognising that for tenant farmers tenant right reflected what they believed to be a proprietorial interest founded in pre-conquest custom. Gladstone worked to accommodate within his legislation this sense of a legitimacy of occupation. In this he ultimately failed, defeated within the cabinet by colleagues alarmed at his belief in what one of them called 'tribal tenure'. Awareness of Gladstone's personal understanding of the issue, however, helped preserve his reputation in Ireland despite the widespread disappointment at the limitations of the Land Act.

Release of the Fenian prisoners was seen by Gladstone as crucial to the success of his Irish venture. While much of the potency of fenianism was owed to the failure of the British parliament to address grievances which had been acknowledged for many years, so the treatment of those who had offended against the law was bound to be seen in the context of that British failure. Gladstone understood this, and a number of Fenian prisoners had been released in the first few months of his taking office. But it soon became evident that the release of a few Fenians was inadequate; as long as any of them remained in prison Gladstone's pacification project would be compromised.

8 The Upas tree is the Javanese tree which yields a milky sap used as arrow poison and which in mythology was thought to be fatal to whatever came near it; hence, its derived meaning of a pernicious influence. 9 Speech at Wigan, *Times*, 24 Oct. 1868.

What then happened was a sustained battle, in private and lasting two years, between Gladstone and the Irish government, in which Gladstone mounted constant and sustained pressure for release and the Irish government, ministers and officials, found ever stronger arguments against and reasons for delay. Many of their arguments were powerful and compelling, but fatally flawed in the context of the immediate circumstances. On 14 September 1870 Gladstone wrote to Lord Spencer, the Irish viceroy:

> your reasons [against release of the Fenians] do not convince me ... In my opinion their release belongs to a policy of confidence, their continual confinement to a policy of mistrust & apprehension. Doubtless we cannot put down Fenianism, but surely what we have to do is gradually to estrange the principles of the Irish people especially of the rising gener- ation as they grow up, from that bad cause. Now I think we know from unexceptional evidence that the sufferings of these Fenians, by which I mean simply their continued imprisonment tend to place in sympathy with them multitudes of men who are not Fenians.[10]

While this represented Gladstone's constant view, it was an object which he finally secured only in January 1871 – two years after he had taken office. By November 1870 public pressure had once more resumed, so that when release occurred the most favourable circumstances from Gladstone's point of view had passed. This failure by Gladstone to carry what he had considered to be politically necessary was a costly one. 'Pacifying Ireland' required a package of measures, closely bound together so as to give a sense of cohesion to a great his- torical task. Speedy release of the prisoners was an executive action which could constitute a token of good faith on the other issues requiring legislation; as J.F. Maguire wrote, 'clemency would shed a glory upon justice'.[11] The failure to release the Fenians cast a retrospective shadow over the hopes which had been raised by the exemplary handling of the church issue, denied for the Land Bill the sympathy which otherwise might have accrued despite its shortcom- ings, and left a wide open field for the government's critics on the university question.[12]

For Isaac Butt the great necessity was the re-establishment of a workable civil polity in Ireland and so for him the Gladstonian initiatives had held great

---

10 Gladstone to Spencer, 14 Sept. 1870, H.C.G. Matthew (ed.), *The Gladstone diaries*, vol. 7 (Oxford, 1987), p. 360. 11 J.F. Maguire to Gladstone, 2 Aug. 1869, Carlingford Papers, Somerset Record Office, 1/59 (microfilm held by the late Professor Colin Matthew). 12 For a fuller account of Gladstone's campaign to secure the release of the prisoners see Philip Bull, 'Gladstone, the Fenian prisoners and the failure of his first Irish mission' in Peter Francis (ed.), *The Gladstone umbrella: papers delivered at the Gladstone Centenary Conference 1998* (Hawarden, 2001), pp 98–114.

promise, representing the possibility that Irish aspirations could after all be met within the framework of Union. In particular, if Gladstone could redress the major grievances of Irish society in a way which did not too adversely affect those on the negative side of some of those reforms, and if this were done through a process of consultation with Irish representative figures, then a beginning would have been made to establishing a new basis for effective Irish governance. Gladstone's approach suggested the possibility of this. His resolution of the church establishment issue was based on widespread consultation, in which care was taken to protect legitimate interests of the Church of Ireland and to ensure its future viability as a voluntary body. As unlikely as it was that landlords would welcome legislation on land tenure, many of them nonetheless recognised its necessity. Gladstone's thoroughness of approach gave some assurance that his solutions would be based both on consultation with interested parties and an understanding of the underlying issues. Settling the university question involved an intractable conflict of irreconcilable interests between his own constituencies in Britain and the Catholic hierarchy in Ireland, but he could not be faulted on the thoroughness of consultation undertaken.

Butt's departure along the home rule path must be understood in the double context of the success of Gladstone's initiatives in creating an unprecedented way forward in Irish affairs and the sudden and transparent collapse of that momentum in 1870. For Butt there were two reasons for this collapse. One was the inadequacies of the Land Act of that year. What Butt had to say of Gladstone's Land Bill is perhaps the best summary judgment there is of the process that had been involved:

> I am bound to say that, imperfect and inadequate as they are, I can trace in its provisions an earnest and sincere desire to protect the Irish tenant – a struggle to escape from principles by which the framers of the Bill believed themselves bound, but which, in favour of the Irish tenant, they made every effort to evade. I fear the result has been only an elaborate failure to do the justice which it was so elaborately attempted to work out.[13]

The other reason, as Butt would have seen it, for this collapse was Gladstone's failure to secure the release of the Fenian prisoners at the time that it would have proved efficacious in terms of Irish opinion; the political importance he attached to this issue is evidenced both in his presidency of the Amnesty Association and in the publication, in the form of an open letter to Gladstone, of the arguments for release.[14] Butt could see, however, that the situation

13 Isaac Butt to Wm Bolster (Limerick Farmers' Club), *Freeman's Journal*, 22 Feb. 1870, quoted in R.D. Collison Black, *Economic thought and the Irish Question, 1817–1870* (Cambridge, 1960), p. 70.   14 Isaac Butt, *Ireland's appeal for amnesty: a letter to the right honourable W.E. Gladstone, M.P.* (London, 1870).

created by Gladstone's failure to sustain the momentum of reform and preserve his position as the focus of Irish hopes left a serious and threatening vacuum in Irish political life. While the expectations raised by Gladstone's 'Justice for Ireland' programme had done much to focus Irish politics, and to give the initiative back to political leaders concerned to strengthen the bonds of constitutional politics, it was essential that some new institutional framework evolve to avoid a relapse into the fragmented public life which had characterised the 1850s and the 1860s. It was to this end that the Home Government Association was formed in May 1870. Helped no doubt by the fact that Gladstone had already significantly breached the old defences of the protestant ascendancy, Butt was now able to provide leadership for a move forward in which the concerns of the majority and those of the minority could be pursued through some new and more accommodating political and civil entities. While – as George Boyce rightly argues[15] – Butt's new party clearly undermined the continuing viability of Liberal electoral politics in Ireland its emergence needs to be seen more as a consequence of the loss of steam in Gladstone's mission than as a cause of the loss of Liberal political initiative.

IV

The endemic tendency to look from the outside at Irish politics in terms of warring factions, of tribal conflict, of religious antagonisms obscures and distorts the reality of a society in which accommodation, compromise and tolerance are at least as sought after as elsewhere. We have only to look at the stereotypes of landlord and tenant in Ireland to understand the way these misrepresentations occur. While the issue of land tenure remained unresolved, conflict, even minor conflict, between landlord and tenant flared into crisis. This meant that what were essentially exceptional circumstances – the murder of a landlord or mass, forced arbitrary evictions – set the tone of how the relationship was characterised. The stereotypes so formed overshadowed the reality of relationships in which each side did all they could, despite intractable underlying problems in the legal assumptions on which they operated, to work together co-operatively. Likewise, in the larger political arena, the constant of the Irish political culture was the aspiration to find the basis, institutionally and ideologically, by which problems could be resolved. In launching the home rule movement Butt was seizing an opportunity for creating a broad institutional basis for a civic polity in place of the Liberalism which had provided this in the 1860s. The 'match' between the dominant political forms of Ireland and the new-style Liberalism emerging in Britain was one of the most notable features

---

15 D.G. Boyce, *The Irish Question and British politics, 1868–1986* (London, 1988), p. 24.

of those years. We see in John Blake Dillon, the returned Young Irelander, the recognition that the future for Ireland lay in accommodating itself to the forms of Victorian Britain, accepting the opportunities which that provided for adding Ireland's own distinctive claims and diversities to the emerging complexities of the larger society, and etching out within the larger context a nationality which could accommodate that diversity.[16] This was met initially with a very full response from within British Liberalism, arising from a growing sense amongst Liberals generally that the relationship with Ireland had been badly mishandled and that it was necessary for compensation and rectification to occur if the Union were to survive. But more particularly it was Gladstone's capacity to articulate, and apparently embody, this aspiration for Irish national cohesion which seemed to provide the conditions in which the body politic of Ireland could be reconstituted.

A closer look at Gladstone's handling of the issue of church disestablishment will do to illustrate the way in which he achieved this standing – indeed function – within Irish politics. While the primary object of the church legislation was to do justice to the rights and sentiments of the majority of the population, it was Gladstone's intent to act with sensitivity to the feelings and interests of the minority for whom the establishment of their church had been a marked and important statement of their identity. He was in a strong position politically: the house of commons had passed a resolution in favour of disestablishment while the Liberals were still in opposition; an election had been fought and won by his party; the government which had opposed disestablishment had given way to his own. He was determined, however, to use that strength to get the leaders of the Church of Ireland, despite resistance, into discussion. Emphasising that the government's determination would not be 'in the slightest degree relaxed by the impolitic opposition which the [archbishop of Armagh had] unhappily decided upon offering', Gladstone mocked the stance which had been adopted: 'A House of Commons has fought and decided – a nation has done the same, & a Ministry has run away, but the Archbishop (how militant he is) waits for the "field of battle"!'[17] Through nurturing the aid of those, both clerical and lay – for example, the bishop of Peterborough (Dr Magee) and Lord Monck[18] – who worked for a more compromising attitude within the Church of Ireland, Gladstone achieved the level of communication which enabled the legislation to accommodate more of the concerns of the church itself. In seeking to do justice to the Church of Ireland, Gladstone was strongly supported by Roman Catholic spokesmen such as J.F. Maguire, who expressed 'the most scrupulous regard for vested interests' and his repudiation,

16 See Brendan O'Cathaoir, *John Blake Dillon, Young Irelander* (Dublin, 1990), especially chapters 10 and 11.   17 Gladstone to Spencer, 23 Jan. 1869, Matthew (ed.), *The Gladstone diaries*, vol. 7, p. 16.   18 See Spencer to Gladstone, 29 Jan. 1869, Gladstone Papers, B.L. Add.MS. 44,306, fs. 40–43.

as an Irish Catholic, 'of sharing in the plunder'.[19] In the end the disestablished Church of Ireland was able to proceed as a voluntary institution in a much more robust and broad-minded manner because of the recognition by Gladstone that majorities alone were not an adequate basis on which to handle the sensitivities of a substantial section of the population. As with the Church of Ireland, so with the issue of land. Gladstone's conception of what was required went to the heart of Irish understandings, and its achievement was made impossible not by Irish concerns so much as English preoccupations with principles of property. While Irish landlords feared what fate might await them through legislation, they understood well enough the claim being made by the tenants and appreciated the historical and cultural bases on which it was founded. The consequence of the failure – the 'elaborate failure' in Butt's phrase – of the 1870 Land Act was to set landlord and tenant more viciously at each others throats, for it took from the one the certainties which had been claimed in the past while denying to the other the security which might have bred contentment.

This was the context in which Butt's Home Rule movement was launched and its intent was not to set out on a path to sever the connections between Ireland and Britain, but to sustain a basis of civil order threatened by the demise of Gladstone's mission. It has been said before that with the abolition of the Irish parliament in 1800 there occurred a vacuum at the heart of the Irish polity which had a major effect on all subsequent developments in the country. The refusal of Catholic Emancipation, the failure to integrate Irish administrative structures to the forms of a Union, the devastation of the Great Famine all contributed to this sense of a void in Irish life. The effects of this can be seen in the recurring tendency to create a substitute focus for national life: O'Connell 'The Liberator', Parnell 'The Uncrowned King', the continuity of the concept of 'alternative authority' stretching from O'Connell's 'Council of Three Hundred', Charles Gavan Duffy's 'Authority', Parnell's mooted 'withdrawal from Westminster', to the elaborate theory of '*de facto* government' evolved through Arthur Griffith's Sinn Féin. Amazingly, Gladstone himself seemed for a while to enter this symbolic pantheon, giving a sense of civic cohesion to Irish life; not here the staunch partisan of the home rule crisis in the mid-eighties, but a figure able to facilitate resolution of problems and a forging of compromise. The loss of momentum for this gave to Butt's leadership and to his new movement its point and purpose. In part Gladstone may have appreciated the need for Butt's policy initiative. In a passage of a letter to Chichester Fortescue in February 1869 Gladstone wrote 'I agree with you that a good Colonial Gov' would probably be the best solution'.[20] A number of Butt's own correspondents

---

19 John Francis Maguire to Gladstone, 'Sunday' [21 Mar. 1869], Gladstone Papers, B.L. Add. MS. 44419, fs. 249–50.   20 Gladstone to Fortescue, 22 Feb. 1869, Carlingford Papers, CP1/35. This is an incomplete letter, and the context of this remark is not explicit. However, it is highly probable that it refers to the problems of Irish government.

in early 1870 connected the inadequacies of the Land Bill to the need to revive Repeal;[21] one of them, R.B. O'Brien, dean of Limerick, wrote that 'Mr Gladstone has closed the line of statesmen in whom I had any hope' and that there was 'only one remaining chance of saving us from coming confusion, and that is to permit us to make our own laws.'[22]

Butt's 'Home Rule nationalism', therefore, can be seen as an extension of the initiatives of Gladstone – an endeavour to stabilise the Irish body politic around forms and institutional structures suited to resolving persistent problems in Irish society. The misfortune was that it was not seen in that way by British governments and the British parliament. There was a propensity, despite the massive evidence of background, ideas and political style, to identify and stigmatise Butt as an extremist, a consequence of his sympathy for the Fenians (especially through his leadership of the Amnesty movement), his apparently radical position on the land question, and his advocacy of the novel and misunderstood concept of Home Rule. As a consequence attention was not paid to the vital propositions with which he was associated. A positive response to his extremely well-informed position on the land tenure issue might have brought early amendments to the Land Act, averting the mounting crisis which was to lead to mass mobilization through the Land League in the late 1870s. Likewise, a willingness to listen to Butt's views on university education and a disposition to use him as an 'honest broker' on that issue might have prevented or minimised the disastrous impact on Gladstone's government of the 1874 bill. And even on the question of Home Rule, on which incidentally Butt was most reluctant to pressure parliament in the early years,[23] a readiness to respond – for example, in terms of Gladstone's idea of a 'good Colonial Gov^t' or even some lesser form of devolution – might have done much to consolidate Butt's position in the country, helping him to hold together the diverse interests which he was able for a while to lead. Any account of Butt's movement must emphasise the many ambiguities on which it was based, but this is part of its importance. Professor Comerford refers to Butt's 'honest and creative attempt to find a balance between the advantages of union and those of self-government' and 'to find an answer to the conflict of interests between landlords and tenants' and he concludes that 'His capacity for seeing both sides of a question and endeavouring to reconcile them marks out Butt as one of the most remarkable Irish public men of the century.'[24]

In other words Butt's capacity, however short-lived it may have proved, to bring together disparate interests and aspirations was his major strength. Amongst the protestant conservatives the desire was less to recover the initiative which Gladstone and the Liberals had gained in the late 1860s than to substitute

21 Isaac Butt Papers, National Library of Ireland, MS. 8692, folder 2.   22 R.B. O'Brien to Butt, 17 Feb. 1870, Ibid.   23 See, for example, William Shaw to Butt, 16 Apr. 1872, Butt Papers, N.L.I., MS. 8694 (4).   24 Vaughan (ed.), *A new history of Ireland*, vol. 6, p. 16.

for it a new and more effective means of carrying through reforms in Ireland which were as accommodating of different interests as was possible. For former Fenians – and indeed former Young Irelanders – there was a ready suspension of their former revolutionary methods and goals in order to embrace, not only a solution, but a process in which less would be sought, with less damage done to cross-community relations in Ireland, and with a greater prospect of it being attained. It is important to recognise that this included a deliberate and principled commitment to a proposed Irish parliament which included an hereditary house of lords with unrestricted powers, intended as a reassurance and a guarantee to the religious minority. This was, as Butt argued, the basis on which the 'Irish aristocracy could learn, as the English have done, to sympathize with, or at all events, to yield to the enlightened and deliberate opinions of the country, while they exercised the powers of control over rash legislation which it is the province of a second chamber to possess.'[25] As Butt's pleas fell on deafer and deafer governmental – Liberal until 1874 and Tory thereafter – and parliamentary ears, the viability of his project was fatally undermined. Protestant conservatives began to withdraw from a position in which they had, but to no avail, taken some substantial political risks, leaving other elements, for whom also compromise had brought few rewards, free to advance upon a path more radical in both nationalist and land reform aspirations. Thus the Home Rule party – enormously strengthened by the results of the 1874 general election – embarked upon a course which was to carry in its train a legacy of polarization and sectarian division.

Far from being a departure from the course which Gladstone had set out into a more radical nationalism, Butt's movement was intended to continue what had now become impossible for Gladstone to carry further. It was a move to fill the gap created by the negative judgment in Ireland of the outcome of Gladstone's reforms, an outcome significantly affected by Gladstone's failure to secure an early release of the Fenian prisoners. A key to understanding what was being sought may be found in the word 'process', a term now in everyday use in relation to the contemporary problem of Northern Ireland. Isaac Butt stands preeminently as someone whose life and politics exemplified those 'bonds of society' in Ireland which transcended sectional divisions, and his early home rule movement – and the major commitment of his career – was to translate these into institutional form, to provide a basis for 'process' in Irish governance.

V

Swift MacNeill and John Redmond set Butt and his movement in a line of continuity from O'Connell through Parnell to Redmond. More correctly, the reins

25 Isaac Butt, *Home government for Ireland: Irish federalism, its meaning, its objects and its hopes* (Dublin, 1871), p. 52.

which Butt put down (or were taken from him) in the mid 1870s were taken up again in 1902 to 1904 by Captain John Shawe-Taylor, William O'Brien, Lord Mayo, Timothy Harrington and Lord Dunraven as they set about the formation and conduct of the Land Conference and in their pursuit of a policy of conciliation in its aftermath. Here again is the recognition of the priority to be given to procedure as distinct from electoral majorities, to pursuing solutions by discourse between the parties principally involved, with British authority acting as a facilitator rather than a principal. The ill-fated Devolution proposals which came out of the conciliation initiatives of these men were a striking example of what Butt had pursued in his formula for a home rule parliament, a shift of decision making to Irish people but with strong arbitrary protections for the minority community. We see the same phenomenon again in the process – this time so described – which emerged in the 1980s and which led to the Anglo-Irish Agreement and subsequent developments. This approach suffered its most significant set-back in 1996 when the Major government lost sight of the need to follow informed, responsible and broadly-based Irish advice and made recourse – given its then dependence on the Ulster Unionist party for a house of commons majority – to that most potent destroyer of conciliation in Ireland, the electoral mandate. It has become a common parlance since the 1980s to speak of the necessity of resolving the problem of Northern Ireland 'within the totality of relationships within these islands'. That is to restate exactly the perspective of Isaac Butt, and – insofar as such a view has now been accepted – has taken us back to the point at which he was.

The modern historiography of Ireland has – at least until recent years – been shaped in large part by the frequently dramatic course of concurrent political developments. Within nationalist historiography this produced what for long became the dominant paradigm of a duality between constitutional and physical force movements. The effect of historical research and writing in the second half of the twentieth century has been to show how inadequate any such division is for the purposes of understanding the complex dynamics of nationalism itself, let alone other dimensions of national history.[26] The more pervasive and much more entrenched polarity of modern Irish historiography has been that of nationalism and unionism, which since independence and partition has become also one of North and South. In the work of historians we can see a developmental relationship. The earlier tradition tended to spawn an heroic history: on the constitutional side drawing on O'Connell and Parnell as models and embodying aspirations for Ireland as a partner in empire – or at least within a British constitutional ambit; on the physical force side reaching back to the

26 This change in historical understanding could be said to have begun with T.W. Moody's 'The New Departure in Irish politics, 1878–9' in H.A. Cronne, T.W. Moody and D.B. Quinn (eds), *Essays in British and Irish history in honour of James Eadie Todd* (London, 1949), pp 303–33.

heroism of 1798, but more particularly focusing on the rise of Fenianism and its outcomes in the revolutionary struggle after 1916. In the years after 1946 a new generation of historians embarked on an exploration of Irish history which involved a much more systematic application of empirical research methodology to various aspects of Irish history, thus breaking away from the dominant earlier modes of conceptualising modern Irish history. This new professionalism embodied a high degree of all-Ireland co-operation, but the focus on intensive research methods effectively produced histories focused on one or other of the dominant political traditions. While T.W. Moody, Conor Cruise O'Brien and F.S.L. Lyons were pioneers on the nationalist side, one of the first and foundational researchers of modern Irish unionism was Patrick Buckland. His fine and thorough expositions of the unionist tradition, both across Ireland as a whole and in Ulster in particular, in a number of volumes and distinguished articles, fit the pattern of quality scholarship which characterised Irish historical research in the later decades of the twentieth century and of which he stands as one of the pioneers.

The last twenty-five years of the twentieth century were as tumultuous for Irish historiography as they were for Irish life more generally. But the most significant aspect of that period has been the collapse of the two world views by which the two parts of Ireland had been sustained for much of the century. The implications of these developments has been far-reaching for historians. The sometimes acrimonious dialogue over different ways of viewing Irish history can be seen in some respects as a working out – often with historians as scapegoats – of the implications of challenges to cherished myths and beliefs about the past. The course of events in relation to the future of Northern Ireland has illuminated, however, principles which suggest an alternative way of evaluating aspects of Irish history which have been critical in shaping Ireland in the modern era. In particular, majoritarian concepts of political authority and legitimation have been rejected as ineffective for a society dominated by fixed communal or ethnic identities which are rarely transcended by shifting voting patterns. One of the tasks now facing the historian is to examine the extent to which historically there are precedents for the approach which has characterised the Northern Ireland Peace Process and what those precedents show us about the dynamics of Irish politics. Central to this paper is the contention that, just as many of those who would wish to be identified as Irish nationalists have embraced the approaches used in attempting to bring stability to Northern Ireland, so a reassessment of nationalism historically is not an exercise in defending imperialism nor an attack on nationalist aspirations as such. Rather, it is a searching out of alternative modes of expressing nationalist aspirations, and in this context the original leader of the home rule movement, Isaac Butt, stands out as an important subject for re-examination.

In general, historians have depicted Butt as – in W.J. McCormack's phrase – 'a transitional figure' between O'Connell and Parnell. In this regard his major achievements have been identified as twofold: the invention, for practical purposes, of the concept of home rule, albeit in a less advanced form than later under Parnell; and the establishment of a political structure which served as a base for Parnell in building a more disciplined and more aggressive successor organization. This does less than justice both to the objectives and to the achievements of Isaac Butt. It is as a nationalist that he should be primarily seen, one cast in a distinctive mould, but very differently from what has come – especially since the 1920s – to be characterised as nationalism. His nationalism was more about nation-building than about the problematic and often divisive issue of national identity. His movement was an attempt to create a framework within which Irish political and social problems could be satisfactorily resolved rather than a precursor to a form of nationalism which tended to make such resolution more elusive by setting in concrete the most fixed positions of opposed interests. Such a view of his movement enables us to set it within a distinctive tradition of Irish political action and outlook which is often neglected, and within which can be included later phenomena like the conciliation movement of the early twentieth century and the mode of conflict resolution being applied in Northern Ireland, as well as phases in the careers of earlier figures like William Smith O'Brien, Charles Gavan Duffy and John Blake Dillon. Providing a more appropriate context for an alternative tradition of nationalism will not only do greater justice to political participants in the past, but also enable a more balanced assessment of the relationship between Ireland and Britain focused less on moments of maximum conflict and more on the normative functioning of government. In such an analysis not only will the objectives of those like Butt who pursued the politics of accommodation better fall into place historically, but fundamental problems in the relationship of the two countries will become easier to understand.

Those who live in societies in which there is, at least at some minimal level, a consensus about the basic institutional structures through which order is sustained often take this for granted and fail to appreciate the significance of its absence in other cases. Indeed, as A.T.Q. Stewart has pointed out, there is a difficulty for them in recognising this difference for the very reason that their own 'superior form of civilized life' is itself a fiction, for 'men in an ordered society quite deliberately deceive themselves about the subject of human nature, wisely perhaps, since such illusions are essential to its health'.[27] Not only had Ireland historically experienced a high level of turbulence in relation to issues of authority and legitimacy, but through the O'Connellite campaigns from the early 1820s to the late 1840s the traditional political leadership of the landed

27 A.T.Q. Stewart, *The narrow ground: the roots of conflict in Ulster* (2nd edn., London, 1989), pp 141–2.

elite had been very substantially undermined. For those of a Conservative disposition – and Butt, like many others of his class and background in Ireland, was deeply Tory – this was seriously threatening to their conception of social and political order. A democratic franchise as a basis of political legitimation was as yet barely on the horizon: in France there had been a long retreat, even amongst progressives, from the more democratic ideals of the early Revolution; and in Britain itself even the advocates of parliamentary reform saw it as a means of stabilising a conservative polity by incorporating the richer middle class interests. In Ireland, for conservatives like Butt, the old landed Protestant elite and its associated professional and ecclesiastical establishments seemed the only viable basis for a political system, and the absence of a substantial and wealthy middle class added credibility to apprehensions about undermining it. Not that Butt was uncritical of that old establishment; he was, for example, an open opponent of the land tenure system and its effect on tenant farmers.[28] Just as Edmund Burke's fierce anger at the Penal Laws against Catholics had been based largely on what he saw as their destructive impact on the bonds of society,[29] Butt considered that a lack of respect for the traditional rights and practices of the tenantry undermined the fabric of society. After the Famine he recognised that there was no longer a social and civic stability to be found in the old order, and his venture in the 1870s was in large part about finding a replacement for it in inter-communal co-operation. That aspiration still preoccupies modern Ireland, and Butt's experience remains relevant to present concerns, as well as forming part of an important commentary on the development and form of Irish nationalism. Any historical review of nationalism should incorporate more fully an understanding of the impact of British responses to Irish issues, and it may help to take into account what Stewart suggests to be the 'fiction' and 'illusions' by which an ordered society such as Britain is itself sustained. In every phase of his life Butt was deeply affected by British failure to understand the effect of their policies in Ireland – and ultimately upon themselves – and rather than leaving Isaac Butt to rest in the sidelines of Irish political history, his experience should be a basis for a more critical analysis of the relationship between the two islands.

28 The work that stands largely alone as an account of Butt's earlier views, and that generally of pre-Famine Irish Toryism, is the regrettably still unpublished PhD thesis by Joseph Spence, 'The philosophy of Irish Toryism, 1833–52: a study of reactions to liberal reformism in Ireland in the generation between the First Reform Act and the Famine, with especial reference to expressions of national feeling among the Protestant Ascendancy', Birkbeck College, University of London, 1991. 29 Edmund Burke, *Letters, speeches and tracts on Irish affairs* (London, 1881), pp 1–69.

'Irish Protestants feel this betrayal keenly …':[1]
Home Rule, Rome rule and nonconformity

ALAN MEGAHEY

Irish Presbyterians in 1913 could look back on three hundred years in Ireland, many of them years of struggle and persecution. At the tercentenary celebrations, the Revd James Heron, Professor of Church History at Assembly's, recalled the first two hundred years as a period when 'our Church had to struggle with a fixed determination on the part of those in power to degrade and exterminate her', and summarised the three centuries as 'a history of incessant labour and poignant suffering and immense sacrifices for truth and righteousness, and to secure the blessings of civil and religious liberty'.[2] Lauding the heroes of the past, he ended by calling on his brethren to emulate 'their fidelity and self-sacrifice … and not surrender lightly what they have won for us at so great a cost'. His colleague at Magee, the Revd F. J. Paul, began by noting that Irish Presbyterians owed 'remarkably little to the favour of princes', and indeed 'seldom enjoyed the sunshine of their smiles'.[3] He ended his critique of contemporary Presbyterianism – and the challenges it faced in education, ecumenism and social service – by peering into the future: 'let me say that in spite of failings and defects, and in spite of dark clouds on the horizon, I believe the prospects before our Church are bright'. But no one who heard his words was unaware of those 'dark clouds'. The third Home Rule Bill would – it seemed – become law within the year. Presbyterians, like most other Protestants in Ireland, believed that their civil and religious liberties were under threat.

English nonconformists, like their Irish brethren, could also look back on a history of persecution and struggle, though the nineteenth century had seen the gradual dismantling of the confessing state, from the repeal of the Test and Corporation Acts in 1828 through the abolition of tithe, the recognition of nonconformist marriages, the opening up of graveyards, and of the universities, and the on-going campaign for disestablishment. It is a mark of their greater confidence that by the end of the nineteenth century the nonconformists were less vocal about disestablishment (as regards England at least) – partly because of the increased dominance in nonconformity of the Wesleyan

---

1 T.W. Russell MP at a Nonconformist Unionist meeting, reported in the *Globe*, 18 Apr. 1888; reproduced as a pamphlet which can be inspected in the Public Record Office of Northern Ireland [PRONI], D 2396/6/2   2 *Addresses on the occasion of the celebration of the tercentenary of Irish Presbyterianism* (Belfast, 1913), pp 15, 20.   3 Ibid., p. 21.

Methodists (who had never been as committed to it as had the 'older' dissenting bodies like the Congregationalists), and partly because it now seemed
almost irrelevant. Even the Liberation Society, so active in mid-Victorian
England, could now feel that it had 'disestablished the Church of England in
that it had established national power and prestige for the Free Churches of
England'.[4] Nonconformists began to assume a higher profile nationally, as they
had done locally in many areas since before the middle of the century and after
the 1867 franchise reform. A significant visual symbol can be seen opposite
Westminster Abbey. In the heart of the imperial capital the Methodists in 1911
opened their huge Central Hall, its Edwardian architecture redolent not so
much of the Christian past as of the political and imperial present - an assertion of confidence in the present age, the nonconformist presence firmly established in Westminster, both in the commons and at central hall. It is significant
for nonconformity generally that by the dawn of the twentieth century, it had
begun to use the term 'Free Churches', with its more positive and up-beat ring.
This shift, no longer 'dissenters', not so often 'nonconformists', but more often
'free churchmen' has been described as 'an important symbolic indication of
the move from negative to positive identification'.[5] It was a term formalised
with the establishment of the National Council of Evangelical Free Churches
in 1896. When C. Sylvester Horne, leading Congregationalist and later a
Liberal MP, wrote his history of the 'free churches' (starting with Wyclif), his
message was much more up-beat and confident than the mood which prevailed
among Irish Presbyterians during their tercentenary. 'The massing of the Free
Church forces for the defence of the interests of religious liberty and Christian
truth', he wrote in 1903, 'is the most influential factor in the present ecclesiastical situation in England.' Indeed, he continued with unbridled optimism, the
free churches, which had 'been so largely instrumental in establishing the principle that the final authority in the State is the people, are now concerned to
establish that the final authority in the Christian church is the Christian people.
They have triumphed in the former issue; they will triumph in the latter.'[6] Free
churchmen were talking the language of their age – progress, prosperity,
reform, freedom – and of course Liberalism. While what Ian Bradley has
termed 'the call to seriousness' had been heard and responded to by evangelical
Protestants both within and without the established church throughout the
nineteenth century, a new focussing of moral earnestness and Christian disci-
pleship is encapsulated in the phrase 'the Nonconformist Conscience'.

The nonconformists had welcomed Irish disestablishment; they had thrilled
to the moral outrage of Gladstone during his Midlothian campaign; they

---

4 W.H. Mackintosh, *Disestablishment and liberation* (London, 1972), p. 329. 5 D.A.
Johnson, *The changing shape of English nonconformity, 1825–1925* (New York, 1999), p. 165.
6 C.S. Horne, *A popular history of the Free Churches* (London, 1903), p. 426.

shared with him, as has been said, 'the same redemptive view of the world'.[7] This did not mean that they had a coherent political programme; indeed, they could not even agree among themselves on many points of theology or church polity. But they could rally round a set of shared principles. They were against promiscuity and gambling and drink; they were anti-Catholic and anti-erastian. They were for temperance and purity and peace; they supported humanitarian action of behalf of the poor, non-sectarian education and freedom, if not full-blown democracy. They had found in the last quarter of the nineteenth century that most of these issues gave them points of contact with Liberal MPs, many of them 'faddists' who campaigned for their own particular pet crusade. Not all nonconformists shared Gladstone's 1885 conversion to Home Rule; many were more receptive than he to Irish Protestant fears, which he seemed incapable of understanding.[8] Probably the majority continued to follow him, both because he was the Grand Old Man, and also because the issue was a matter of 'freedom'. Some prominent nonconformist leaders opposed Home Rule. The great Birmingham Congregationalist, R.W. Dale, stayed loyal to Chamberlain and (somewhat distressed) opposed Gladstone, largely because he firmly believed in 'the unity of Great Britain and Ireland',[9] or, as Chamberlain would increasingly come to see it, in maintenance of the integrity of the empire. Newman Hall, another leading Congregationalist, made a similar point when he wrote to Gladstone in 1886 pleading for the continuance of 'the supreme authority of the Imperial Parliament of a united Empire'.[10] He, and other non-conformist opponents of the Grand Old Man's Irish policy, tended to feel obliged to affirm their reverence for the Liberal leader. As Hall put it in 1893: 'I had long enjoyed Mr Gladstone's friendship. The better I knew him the more I honoured him. I felt, and still feel that, however opinions may differ as to his judgment of methods, he is absolutely sincere in his desire to do justice to Ireland.'[11] C.H. Spurgeon, the Baptist colossus, sought to keep private his opposition to Gladstone's 1886 Bill, but it became known – and indeed, according to his biographer, 'materially contributed to the great leader's defeat in 1886'.[12] His opposition was rooted in his fears of Roman Catholic influence, so his stance was close to that of his brethren in Ireland, with whom he was close doctrinally as well: they had supported his stand against theological liberalism during the 'down-grade controversy'. James Guinness Rogers, an Ulsterman by birth and minister to the most socially up-market Congregational church in

7 J.P. Ellens, *Religious routes to Gladstonian liberalism* (Pennsylvania, 1994), p. 268.   8 See J. Loughlin, *Gladstone & the Ulster Question, 1882–93* (Dublin, 1986), especially pp 241 and 289.   9 A.W.W. Dale, *The life of R.W. Dale* (London, 1898), p. 471.   10 N. Hall, *An autobiography* (London, 1898), p. 281.   11 N. Hall, 'Nonconformists and unionism', *Fortnightly Review*, new series, xlix, no. ccxc (Feb. 1891), 321–2.   12 Spurgeon's own autobiographical writings are interlarded with comments such as this by his editors, Susannah Spurgeon and Joseph Harrald; C.H. Spurgeon, *Autobiography: volume 2; The full harvest* (Edinburgh, 1973), p. 377.

England, also worried over the Home Rule policy, but as D. W. Bebbington has said, the 'magic of Gladstone' kept him back 'from the brink of opposing Home Rule'.[13] Whether nonconformists supported or opposed Home Rule, they did so as a matter of conscience. They were steeped in the protestant belief in individual judgment and personal accountability. Many were outspoken proponents of what came to be called the nonconformist conscience.

The term 'nonconformist conscience' was first popularised in 1890 during the campaign to depose Parnell as Irish leader after his appearance in the divorce court. Its leading exponent was the Revd Hugh Price Hughes, leader of the Methodist 'Forward Movement', editor of the *Methodist Times*, and convinced Home Ruler. After his declaration that 'what is morally wrong can never be politically right', a controversy ensued in the pages of *The Times* under the heading, 'Nonconformist conscience'.[14] Maybe 'a new political term was born',[15] but only in the sense that in the period 1890 to 1914 a more self-confident nonconformity is in evidence, and moreover one which increasingly looked to the government to abate social ills. Their 'conscience' had obviously profound political implications, as was evident in the call to unseat Parnell, though nonconformists were still not unanimous in their support of Home Rule. At the end of the century they were also divided over the Boer War, though in that case only a small minority were 'pro-Boers'. But the Conservatives' 1902 Education Act did much to reunite nonconformity behind the Liberal party, as (to a lesser extent) did the issue of 'Chinese slavery'. The 1906 election was a milestone, and as Stephen Koss has noted, the free church leaders 'promoted Liberal candidates' even if they 'bestowed their blessing selectively, and often with gnawing doubts'.[16] But they could feel gratified that some 200 nonconformists sat on the Liberal benches, outnumbering the Unionists, of whom a mere half dozen were free churchmen. 'We have been put into power by the Nonconformists', said the new prime minister, Henry Campbell-Bannerman.[17] In 1911, Henry W. Clark, surveying nonconformity in England (since 'Wiclif') expressed some doubts about its 'politicization' during the previous forty years. He was echoing the sentiments he had expressed in his anonymous and widely-read book, *Nonconformity and politics*, published two years earlier which called for less political and more spiritual dedication. Its 'drugged spiritual passion and dying spiritual power should be enough to show how heavy a payment Nonconformity is being called upon to make (and this is by the inevitable law of things) for its intrusion into the political field', he declared gloomily.[18] But Clark could still end

---

13 D.W. Bebbington, *The nonconformist conscience* (London, 1982), p. 88. 14 There is a good examination of Hugh Price Hughes, the nonconformist conscience and the fall of Parnell in C. Oldstone-Moore, *Hugh Price Hughes* (Cardiff, 1999), pp 209–19. 15 Oldstone-Moore, op. cit, p. 216. 16 S. Koss, *Nonconformity in modern British politics* (London, 1975), p. 76. 17 Quoted in Ibid., p, 74. 18 'A Nonconformist minister', *Nonconformity and politics* (London, 1909), pp 158–9.

his history of nonconformity declaring that the ideal of a 'free church in a free state' was on the horizon and 'that the full homeward journey will be accomplished by Nonconformity's massed bands erelong'.[19]

So English nonconformists could look forward with confidence and hope; but Irish nonconformists did not. They believed that the very 'civil and religious liberties' which had been won so painfully were now threatened. Of course they were technically not 'nonconformists' at all. Disestablishment had placed all the churches in Ireland on the same legal footing. Nevertheless, Irish Presbyterians, Methodists, Congregationalists and Baptists had a number of good reasons for feeling 'nonconformist'. They felt they were battling still with an establishment which retained its Anglican ethos, or which was now all too sympathetic to Roman Catholic claims. The Presbyterian newspaper, the *Witness*, was complaining in 1881 about 'the "boycotting" to which Presbyterians have been subjected in regard to public appointments'.[20] Over twenty years later it was still asserting that 'Presbyterians have not received their fair share'.[21] Almost as numerous as Irish Anglicans, Presbyterians felt their voice was not given equal weight. They still did not enjoy 'the favour of princes'. The nationalist MP Jeremiah MacVeigh produced a pamphlet attacking the Presbyterians for appealing to their 'fellow Nonconformists', on the grounds that 'where there is no Establishment there can be no Nonconformity'; nevertheless a few pages later he was trying to split the united Protestant front by claiming that 'the Presbyterians and Methodists suffer nearly as much under Ascendancy as Roman Catholics'.[22]

There was of course another, more positive, aspect to the Irish 'nonconformist' identity: their close theological and structural links with British nonconformity. They shared the same Bible based evangelical message, even if they tended to give it a more conservative and individualistic spin than was now fashionable in Britain. In Methodism, the British president presided at the Irish Conference, and fraternal greetings were exchanged annually. The Presbyterians exchanged annual greetings with their Scottish brethren, and a small but significant number of the clergy in both these churches received at least part of their training in Britain. The Irish Baptists and Congregationalists also kept up links across the Irish Sea, while eschewing the 'advanced' opinions, theological and political, of many in the British churches. In their hour of crisis – and 1913 was surely that – Irish nonconformists turned to their brethren in England and Scotland for support. They had done so before. In 1888 the Nonconformist Unionist Association had been launched in London, largely thanks to the efforts of the prominent Wesleyan Conservative, Sir George Chubb. At its inaugural meeting T.W. Russell, the Ulster (though Scots born)

19 H.W. Clark, *History of English nonconformity* (2 vols, London, 1911), vol. 2, p. 426. 20 *Witness*, 4 Feb. 1881. 21 Ibid., 30 Dec. 1904. 22 J. MacVeigh, *Home Rule or Rome rule* (Home Rule Council, London 1912), pp 21 & 29.

liberal unionist, trumpeted his distress that "the Nonconformists of England should have deserted their brethren in Ireland on a question of the most vital concern to both", calling it a 'betrayal' and 'one of the most amazing phenomena of the day'.[23] As a Presbyterian with working-class credentials, he was to "win fame as an eloquent and populist representative of loyalism in Britain' in the years between 1886 and 1900.[24] In the new century Russell would become an opponent of conservatism and unionism in Ireland, ending up after 1906 depending almost entirely on the Roman Catholic vote, at a time when the British nonconformist 'betrayal' of their brethren in Ireland constituted an even greater threat. But for the moment his eloquence was channelled into the Herculean task of trying to detach nonconformists from their Liberal allegiance. Lord Abercorn expressed his satisfaction at the new initiative: 'it is an encouragement to think that the unionist Nonconformists in England have really organised themselves and are at last going to play an important part ... on behalf of the Union of England and Ireland'.[25] But it was the initiatives taken at the Irish end which were most effective. Lord Ranfurly, of the Irish Unionist Alliance, called in 1893 for a list of Irish nonconformist ministers to be sent to him, so that they might be dispatched to visit ministers in England and Scotland.[26] Guinness Rogers was moved to draw attention to 'another Ulster Presbyterian invasion'.[27] By 1908 thirty clergy were actively involved in speaking engagements in Britain – 18 Presbyterian, 4 Methodist, 2 Independent, and 9 clergy of the Church of Ireland.[28] Did they have any impact? R.D. Bates, Unionist campaign organiser, reckoned that in at least three, and probably more, seats in Britain during the 'khaki' election 'the influential advocacy of our cause by the Presbyterian and Methodist ministers' had tipped the balance – though we might be tempted to say that it was after all the 'khaki' election, and Bates did have an axe to grind. On the eve of the first 1910 election, eleven former moderators of the Presbyterian general assembly 'took the unprecedented step' of publishing a manifesto in support of the union, a move calculated to speak to the electorate in Scotland in particular.[29] After the two 1910 elections, which left the Liberals dependent upon nationalist (and Labour) support, the Nonconformist Unionist Association assured the Ulster Unionist Council that 'large numbers of Nonconformists in Great Britain will

---

23 T.W. Russell MP as reported in the *Globe*, 18 Apr. 1888; PRONI, D 2396/6/2. **24** A. Jackson, 'Irish unionism and the Russellite threat, 1894–1906', *Irish Historical Studies*, xxv, no. 100 (Nov. 1987), 376–7. **25** Lord Abercorn to W.E. Ball, secretary of the Nonconformist Unionist Association, 23 June 1888; PRONI, D/2396/3/2. **26** Irish Unionist Alliance: Executive Committee Minute Book, 22 Mar. 1893; PRONI, D 989/2. **27** In the mass circulation *Christian Weekly*, 2 Mar. 1893; quoted in Bebbington, *Nonconformist Conscience*, p. 92. **28** Unionist Associations of Ireland, Speakers Book; PRONI, D 1327/2/4. **29** See Holmes, '"Ulster will fight and Ulster will be right": the Protestant Churches and Ulster's resistance to Home Rule', in W.J. Sheils (ed.), *The churches and war* (Oxford, 1983), p. 322.

place religion before party when another General Election comes on the question of what is called Home Rule'.[30] But the English Congregationalist R.F. Horton, a life-long Home Ruler, felt compelled to admit that the 'bitter cry of our Protestant brethren in Ireland, directed to those who are closely allied with them in faith and practice on this side of the Channel, seems to fall upon deaf ears. Presbyterians and Methodists, Friends and Congregationalists, appeal to us to arrest the dreaded disaster of Home Rule; and we make no, or at best only a fainthearted reply'. The reason was simple: 'We the Nonconformists of England and Wales, in the main, feel impelled by political principle to support Home Rule for Ireland.'[31] Horton had chosen his words carefully. *The bitter cry of outcast London* had been a wake up call to the churches in 1883, when another Congregational minister, the Revd Alfred Mearns, had successfully called for a greater focus on social problems, thus helping to launch all the churches in a new departure which would be dubbed 'the social gospel'. The 'bitter cry' of Irish nonconformists, Horton was warning, would have no such effect. It was a significant statement from a man who had been taken to court in 1910 by Lord Alfred Douglas because he had described Oscar Wilde's erstwhile lover's publication, the *Academy*, as a 'Catholic journal'. (Horton won the case, and Douglas soon afterwards became a Roman Catholic.) Horton was the man who had heard a sermon by a curé in rural France on 'The gates of Hell shall not prevail against it', an exposition of the power of the Catholic Church. That sermon, Horton claimed, 'gave a special force to the brochure which I published this year [1910] with Joseph Hocking, *Shall Rome reconquer England?* To the curé of Mégève it seemed certain that she would …'[32] Horton was no friend of Romanism, but he was and remained a supporter of Home Rule. In this he was not unlike the majority of his fellow-nonconformists; their anti-Catholicism was still strong, but they held nevertheless to the Liberal commitment to Home Rule.

M.J.F. McCarthy, the Irish Roman Catholic lawyer, propagandist and writer of immensely popular anti-Catholic books, was appalled at this lack of response from English nonconformists. He had touched on the subject in 1904, complaining that they 'neglected the interests of nonconformity, and abandoned themselves to what was in reality the cause of Irish-Roman superstition'.[33] Eight years later he devoted a whole book to the subject. In *The nonconformist treason: or The sale of the Emerald Isle* he proved himself as usual to be a master of excoriation:

> The typical representatives of political Nonconformity to-day have deserted the great principle of religious freedom for which Bright and

30 Ulster Unionist Council, Executive Minute Book, 26 Jan. 1911; PRONI, D 1327/1.2. 31 *Church of Ireland Gazette* (Letter to the editor), 10 Feb. 1912.   32 R.F. Horton, *An autobiography* (London, 1918), p. 300.   33 M.J.F. McCarthy, *Rome in Ireland* (London, 1904), p. 205.

Chamberlain stood, and, in alliance with Irish political Romanism, are stumping the country, week-days and Sabbath days, for the purpose of forcing the Lords and the Sovereign to put Ireland under the sway of that greatest of all sacerdotal tyrannies from which they themselves have escaped with infinite difficulty! They are about to force the Protestant Irish, twenty-five per cent of Ireland's population, to swallow the camel of Romanism, while they themselves in England straining at the gnat of Anglicanism![34]

Then followed three hundred pages of detailed criticism, ending with a denunciation of the Liberal Government's resolve to sell and betray Irish Protestants. 'And Mr Asquith and his friends', he says in the closing paragraph which conjures up an unlikely image, 'cry out as they proceed with the sale, like the chief priests and elders of Jerusalem, "THEIR BLOOD BE UPON US AND ON OUR CHILDREN".'[35]

As the book makes clear, the ministers of the crown were not the only villains. All too many British nonconformists were prepared to commit 'treason'. Joseph Hocking, co-author with Horton of *Shall Rome reconquer England?*, was one such traitor. A tin-mine owner's son from Cornwall, he was ordained as a minister of the Independent Methodist Free Church in 1884, and from 1888 until 1910 ministered at Woodford Green Chapel, in Essex. He was known to the public as a prolific writer of novels – over fifty of them, usually with religious themes and 'a tendency towards preachiness', which, nevertheless, 'a large number of readers in fact found highly entertaining'.[36] His serialisations in the *British Weekly* were popular – and remunerative. His brother, Silas, also a writer and minister, 'drifted out of the Methodist ministry' and became a Liberal party activist in the pre-war years.[37] Joseph thus had not only had a wide public audience, but also family links into a network which Silas assiduously developed in the first fifteen years of the new century, not least in his connections with Lloyd George. So Joseph Hocking was in a good position to speak to the nonconformist masses in England on the question of Home Rule.

The tenor of his message is well illustrated in his novel, *The woman of Babylon*, published in 1906. The advertising 'puff' for the book describes how Hocking 'has given himself the arduous task of exposing the intrigues that may be resorted to by scheming Romish priests who wish to secure dominating influence in the home' and had revealed 'the present condition of conventual life, and the sloth of the English law in tolerating certain high-handed actions performed in the name of the Roman church'.[38] Further issues were exposed in

---

34 M.J.F. McCarthy, *The nonconformist treason or The sale of the Emerald Isle* (London, 1912), pp 5–6. 35 Ibid., p. 340. 36 J. Sutherland, *The Stanford companion to Victorian fiction* (Stanford, 1989), p. 301. 37 See S.K. Hocking, *My book of memory* (London, 1923), p. 177. 38 Page 7 of the advertisers appendix in the first edition of *The woman of Babylon* (London, 1906).

The Jesuit, published in 1911, a fictional 'autobiography' of Kerry Trevanion Killigrew. Son of a puritan Cornish father and a Roman Catholic Irish mother, Killigrew (whose middle name was the name of Hocking's house in Woodford Green) is a Liberal MP. He is persuaded to join in the campaign to change the Coronation Oath. 'If there is one thing I hate', he declares, 'it is that distinctions should be made by the state between men who hold different faiths'.[39] However he discovers that the group he has been associating with has a darker agenda. Simon Maynooth (appropriately named) reveals the horrific plot when he asks: 'with a Catholic King on the British throne – a Catholic King, subservient to, obedient to, and taking his orders from Rome – shall we not have fulfilled that commission which Manning sketched so eloquently? Shall we not have gone far to subdue, to conquer and to rule, an imperial race?'[40] Killigrew realises that the campaign to change the Coronation Oath is part of a wider conspiracy to undermine Protestant England, and he backs off. But woven into the story is another aspect: the hero's love for an Irish Roman Catholic girl, Kathleen, who has been hidden away in a convent, but with whom he is finally united.

These two novels reveal some of the concerns of nonconformists, and some of the features of their anti-Catholicism. The broad, underlying thrust of both novels is anti-Catholic polemic, dealing through the medium of fiction with the issues which Michael McCarthy sought to present through statistics, observation and history. Such anti-Catholic polemic was a defining feature of the Free Church movement. It was this that brought British and Irish nonconformists into closest harmony. What is anti-Catholicism? 'It is', in the recent rather portentous words of R.D. Tumbleson, 'the ghost in the machine … a myth of iniquity whose pitiless prelatic villain has remained consistent for half a millennium, from John Foxe's martyrology to Dostoyevsky's Grand Inquisitor'.[41] Any nonconformist would have recognised the Foxe allusion, and Irish sensibilities on that score were even more alive and more recent than English ones. A strain (or stain) of violence runs through Irish history, that 'narrow ground' where 'violence would appear to be endemic'.[42] Irish Protestants, outnumbered in the whole island by three to one, lived with a level of violence which chimed in with their reading of sixteenth-century persecutions, burnings at the stake and alien despots. Reformation martyrology, familiar also to English Protestants of course, was felt by the Irish to be a living reality. Little wonder that Amy Carmichael, the Ulster missionary in India, 'constantly read stories from *Foxe's Book of Martyrs*' to her Indian female pupils in the 1900s.[43] Robert Harbinson remembered his Belfast schooldays three decades later when he

39 J. Hocking, *The Jesuit* (London, 1911), p. 197.   40 Ibid., p. 229.   41 R.D. Tumbleson, *Catholicism in the English Protestant imagination* (Cambridge, 1998), p. 13.   42 A.T.Q. Stewart, *The narrow ground* (London, 1977), p. 113.   43 F. Houghton, *Amy Carmichael of Dohnavur* (London, 1953), p. 342.

learned about 'our glorious Protestant heritage' not from the clergyman, but from his teacher ('Coughdrop') reading aloud from *Foxe's Book of Martyrs* – 'that and nothing else'.[44] But while more alive and vivid to Irish Protestants (and remaining so into the twenty-first century), the anti-Catholic tradition was strongly present also among their English brethren.

At the 1900 opening session of the National Council of Free Churches Council in Sheffield the new president (a Wesleyan) identified 'Popery' as the 'one dangerous foe to the religious liberty of the Empire' and warned 'all Free Churchmen to be true to their Protestantism'.[45] There were plenty of issues to engage their attention. The proposed opening up of convents to government inspectors had been hotly debated in late 1860s and 70s and could still get an audience excited with suggestions of the dark goings on behind closed walls. The campaign by Irish nationalists to exclude convents from the workshops inspection bill in 1901 proved that they were 'serfs of the church'.[46] Even Colonel Saunderson, redoubtable Irish unionist leader, was attacked in 1902 for having failed to support the opening up of convent laundries to government inspectors – though as Alvin Jackson assures us, he 'was in fact free from any such lapse into broadmindedness'.[47] At the Free Church Council in 1909, Silas Hocking denounced nonconformist MPs who had voted against inspection of nunneries, with the result that men in the audience 'leapt to their feet in a frenzy of feeling and some shouted themselves hoarse with cries of "Traitors, traitors". It was said to be "the wildest and most exciting scene" ever witnessed at the Free Church council'.[48] In 1908, under pressure from Protestant organisations, the Liberal government banned the wearing of vestments and the carrying of the Host in public procession at the Eucharistic Congress held in London. This episode was not so uncharacteristic of 'secular' Britain as a recent commentator has suggested.[49] It followed hard on the heels of what has been called 'the last Victorian anti-ritualist campaign' in the years 1895 until 1906, when Protestants attacked the 'popish' practices of some clergy in the Church of England.[50] Free churchmen were as concerned about 'creeping Romanism' within the Established Church as they were about Popery: both undermined the Protestant identity of Britain. The Coronation Oath controversy also aroused much passion, touching as it did on the nature of the constitution and on the doctrines of the Church of England, and on what were seen

---

44 R. Harbinson, *No surrender: an Ulster childhood* (London, 1960), p. 201. **45** *The Free Church Year Book and Official Report* (London, 1900), p. 17. **46** *Irish Protestant*, Sept. 1901 **47** A. Jackson, *Colonel Edward Saunderson* (Oxford, 1995), p. 144. **48** D.W. Bebbington, 'Nonconformity and electoral sociology, 1867–1918', *Historical Journal*, 27, no. 3 (1984), 648–9. **49** C.A. Devlin, 'The eucharistic procession of 1908: the dilemma of the Liberal government', *Church History*, 63, no. 3 (Sept. 1994), 407–25; but see also G.I.T. Machin, 'The Liberal government and the eucharistic procession of 1908', *Journal of Ecclesiastical History*, 34, no. 4 (Oct. 1983), pp 559–83. **50** G.I.T. Machin, 'The last Victorian anti-ritualist campaign, 1895–1906', *Victorian Studies*, 25, no. 3 (Spring 1982), 277–302.

as the attacks on it from without (by secularists, Roman Catholics, and indeed nonconformists) and from within (by the ritualists).[51] When the declaration was amended in 1910 before George V's coronation, Ulster unionists, fiercely opposed the change, not realising that the king himself had been instrumental in removing the more anti-Catholic aspects of the declaration he was expected to make.[52]

C. Sylvester Horne, elected as a Liberal MP in 1910, could claim that 'If anyone ever doubts the truth of the famous saying that every political question is at its roots a religious question, let him come to the House of Commons.'[53] Among the topics he listed were slavery, education, marriage, the royal oath, disestablishment, and 'the pros and cons of the *Ne temere* decree'. That issue, and the whole question of interference by Roman Catholic priests in the area of mixed marriages – so central to Hocking's *The woman of Babylon* and *The Jesuit* – became a *cause célèbre* in 1911 with the McCann case, in which a Belfast priest was accused of having suborned a Roman Catholic husband to leave his Presbyterian wife, taking their children with him – ostensibly as a result of the implementation of the *Ne temere* decree. The case caused what has been called a 'moral panic', in a national atmosphere destabilized by the constitutional crisis, strikes and the Agadir incident, and during the hottest summer of the century. William Corkey, a young Presbyterian cleric (and much later a Stormont MP) whose parishioner Mrs McCann was, helped to make it a national issue by a speech in Edinburgh on the very day that Asquith introduced the Parliament Bill into the house of commons.[54]

Joseph Hocking was kept fully informed about the case by an Ulster correspondent, W. J. McKeown of Glenavy. Receiving from him a clutch of cuttings on the affair, Hocking wrote in outraged terms that 'the act of separating the man & wife, and of robbing the young mother of her husband and especially of her child – now seems to me little short of fiendish. The real crux of the matter does not lie in the action of the man, or the advice of the priest; but in the system which lies at the back of it all.'[55] Hocking had already made clear to McKeown, back in 1908, that he did not believe in Home Rule for Ireland. 'I believe Home Rule would mean Rome Rule', he had written, '& I believe it would be the oppression of Protestants in your country. I believe this too, that if the Liberal Government were to introduce a Home Rule Bill on Mr Gladstone's lines it would wreck the Government even as it wrecked his.

51 See, for example, J.H. Round, 'The Protestant declaration', *Contemporary Review*, lxxix (Apr. 1901), 514–23. 52 J. Loughlin, *Ulster unionism and British national identity since 1885* (London, 1995), p. 58. 53 C.S. Horne, *Pulpit, platform & parliament* (London, 1913), p. 200. 54 More details of the McCann case, and references to the growing amount of material relating to it, may be found in my book, *The Irish Protestant churches in the twentieth century* (London, 2000), 25–6. 55 The Revd Joseph Hocking to W.J. McKeown, 24 Jan 1911, McKeown Papers, PRONI, D/2185/1.

Moreover I am sure that the Nonconformists of England are far less Home Rulers than they were at that time'.[56]

In the course of 1911, however, while McCarthy was gathering evidence for his critique of English nonconformity, Hocking began to have doubts about his own stance on Home Rule. He spelt these out to McKeown in March, and while maintaining that 'I have never been able to see my way to Home Rule for Ireland', he pointed out that he was in a minority among English Nonconformists, who while 'not cold towards Protestantism ... cannot see that Home Rule has anything to do with Rome Rule'. And he also noted that 'they look with doubt on the Orangeism of Ulster. 1. Because of the wild threats made such as taking up arms &c. 2. Because Ulster Protestantism seems to spell enmity to Liberal Principles. And one of the greatest enemies to religious justice in England is the Conservative Party.'[57] During the summer Hocking was asked to send a message from English nonconformists 'to support the Ulster Unionists in their fight'. He declined to do so.[58] When approached by a newspaper shortly afterwards, in the same vein, he wrote a letter which was widely quoted, calling on Ulster to send 'a large number of its best speakers and lecturers to England'. 'Let them prove to the English nonconformist', he wrote, 'by reasoning, by facts from history, and from the very nature of Romanism, that Home Rule means Rome Rule, and no English parliament will dare to pass it.' But, he warned, they must avoid talk of armed resistance; and they must not abuse the Liberal government.[59] In a follow-up letter he declared that he wanted 'to lift the question of Home Rule out of the realms of party politics'.[60] That was precisely the point made by *The Witness* when it declared in 1906 that 'Unionism in Ireland, and especially in Ulster, is not on party lines at all, it is simply and solely opposition to a separate Irish parliament, which we conscientiously believe would be disastrous to the country'. And again, six years later but more stridently, the newspaper declared: 'To call this a mere political question, a mere political incident, a mere question of franchise or income tax, is to ignore the real gravity of the issue, and to bring great Constitutional principles to the level of a question about a parish pump or a poor law guardian.'[61] One Presbyterian minister put it like this: 'Of course when the Home Rule battle was being fought I took my part in it, but I regarded that as a religious and not a political question, a struggle for freedom and for the Protestant religion. But in ordinary political questions I took no part and expressed no opinion.'[62]

Joseph Hocking, having dispensed advice about Irishmen visiting England, now decided to pay a visit to Ireland in January 1912. The result, later that year,

---

56 Hocking to McKeown, 14 Sept. 1908, McKeown Papers, op.cit.   57 Hocking to McKeown, 7 Mar. 1911; McKeown Papers, op.cit.   58 J. Hocking, *Is Home Rule Rome rule?* (London, 1912), p. 11.   59 Ibid., p. 13.   60 Ibid., p. 15.   61 *Witness*, 12 Jan. 1906; 19 Jan. 1912   62 R. Barron, *The God of my life; an autobiography* (Belfast, nd [1928?]), p. 105.

was the publication of *Is Home Rule Rome Rule?*, its cover suitably (even garishly) decorated with shamrocks, and the papal triple crown and crossed keys. The cover gave little clue as to his answer. In the first half of the 192–page book, Hocking writes as if his anti-Catholic prejudices have been confirmed, and his sympathy with Ulster's position appears to have deepened. Belfast is not, he discovered, 'identical with a sour, morose, bloodthirsty Orangeism', though the people there 'dread the thought of Home Rule; they hate it, and they vow that they will fight it to the death'.[63] He finds – hardly surprising for the author of *The Jesuit* – that 'the power of the priest is simply enormous'.[64] He meets with Mrs McCann at Corkey's house. Here, in the flesh, was a young woman misused by the priests, just as his fictional Kathleen had been. Thus far, his argument would have gladdened the heart of any Irish Protestant. But then, half way through the book, a different picture begins to emerge. 'I believe', he states categorically, 'the Church of Rome dreads and fears Home Rule'.[65] And this is what makes him change his mind. Utterly convinced that the Roman church did not want Home Rule, that was to him sufficient reason to become a Home Ruler. The book ends with a ringing declaration of his usual antiCatholic stance, but set now within a different context: 'I cannot believe, therefore, that Home Rule means Rome Rule; on the contrary, I firmly believe that it will be the first step in the way of freedom from the bondage of Rome. It will break the shackles of the past and usher in a new era of liberty. And in my heart of hearts is the conviction that it will prepare the way for the coming of the evangel, for which Ireland has so long waited.'[66] A year later, in a letter to his Ulster correspondent, he spelt it out again: 'The thing which faced me when visiting Ireland was this – Ireland has Rome Rule now ... My desire is to destroy that power, and I argue from what I saw ... that the only power that will break the tyranny of Rome is to make the Irish Roman Catholic free.'[67]

He was not alone in this treatment of the subject. George Moore had scandalised public opinion in Ireland when in 1903 he declared himself a Protestant, and asserted that 'English rule has not prevented the Roman priests from absorbing all the wealth of Ireland. Why should Rome desire change? Home Rule cannot better Rome's position in Ireland.'[68] Quirky and unstable Moore might have been, but others felt the same. Three years later, Douglas Hyde was writing to the Revd J.O. Hannay warning that the Gaelic League must avoid a clash with the Roman Catholic clergy, who 'are, and will be for the next 50 years (unless a strong Home Rule bill is passed) the dominating factor in Irish life'.[69] The Irish hierarchy, the journalist Sydney Brooks declared in

63 J. Hocking, *Is Home Rule Rome rule?*, pp 20, 33. 64 Ibid., p. 50. 65 Ibid., p. 108. 66 Ibid., p. 192. 67 Hocking to McKeown, 15 Jan. 1913, McKeown Papers, op. cit. 68 See T. Gray, *A peculiar man: a life of George Moore* (London, 1996), p. 228. 69 Quoted in P. Murray, 'A sectarian skeleton in the Gaelic League's cupboard?', *Studies*, 82, no. 328 (Winter 1993), 483.

1912, 'does not want Home Rule, will not lift a finger to get it, and will be heartily relieved if it escapes being compelled to accept it'.[70] At the end of that year, Cardinal Logue was telling a correspondent that 'on the whole, as far as religious interests are concerned, I would rather live under the Imperial Parliament than under a Home Rule Parliament'.[71] That is why Hocking now looked forward to a Home Rule parliament in Dublin. As he wrote, quoting George Bernard Shaw, 'the Roman Catholic Church – against which Dublin castle is powerless – would meet with the one force that can cope with it victoriously. That force is democracy.'[72] This line of argument was incomprehensible to most Irish Protestants. J. P. Mahaffy, soon to be provost of Trinity, considered the proposition and came to the conclusion that 'there is no probability that those who throw off the bondage of the Roman Catholic Church will tolerate the restrains of any creed'.[73] In other words, Home Rule would mean either Rome Rule or godless freethinking. Both were to be abhorred. The Irish evangelist T.C. Hammond similarly believed that Hocking's thesis was a dangerous invitation to anti-clericalism, as if that 'were a blessing second only to sound religion'.[74]

The Revd William Crook was a leading Irish cleric; he just missed by a couple of years being the Methodist vice-president when Hugh Price Hughes crossed from England during his own English presidential year to preside (as was customary) at the Irish Conference.[75] Probably it was a fortunate near miss. In the initial phase of taking the anti-Home Rule message to England in 1888, he wrote a 'Letter to an enquiring English Liberal' which spelt out the position from which he and his fellow-nonconformists did not waver thereafter. His letter (published as a pamphlet) ended thus:[76]

> In conclusion, Home Rule, as demanded by Irish Romanists, and conceded by Mr Gladstone's Bill, means ROME RULE OVER IRELAND, AND THE ENSLAVING OF PROTESTANTISM UNDER THE IRON HOOF OF A NEW AND DISLOYAL ASCENDANCY, and hence should be opposed to the death, and will be over here, whether English Methodists desert us, as Mr Gladstone deserted the brave an loyal Gordon, or have the backbone to stand by the old Liberal standard.

70 S. Brooks, 'Aspects of the "religious" question in Ireland', *Fortnightly Review*, new series, xci, no. dxlii (Feb 1912), 395.   71 Cardinal Logue to Bishop O'Donnell, 6 Dec. 1912; quoted in M. Harris, *The Catholic Church and the foundation of the Northern Irish state* (Cork, 1993), p. 47.   72 Hocking, *Is Home Rule Rome rule?*, p. 178.   73 J.P. Mahaffy, 'Will Home Rule be Rome rule?', *Blackwood's Magazine*, cxcii, no. mclxii (Aug. 1912), 158.   74 T.C. Hammond, 'The religious question in Ireland', *Nineteenth Century*, lxxiii, no. 432 (Feb. 1913), 354.   75 Crook was Irish vice-president in 1883–4 and again in 1896–7; Hughes presided at the Irish Conference in 1899   76 W. Crook, *The Irish Question* (Belfast, 1888), p. 6.

That remained the Irish Protestant position, whatever other arguments – economic, strategic, imperial – might be tacked onto it. There was simply no meeting of minds with British nonconformists, the 'overwhelming majority' of whom, as Hugh Price Hughes claimed before the 1892 election, were committed to home rule and even were Mr Gladstone to go down in defeat would 'still continue, as their fathers did before them, to advocate what they believe to be the true principles of Evangelical Protestantism, and of civil and religious freedom'.[77] The very same principles that Irish nonconformists appealed to in opposition to home rule were paraded as arguments for it by their British brethren. Similarly, Hocking's opposition to Roman Catholicism was expressed in the same highly-coloured and emotive language as William Crook used, but in 1912 he came to that startlingly different conclusion as to the best way of combating the perceived evil. So Hocking, like most nonconformists, was guilty of 'betrayal', of 'treason'. Half a century later the Revd Ian Paisley still pointed to the same dangers: 'the same terrorism, the same tyrannies, the same superstition, the same episcopacy, the same prelacy, the same Popery are rife in our land today. Give us the spirit of the Covenanters!'[78] But such nonconformist rhetoric no longer evoked any response in England. Before the first world war, British nonconformists could empathise with the anti-Catholicism, even if they parted company with their Irish brethren politically. After the war, even the rhetoric evoked no response.

By then, both the Liberal Party and the Free Churches had changed. Indeed, Bebbington would predate the change for the latter, claiming that by 1910 'the period of the Nonconformist conscience had come to an end'.[79] Certainly after the war, moral force arguments and hopes of the Kingdom of God on earth were more likely to find a political outlet in support of the Labour party, most of whose founding fathers came from nonconformist backgrounds. The Liberal party was a spent force. The southern unionists had been betrayed. The Ulster protestants held power in their citadel at Stormont. But the 'betrayal' theme would live on in their memory, and come to the fore again when the 'factory of grievances' was in danger of being dismantled. In the context of a 'liberalising' Stormont government, Ian Paisley could declare in 1964 that 'our leaders in church and state today have either lost the great vision of our protestant heritage or else are practising deliberate treachery to that which our fathers won for us at such a tremendous price'.[80] A new litany of betrayal (or imagined betrayal) unfolded in the subsequent decades: the disbanding of the Ulster Special Constabulary (the 'B Specials') in 1970, direct rule in 1972, Harold Wilson's 'spongers' speech in 1974 and the Anglo-Irish Agreement of 1985.

77 H.P. Hughes, 'The Ulster Protestants and Home Rule', *New Review*, 7, no. 38 (July 1892), p. 21.   78 Quoted in M.A. MacIver, 'Ian Paisley and the reformed tradition', *Political Studies*, xxxv, no. 3 (Sept. 1987), p. 366.   79 Bebbington, *Nonconformist conscience*, p.160.   80 MacIver, op. cit., p. 367.

Then in the nineties came the demise of the Ulster Defence Regiment, the Drumcree stand-off and the Good Friday Agreement. The words 'betrayal', 'bitterness' and 'treachery' could still be used to define much Ulster protestant thinking in the last decade of the twentieth century, as in the first.[81] But just as Hocking examined the evidence and came up with what had seemed to many to be a jarring conclusion, so at the end of the twentieth century an Irish Catholic living in England could look at the 'most childish of all myths, that Home Rule is Rome Rule', and conclude that 'the rank and file loyalists' were the victims of poor leadership. 'They have been betrayed, misused, misled, blinded to their best interests and even cajoled out of their identity.'[82] Patrick Buckland touched on this point in his assessment of James Craig, when he wrote that 'the failures of Northern Ireland were not the failures of leadership alone, for it is doubtful whether greater determination on his part would have fundamentally altered the course of events and secured the ultimate survival of Stormont'.[83] Elsewhere, considering the demise of southern unionism – and this may be relevant to considerations of 'betrayal' - he has also reminded us of an old Irish proverb: 'Beware the teeth of a wolf, the heels of a horse, and the word of an Englishman.'[84]

81 See, for example, J. Loughlin, *Ulster unionism and British national identity since 1885* (London, 1995), p. 212 and *passim* 82 A. Pollack (ed.), *A citizens' inquiry: the Opsahl Report* (Dublin, 1993), p.161. 83 P. Buckland, *James Craig* (Dublin, 1980), p. 124. 84 P. Buckland, in D.G. Boyce (ed.), *The revolution in Ireland, 1879–1923* (London, 1988), p. 90.

'The country's true place of reformation': the contemporary Irish history play

SHAUN RICHARDS

The history play has been central to the initial revival and subsequent reappraisal of the Irish nation from the establishment of a self-consciously Irish 'national' theatre in the period of the Literary Revival at the turn of the nineteenth century. Its overall status is captured in Lady Gregory's vision 'of historical plays being sent by us through all the counties of Ireland. For to have a real success and to come into the life of the country, one must touch a real and eternal emotion, and history comes only next to religion in our country.'[1] However, as subsequent events were to demonstrate, history was as multiple in its articulations as was faith, and accusations of heresy were not reserved for religion alone.

History's centrality to the establishment of the Irish state is clear. The declaration of the Republic in 1916 based its legitimacy on rights established by 'the dead generations' who 'six times during the past three hundred years' had asserted their right to national freedom and sovereignty.[2] The function of history was to inspire the population; not to reflection but to action, and mobilisation of a national consciousness was not necessarily to be achieved by scrupulous scholarship and objective judgement. As observed by Sir Charles Gavan Duffy in an address of June 1893, 'Big books of history' are not read by the people, but 'they will read picturesque biographies, which are history individualized, or vivid sketches of memorable eras, which are history vitalized.'[3] History vitalized and individualized was also the accepted subject for history plays and their function was equally utilitarian. For whether history was presented on the page or the stage it was, in Oliver Macdonagh's phrase, 'politics by other means.'[4]

The conclusion drawn by Stephen Watt from his examination of plays by late-nineteenth century Queen's Royal Theatre dramatists such Dion Boucicault and J.W. Whitbread that 'there *was* an Irish drama before Yeats: a

---

1 Lady Gregory, *Our Irish theatre* (Gerrards Cross, 1972), pp 57–8. 2 'The proclamation of the Irish Republic', in Vivian Mercier and David H. Greene (eds), *1000 years of Irish prose* (New York, 1961), p. 245. 3 Charles Gavan Duffy, 'What Irishmen may do for Irish literature', in Sir Charles Gavan Duffy, Dr George Sigerson, Dr Douglas Hyde, *The revival of Irish literature* (London, 1894; reprinted New York, 1973), p. 24. 4 Oliver MacDonagh, 'Time's revenges and revenge's time: a view of Anglo-Irish relations', *Anglo-Irish Studies*, iv (1979), 6.

political, in numerous respects anticolonial, drama'[5] accords with Seamus de Burca's assertion that the Queen's was 'the real national theatre - certainly up to 1916.'[6] In P. J. Bourke's plays which were produced at the Queen's in the years immediately before Easter 1916, these appeals to national endeavour were frequently based in the past; specifically the rising of 1798. *The Northern insurgents* (1912), sub-titled *A romantic Irish drama of Ulster in 1798*, closes on the heroine's revolutionary blessing on her lover: 'Go then, in God's name, to meet the French, and may God send you back safe to me, Neil, and may we be reunited in a free Ireland.'[7] Yeats and Lady Gregory's *Cathleen Ni Houlihan* (1902) also took 1798 as its setting and specifically echoed earlier risings in an attempt to encourage future resistance. But if the overall function of history plays in the pre-1916 period was to encourage the nation's realisation of its 'august destiny'[8] any subsequent dramatic interpretations which disrupted the first flush of post-independence triumph were faced with significant opposition. Hannah Sheehy-Skeffington, who led the protests of Republican women against O'Casey's *The plough and the stars* in February 1926, asserted that their protest was based 'on national grounds solely, voicing a passionate indignation against the outrage of a drama staged in a supposedly national theatre, which held up to derision and obloquy the men and women of Easter Week.'[9] The evident expectation was that O'Casey's dramatisation of history should match society's psycho-political requirements. Historical iconoclasm was not to be tolerated; hence the Abbey was only 'supposedly' a national theatre.

The approved history and history play which pre- and immediately post-dated the founding of the state were intent on reversing a colonial history based on what Alice Stopford Green described in 1912 as the 'Moral Tale' of 'the good man (English) who prospered and the bad man (Irish) who came to a shocking end.'[10] Accordingly, history was written along teleological lines charting the nation's emergence from servitude; a tendency whose longevity is exemplified in P.S. O'Hegarty's 1952 history of 'a people coming out of captivity, out of the underground, finding every artery of national life occupied by the enemy, recovering them one by one, and coming out at last into the full blaze of the sun.'[11] More sophisticated historical methodologies had been in evidence from the establishment of the journal *Irish Historical Studies* in 1938 and its section of essays dedicated to 'Historical Revisions' which 'were

5 Stephen Watt, *Joyce, O'Casey, and the Irish popular theater* (Syracuse NY, 1991), p. 88.
6 Seamus de Burca, 'An interview with Seamus de Burca', conducted by Kurt Jacobsen, *Journal of Irish Literature*, xiii, nos. 1 & 2 (1984), 78.   7 P.J. Bourke, *The Northern insurgents, Journal of Irish Literature*, xiii, nos. 1 & 2, (1984), 74.   8 'The proclamation of the Irish Republic', in Mercier and Greene, p. 246.   9 Letter to the *Irish Independent*, 15 February 1926. Quoted in Robert G. Lowery (ed.), *A whirlwind in Dublin* (Westport, Conn.,1984), p. 58.   10 Quoted in Roy Foster, 'History and the Irish question', in Ciaran Brady (ed.), *Interpreting Irish history: the debate on historical revisionism 1933–1994* (Dublin 1994), p. 122.
11 Quoted in ibid., p. 143.

intended to refute received wisdom or unquestioned assumptions concerning well known events, persons or processes by means of the findings of new research'.[12] While *The plough* clearly does not engage with 'the findings of new research' its first audience's response to O'Casey's iconoclasm anticipates what Desmond Fennell later described as the deleterious effect of historical revisionism 'which, far from sustaining, energising and bonding the nation, tended to cripple, disintegrate and paralyse it.'[13] Fennell's demand that history 'serve the nation's well-being'[14] opens up recent historiographical debate and its relevance to contemporary history plays. For exactly how history and the history play are to serve the nation's well being is not as self-evident as Fennell suggests.

Theatre cannot be said to occupy the same social centrality in a multi-media age as it did in the period of the Revival, but its engagement with history and the historical process can still make a profound contribution to both the advancing, and retarding, of a creative collective historical memory. Indeed, as argued in Richard Kearney's paraphrase of Paul Ricoeur, 'without the backward look a culture is deprived of its memory, without the forward look it is deprived of its dreams'.[15] The task is then to produce a history and historical drama which 'does not reproduce conditions, but, rather, reveals them.'[16] And it is in the context defined by Walter Benjamin and acted on by Bertolt Brecht that one can define a movement within the Irish history play concerned with 'laying bare society's causal network'.[17] It is this which informs Tom Murphy's *Famine* (1968) which directly engages with the determining power of the Famine of the 1840s

Murphy's prime objective is to establish the historical cause of what he saw as the famine of the spirit and imagination of the 1960s Republic and, somewhat prophetically, the violence of the north. While accusations as to the cause and violent course of the Famine are made within the play with the peasants' farming failures attributed to the fact that they were 'moulded and shaped that way by England and by England's tools, the landlords, over the past five or six hundred years',[18] Murphy's concern is less with centuries-old culpability for past disasters than with their baleful influence on Ireland's future social development. The play closes on Liam's bleak hope that when things get better 'we'll be equal to that too'[19] as Murphy projects a future in which the inheritance of a famine mentality denies self-expression and realisation as unhealthy deviations

12 Ciaran Brady, '"Constructive and instrumental": the dilemma of Ireland's first "New Historians"', in Brady (ed.), *Interpreting Irish history*, p. 4.   13 Desmond Fennell, 'Against revisionism', in Brady (ed.), *Interpreting Irish history*, p. 189.   14 Ibid., p. 187. 15 Richard Kearney, *Poetics of modernity. Toward a hermenuetic imagination* (1995), p. 77. 16 Walter Benjamin, *Understanding Brecht* (London 1973), p. 4.   17 Bertolt Brecht, *Brecht on theatre* (London 1964), p. 109.   18 Tom Murphy, *Famine*, in *Tom Murphy: Plays One* (London, 1992), p. 57.   19 Ibid., p. 89.

from the basics of survival. Such paralysis of the spirit may have been displaced
by the vigour of the Celtic Tiger, but in *Famine* the past wills to the future not
only resignation but also physical force as, through Malachy, Murphy suggests
that there is a 'violent *consequence* of famine' which leads in a direct line through
the Land Wars to Michael Collins.[20] Through his decision not to take Malachy's
story to closure, but leave him as a vengeful ghost of the diaspora, Murphy suggests that 'the result of a shameful present is a violent future'[21] as Liam's
resigned 'this country will never see him again' is countered by Maeve's 'It'll see
his like.'[22] Here the causal network is presented in the starkest of terms.

The play was first produced in March 1968 some months before the start
of the Civil Rights protest marches whose suppression led into the Troubles.
In retrospect Murphy saw how, 'though undesignedly', the play was 'anticipating the outbreak of hostilities in Northern Ireland.'[23] Clearly, the immediate cause of the Civil Rights marches was local injustice rather than memories
of the Famine but this late-sixties moment forcibly revealed the power of
unresolved and unaccommodated history to return. In 1966 the fiftieth
anniversary celebrations of Easter 1916 could regard the Rising as significant
enough to be celebrated yet distant enough to be unproblematic, but the outbreak of the Troubles marked any subsequent anniversaries as times of deep
dissension. In a strongly-felt response to the poverty of commemoration of
the seventy-fifth anniversary in 1991 Declan Kiberd noted that 'If, in fact, the
Christian brothers had brainwashed one generation with a set of nationalist
myths, then their products-in-revolt could administer an equally simplified
antidote' in which any ceremony was queried as it might provide comfort and
succour to the IRA.[24] And for this reason the interpretation and dramatisation
of 1916 is a key moment in contemporary historical debates. Roy Foster's
claim that contemporary Irish historians 'have gone so far as to dismiss most
of the canon of Irish history as conceived by the generation of 1916'[25] being
contested by John Arden and Margaretta D'Arcy's *The non-stop Connolly
show* (1975).

The play's twenty-four hour playing time has ensured limited productions
but it is noteworthy for its theatrical brio and ambition and explicit historical
agenda. The radical tone of the play's sub-title, 'A dramatic cycle of continuous struggle in six parts', is developed in the authors' assertion that 'our aim
was primarily to counteract ... the "Conor Cruise O'Brien historical revisionism", currently much in vogue in Irish intellectual circles', the main tenets of
which they identify as a belief that 'the 1916 Rising was unnecessary' and that

20 Tom Murphy, 'Introduction', in *Tom Murphy: Plays One*, p. xvii. 21 Ibid.
22 Murphy, *Famine*, p. 89. 23 Murphy, 'Introduction', in *Tom Murphy: Plays One*, p. xvii.
24 Declan Kiberd, 'The elephant of revolutionary forgetfulness', in Máirín Ní
Dhonnchadha and Theo Dorgan (eds), *Revising the Rising* (Derry, 1991), p. 3. 25 Roy
Foster, 'History and the Irish question', in Brady (ed.), *Interpreting Irish history*, p. 140.

'the present anti-imperialist struggle in the country has ... no historical valid-ity'.[26] The play's conclusion confronts both revisionist denials of the Rising's necessity and the Republic's preference for its closure, as Connolly is portrayed as a revolutionary socialist whose actions fuelled subsequent revolutions 'in Russia, China, Cuba, Africa, Vietnam' and provided the dynamic for what the logic of the play suggests is the armed struggle in Northern Ireland: the play closing on the line:

> we were the first. We shall not be the last.
> This was not history. It has not passed.[27]

Few plays have matched the agit-prop ardour of *The non-stop Connolly show* but the relationship between 1916 and the present was also engaged with in Tom Murphy's *The patriot game* (1965; first produced 1991) which explored the Rising's impact on the consciousness of a modern generation. Given the varying expressions of frustration and disillusion with the national recognition of the Rising what is striking about Murphy's play, which was written to be tel-evised by the BBC on the Rising's fiftieth anniversary in 1966, is that when translating the television script to stage form for its 1991 theatre premiere Murphy determined to maintain 'the original artistic intention' which he described as 'a commemoration, a celebration of 1916.'[28]

The play draws attention to its construction as performance so underlining the fact that 'history' is discourse rather than event; the drama of the Rising being played out before an initially cynical young female Narrator who informs the audience that an actor is 'playing Patrick Pearse' in 'The Disgraceful Story of 1916.'[29] The opening stage directions are explicit as to her response to the drama, for while she will provide the narration it 'appears to her to belong to another age' from which she is clearly distanced by her 'modern day image (leather-jacket and white dress)'.[30] Murphy is literally presenting 1916 as history, setting up a gulf between the narrated events and the contemporary moment occupied by both the Narrator and audience. The Narrator 'doesn't like the emotion of nationalism' and her first reaction to Pearse is the dismissive 'Stupid!'[31] However, her resolve 'to keep control of herself', which initially means not voicing her cynicism, is progressively affected by the events of the Rising so that her confident 'I hate nationalism. It doesn't exist ... And I'm not getting involved' is overwhelmed.[32] At the moment of the execution of the leaders the command 'FIRE' is met by her defiant 'UP THE REPUBLIC' to which

26 Margaretta D'Arcy and John Arden, 'Authors's preface', in *The non-stop Connolly show* (London, 1977), pp v and vi.   27 Ibid., p. 448.   28 Tom Murphy, '*The patriot game*, Author's Note', Programme for *The patriot game*, Abbey Theatre, Dublin, May 1991. 29 Tom Murphy, *The patriot game*, in *Tom Murphy: Plays One* (London, 1992), p. 93. 30 Ibid.   31 Ibid., p. 93.   32 Ibid., p. 129

Pearse ironically responds '... And you were only playing the narrator.'[33] The play's closing words take on a particular resonance when considered in the context of Murphy's other plays with their frequent focus on psychically sustaining returns 'home'. For Pearse's 'Come on. Come on home'[34] embraces both Narrator and audience in the invitation to re-engage with their historical past and prioritize remembrance and celebration over denial and shame.

In the 1992 introduction to the play Murphy stated 'I believe that nationalism is an elemental and dangerous emotion, intrinsic to us all: but I believe that it is more dangerous not to acknowledge it or pretend otherwise.'[35] The nature of the need to acknowledge nationalism and its history carries a particular force in the 'revisionist' context of 1990s Ireland where Murphy's decision not to revise the play's 1960s sentiments is not so much an indication of unreconstructed nationalism as a recognition of the positive function to be played by a collective historical memory which is threatened by the 'corrosive and inquisitorial scepticism' of Revisionism. The terms are Kevin Whelan's, for whom such attitudes 'leads to an alienation of Irish people from their ancestors, and makes them strangers in their own country, cut off from the nourishing sense of a national identity'.[36] This defence of a deep historical memory is erected against revisionism, but Richard Kearney's parallel argument that 'The kind of imagination required to meet the challenge of postmodernism is, then, fundamentally *historical*'[37] widens the range of debate and provides an extra urgency, for the cost of postmodern history's ludic nature is an abandonment of the past's claims for, if not fulfilment, at least acknowledgement, in the present. For some twenty years historians have been flirting with the 'textuality' of their practice: the 1975 claim that 'Historical events do not exist and can have no material effectivity in the present,'[38] echoed in the late 1980s assertion that 'historical knowledge is a tissue of remnants and fabrications concealing an essential absence'.[39] This takes Hayden White's declaration that 'Historians and philosophers of history [are] freed to conceptualize history ... in whatever modality of consciousness is most consistent with their own moral and aesthetic aspirations'[40] to a point where history has no apparent referent beyond the textual construct; a position countered by Fredric Jameson's concern with combating '[the] threat of infinite relativization'[41] and asserting the lived material reality of history.

While Brian Friel's *Making history* is alert to debates on the narrativity of history its setting in the late-fifteenth and early-sixteenth century demonstrates

33 Ibid., p. 149. 34 Ibid. 35 Murphy, 'Introduction', in *Tom Murphy: Plays One*, p. xviii. 36 Kevin Whelan, 'Come all you staunch revisionists, towards a post-revisionist agenda for Irish history', *Irish Reporter*, 2 (1991), 23. 37 Richard Kearney, *The wake of imagination* (London, 1987), p. 392. 38 Barry Hindess and Paul Hurst, *Pre-capitalist modes of production* (London, 1975), p. 312. 39 David Harlan, 'Intellectual history and the return of literature', *American Historical Review*, 94, no. 3 (1989), 581. 40 Hayden White, *Metahistory* (Baltimore, 1973), p. 434. 41 Fredric Jameson, 'Marxism and historicism', in *The ideologies of theory: essays, 1971–1986*, vol. 2 (London, 1988), p. 159.

a far clearer concern with historians' debates as to the degree of national consciousness operating in that period. Steven Ellis argued that 'the adoption for late medieval Ireland of an anachronistic, Hibernocentric perspective, with associated nationalist themes, is a conceptual trap'.[42] This resulted in Brendan Bradshaw's riposte that, with regard to the accurate periodisation of national consciousness, it is more useful to consider 'the intellectual viability of investigating historical entities in a state of potential rather than actual existence'.[43] While the play acknowledges the fractious nature of the Irish polity in the period, the historian, Peter Lombard, speaks to O'Neill of 'those early intimations you must have had of an emerging nation state' and the fact that under his leadership 'suddenly the nation state was becoming a reality'.[44] While Lombard uses the language of Hayden White with regard to the narrativity of history his arguments as to its function are more closely aligned to those of Desmond Fennell. Their moment, he tells O'Neill, is that of 'a colonized people on the verge of extinction'[45] with the purpose of history being to sustain and advance their cause. While Lombard's discourse is that of postmodern relativism his choice of narrative is informed by a national 'state of potential'. And as with Lombard so with O'Neill, for while he has consciously varied his accent from English to Tyrone throughout the play, it closes on a subdued moment of personal truth when 'his accent is pure Tyrone'.[46] Friel constructs a dialogue of anachronistic self-reflexiveness but never takes a Pirandellian turn into an absolute removal of certainty. His final referent is an essential Irish actuality. However it would be an error to read this affirmation as motivated by narrow exclusivity. For what is omitted from Lombard's nationalist history is the truth of O'Neill's marriage to Mabel Bagenal, his wife of English planter stock.

In an echo of Jimmy Jack's warning against marrying outside the tribe in *Translations* (1980), Mabel's sister, Mary, counsels against the cross fertilisation of seeds. However, at the close of the play, while Lombard's narrative of O'Neill's history becomes ever more celebratory, so the trajectory of O'Neill's personal story becomes ever more subdued; his addressee being the abandoned wife rather than Lombard's colonized people. Friel is affirming the reality of an emerging Irish nation but his objective is to accommodate all strands of the national narrative and recognize that while Mabel might be omitted from history as simply 'a domestic story'[47] this personal story is political, its historical truth affirmed for audiences through the realist style of its presentation.

While *Making history* has been criticized for historical inaccuracy[48] Friel's objective is clearly to use history to suggest that the hybridity of the Irish past

42 Steven G. Ellis, 'Nationalist historiography and the English and Gaelic worlds in the late middle ages', *Irish Historical Studies*, xxv, no. 97 (1986), p. 18. 43 Brendan Bradshaw, 'Nationalism and historical scholarship in modern Ireland', in Brady (ed.), *Interpreting Irish history*, p. 193. 44 Brian Friel, *Making history* (London 1989) p. 64. 45 Ibid., p. 67. 46 Ibid., p. 70. 47 Ibid., p. 69. 48 Cf. Hiram Morgan, 'Making history: a criticism and a manifesto', *Text and Context*, iv (1990), 61–5.

is a valuable antidote to its sectarian present. The position is amplified in Terence Brown's Field Day pamphlet which suggested that an appreciation of the complexity of the protestant past would suggest modes of self-definition whose 'rich and complex tradition challenges the dominant historical myth of the whole protestant community'[49] and open up its own radical past. Here, an elided history becomes the source of what Marianne Elliott termed 'inter-communal alliances and radical solutions', but it is her conclusion 'that the protestants also need to be conciliated'[50] which raises the crux of the problem. For as Edna Longley observed with regard to the Field Day project in general, Northern Protestants are written out of history 'unless prepared to go back and start again in 1798';[51] so that even the accommodation is marred by exclusivist assumptions. The issue is then to understand the felt legitimacy of historical difference, with *Observe the sons of Ulster marching towards the Somme* (1985) by Frank McGuinness standing as an exemplar of an empathically rendered account of the legitimacy of alternative historical narratives.

At the play's opening, Pyper, the now elderly survivor of a band of Ulstermen who died at the Somme, declares that he is 'angry at your demand that I continue to probe' and resists 'your insistence on my remembrance'.[52] His sole presence on stage and the constant use of 'you' in his monologue positions the audience as those for whom he is 'not your military historian'[53] and even when it become clear that his addressees are the ghosts of his dead companions the audience remain implicated as those for whom his enacted memories have an emotional intensity not found in the 'sufficient records.'[54] For McGuinness, the play's objective was to lead Pyper to say 'I love my Ulster', the line which, he said, informed the whole work and whose emotional legitimacy the audience was invited to accept.[55] The full import of accepting this territorial claim coming in the force of Pyper's denial of other claimants, namely those whom he terms 'Fenian cowards'.[56]

Unearthing what McGuinness termed 'the very powerful historical roots'[57] fuelling contemporary animosity is the play's objective, but this does not necessitate a sanitisation of the insular and self-destructive nature of the mentality which is staged. For what is replayed through Pyper's memory are the crucial stages of 'Pairing' and 'Bonding' prior to the battle of the Somme through which he is translated from the cynical dilettante who had 'escaped Carson's

49 Terence Brown, *The whole Protestant community: the making of an historical myth* (Derry, 1985), p. 19. **50** Marianne Elliott, *Watchmen in Sion; the Protestant idea of liberty* (Derry, 1985), p. 27. **51** Edna Longley, *Poetry in the wars* (Newcastle upon Tyne, 1986), p. 192. **52** Frank McGuinness, *Observe the sons of Ulster marching towards the Somme* (London, 1986), p. 9. **53** Ibid. **54** Ibid. **55** John Waters, 'Alone again, naturally' (interview with Frank McGuinness), *In Dublin*, 14 May 1987, p. 18. **56** McGuinness, *Observe the sons of Ulster*, p. 11. **57** Charles Hunter, 'Strange passion about the Somme' (interview with Frank McGuinness), *Irish Times*, 15 Feb. 1985, p. 12.

dance'[58] to one who can declare 'There would be, and there will be, no surren-der.'[59] However, rather than reacting simply to the intransigence, audiences would ideally understand what McGuinness termed 'the internal history, the spirit of the people we call Protestants' and while this would not create politi-cal unity it could produce 'an imaginative unity, an imaginative understanding of why people were behaving the way they did.'[60] Here McGuinness, like Friel, uses the history play to confront the one dimensional 'folk memory of the Irish' which, for McGuinness, 'is a lethal cultural weapon. At its most destructive it can reduce history to goodies and baddies, the sanctified "us" versus the demonic "them".'[61]

History then has a dual presence in *Observe*, for while the staging of alter-native histories provides audiences with the opportunity to acknowledge the plurality of the past it simultaneously shows Pyper's progressive entrapment by the accumulated weight of historical narratives. The elder Pyper's assertion that 'The sons of Ulster will rise and lay their enemy low as they did at the Boyne, as they did at the Somme, against any invader who will trespass on to their homeland'[62] obliterates his youthful mockery of 'The war of the elect upon the damned'.[63] And while nationalist historical narratives are deflated in the soldier's story of Pearse, 'The boy who took over a post office because he was short of stamps',[64] the same demystification is not applied to their own Protestant history which, as in their enactment of battle of the Boyne before the Somme offensive, allows no deviation: 'we know the result, you know the result, keep to the result'.[65] It is this inflexibility and subsequent denial of other narra-tives, both of individuals and alternative traditions, which McGuinness seeks to critique. Audiences are invited to understand, and even admire, Pyper's fidelity to the principles of his dead comrades, but then engage with a more expansive understanding in which his historical narrative is given neither a dominant or subordinate position, but allowed equality of esteem in a situation of democratic plurality.

Pyper's condition confirms the perception that 'To be Irish is to endure the nightmare of historical stasis'[66] and in this *Observe* is paradigmatic of the con-temporary history play which, as McCracken in Stewart Parker's *Northern Star* (1984), tends to the view that 'History was a dungeon. The people were locked into their separate compounds., full of stench and nightmare.'[67] The proviso, however, is that audiences are able to act against the entrapment experienced by the on-stage characters as a direct result of their apprehension that, as in the

58 McGuinness, *Observe the sons of Ulster*, p. 56.   **59** Ibid., p. 80.   **60** Ibid.   **61** Frank McGuinness, 'The artist as a young pup' (review of Bob Geldof's *Is that it?*), *Irish Literary Supplement*, Fall 1986, p. 9.   **62** McGuinness, *Observe the Sons of Ulster*, p. 10.   **63** Ibid., p. 36.   **64** Ibid., p. 64.   **65** Ibid., p. 70.   **66** Terence Brown, 'Awakening from the night-mare', in *Ireland's literature: selected essays* (Mullingar, 1988), p. 246.   **67** Stewart Parker, *Northern Star*, in *Three plays for Ireland* (Birmingham, 1989), p. 65

pastiche of major Irish playwrights in *Northern Star*, they are playing roles in a
pre-scripted play. 'Citizens of Belfast,' declares McCracken, 'you rehearse all
of your chosen parts and you play them with the utmost zeal – except that
maybe they're really playing you.'[68] Liberation occurs when audiences are able
to see the pre-scribed script of the past as only a draft and open to re-writes
according to the exigencies of the moment.

As indicated above, *Northern star* works through sequences written in the
style of Irish playwrights from Farquar to Behan which are signalled as a pro-
gression from an Age of Innocence to a final Age of Knowledge. This is what
Parker termed the Irish 'comedy of terrors' in which the knowledge acquired
by McCracken is only as to the failure of 1798: 'Our own fault. We botched the
birth.'[69] What has been lost, he acknowledges, is the proto-socialism of Jimmy
Hope, 'The steadfast light, the real Northern Star.'[70] But Hope's credo that
'The moral force of the labouring class will prevail, whatever comes or goes'[71]
deserts the play with him in the fifth of the seven Ages, leaving the despairing
McCracken with the realisation that, far from liberating people from the
dungeon of history, their achievement was 'to reinforce the locks' as 'the cycle
just goes on, playing the same demented comedy of terrors from generation to
generation, trapped in the same malignant legend'.[72]

Both *Observe* and *Northern Star* are staged as the memories of their respective protagonists as they look back over their individual failures and final
entrapment in histories other than those they wished to advance. In this sense
they are both, in the title of Ron Hutchinson's 1991 play, *Pygmies in the ruins*,
seemingly fated to layer one more bloody level on a structure whose overall
design is beyond their power to determine. Past and present become inter-
twined and, as in *Pygmies in the ruins*, though violent acts may be separated by
a hundred years, they are 'all part of the same bloody knot of rope and it's never
going to get unravelled'.[73] This judgement by Washburn, the disillusioned
police photographer in Hutchinson's play, leads to his emigrating in order to
claim 'a greater inheritance than this';[74] a repetition of Pyper's early attempt to
escape 'the call of my Protestant fathers'.[75] But whether the response is the
retreat of Washburn, Pyper's acceptance of the Orange sash of his once derided
'interfering' ancestors, or McCracken's resigned acknowledgement that 'the
entire pattern of depravity just goes on spinning on out of control',[76] the result
is an abandonment of society to the vicious cycle which they recognize but on
which they are unable to act. In this sense the plays by McGuinness and Parker
act as bleak companion pieces in their insights into contemporary realities, with
the frustrated non-sectarian ideals of McCracken in 1798 degenerating in the

68 Ibid., p. 34. 69 Ibid., p. 75. 70 Ibid., p. 58. 71 Ibid. 72 Ibid., p. 65. 73 Ron
Hutchinson, *Pygmies in the ruins*, programme/playtext, Royal Court Theatre (London,
1992), p. 29. 74 Ibid. 75 McGuinness, *Observe the sons of Ulster*, p. 57. 76 Parker,
Northern Star, p. 65.

contemporary moment into the absolute intransigence of the elder Pyper. But their relationship to their respective historical moments of 1916 and 1798 is perhaps even more significant.

The distinction is frequently made between history and collective memory in which the latter has the effect of providing the group with an organic sense of cohesion; frequently in opposition to groups with other priorities and historical perceptions. As noted above, the gap between what a nation is judged to require from written history, conceived as a confirmation of collective memory, frequently clashes with history conceived as conclusions drawn from fresh evidence. In *Observe*, Pyper individualizes the emotional aftermath of the battle for those bound irrevocably to ideals for which their companions died. Through his empathic dramatisation of Pyper's consciousness McGuinness is attempting to insert the collective memory of one group into the consciousness of those who would previously have denied its legitimacy. Here, history as record and history as memory overlap, for now two significant events of 1916 are deemed worthy of commemoration and the culturally determining effect of the Somme given parity with that of the Easter Rising. The ability to recognize the emotional equivalence of two parallel narratives within the same historical moment then becomes the model for accepting the validity of their outcomes within two contemporary cultures.

As a history play, *Northern Star* is concerned with what was, yet is far more engaged with what could have been and what still might be. In this sense the relationship between the stage and history ceases to be one of fixed determinacy and becomes far more one of speculative possibility; a means of staging alternatives which, untaken or unfulfilled in actuality, break down the monolithic absoluteness of the past and present the history play as a literal playground where other narratives can be apprehended. This constructively ludic turn is manifest in Frank McGuinness' *Mutabilitie* (1997), the drama of Shakespeare's sojourn in Ireland which explicitly raises the question as to whether the theatre cannot be 'a temple where the remembered dead rise from their graves'; the 'country's true place of reformation'.[77]

While the premise that Shakespeare was shipwrecked in Ireland owes more to imagination than record, locating his arrival in the immediate aftermath of 'the late wars of Munster' positions the play on the cusp of a new century as, following the failed rebellion of Hugh O'Neill, the Irish seek desperately for a saviour; one they believe they have found in the destitute Shakespeare. Indeed McGuinness' play becomes that which the Irish wonderingly comment on when they hear of how theatre functions: 'It is a most extraordinary place. They can do and say and go anywhere in it.'[78] For what McGuinness is intent on doing, and which his reprise of the split staging technique of *Observe* frequently

77 Frank McGuinness, *Mutabilitie* (London, 1997), p. 56.   78 Ibid., p. 26.

contributes to, is emphasising the fluidity of experience and perception which also extends to racial, religious and gender categories. The madness-inducing rigidity of the colonist-poet Spenser in whose castle Shakespeare stays, is contrasted with the playwright's multifaceted and subversive identity which, on stage, has seen him act 'a king and his queen and a boy and his lover and a clown'[79] and in life (or on McGuinness's stage) to be both Catholic and gay. This performative aspect of identity, with theatre as its crucible, stands as a radical liberation from essentialist limitations. And the liberation is transcultural, for in Ireland Shakespeare learns to return to his denied faith and the theatre, while File, the Irish poet, acknowledges that his gift to her is the recognition that 'I am what I imagined'.[80] Imagination is then paramount, and the play closes on McGuinness's 'imagined' point of harmony as File, and her previously estranged husband, adopt Spenser's abandoned son, her gift to him of their 'little milk' countering her earlier refusal of sustenance to the child. Far from her opening declaration that 'our duty is no longer to each other. It is to our race',[81] File has accepted a inclusive, humanist alternative to exclusivity by not taking a hostage, but embracing a child. This reconciliation of erstwhile opposites is why, as the final stage directions indicate, 'The Irish move with a new freedom.'[82]

As the engravings and photographs in the programme from *Mutabilitie*'s premiere at London's National Theatre indicates, it was written with an awareness that, despite the imminent quodrocentenary of the Munster wars, nothing had changed; images of Elizabethan conflicts opening a sequence which closes with Tony Blair on the streets of Belfast. The File's query as to whether the conflict must continue as 'We approach the end of this century' takes on bitter aftertaste as her reiterated 'Must it continue for another hundred years?'[83] reaches the seemingly impossible twentieth century in which violence of Elizabethan origin becomes the matter of nightly television news. The difference between McGuinness' history play and those we have observed above is that it claims no base in record for its veracity, rather it attempts 'to expand human options by reconfiguring the past and transcending it through creative improvisations'.[84]

While it is understandable that the preoccupation of the Irish history play has been with conflict and trauma, such work runs the risk of narrowing down debate into reflections on established and limiting binaries, most specifically those of the colonial conflict and its aftermath. Given the centrality of Easter 1916 to historical controversy and dramatic productions, the description of it by an old North American Indian in an Ohio whorehouse in Sebastian Barry's *White Woman Street* as 'Some big mail depot or someplace' which is 'burning

79 Ibid., p. 20. 80 Ibid., p. 93. 81 Ibid., p. 11. 82 Ibid., p. 99. 83 Ibid., p. 58. 84 Ashis Nandy, 'History's forgotten doubles', in Philip Pomper, Richard H. Elphick, and Richard T. Vann (eds), *World history, ideologies, structures and identities* (Oxford, 1988), p. 178.

like Richmond'[85] decentres the event and opens up a panorama of other historical narratives. Indeed, Barry's focus for much of the play on the US Cavalry
memories of his ageing protagonist, the Sligo-born Trooper O'Hara, reinforces
the overall objective of establishing the kaleidoscopic quality of Irish historical
experience. In O'Hara's reflective 'The English had done for us, I was thinking,
and now we're doing for the Indians,'[86] Ireland's emiseration is given a global
perspective in which it is both victim and victimiser, while O'Hara's fateful
intention of spending Easter 1916 robbing a gold train not only provides an
ironic context for rising of the insurgents but recognizes the possibility of diasporic histories. Such conscious complexities are central to Barry's overall intention of rendering untenable any singular version of Irish history. This is seen
specifically in his plays set in Ireland, where lives which run counter to the flow
of the national narrative are given an even clearer profile.

Barry's urge to record alternative lives is evident in *The steward of Christendom*
(1995) and *Our Lady of Sligo* (1998) where the male protagonists, while 'part of a
vanished world',[87] assert respectively that 'I know my own story of what happened, and I am content with it'[88] and 'All those things were true once and they
still are true. I'm saying it and I should know.'[89] The timorous question of
Thomas Dunne in *The steward of Christendom* 'it *was* me, wasn't it, Matt?'[90] captures both the resolution and fragility of individual memory when set against
official discourse. For what both plays seek to record are lives which are simultaneously implicated in, yet apart from, the dominant history of their times. In *The
steward of Christendom* this encompasses the fraught period leading up to the creation of the Free State during which Thomas Dunne has been chief superin-
tendent in the Dublin Metropolitan Police. While his life in the state of 1932 is
one of marginalisation and memory loss spent in a mental home, the fleeting
moments of clarity and visitations from his past establishes a life of pride and
profundity in which he lost a son in the British Army in World War One and,
from some perspectives treacherously, gave his love and loyalty to Queen
Victoria. While occasionally chastized by his male nurse as a 'big gobshite ... that
killed four good men and true in O'Connell street in the days of the lock-out',[91]
Barry is concerned to provide Dunne with a discrete individual history which
encompasses his emotionally rendered memories of childhood and his adult
experiences of childbirth and child-loss. This is evoked through Dunne's history,
which not only runs in grooves alternative to those predominantly approved but,
as it is possessed of an profound emotional intensity, imprints itself onto consciousnesses perhaps previously impervious to the record of 'Castle Catholics'.

85 Sebastian Barry, *White Woman Street*, in *The only true history of Lizzie Finn, The steward
of Christendom, White Woman Street, Three plays by Sebastian Barry* (London, 1995), p. 175.
86 Ibid., p. 158.   87 Sebastian Barry, *The steward of Christendom*, in *Three plays by
Sebastian Barry* (London, 1995), p. 78.   88 Ibid.   89 Sebastian Barry, *Our Lady of Sligo*
(London, 1998), p. 22.   90 Barry, *The steward of Christendom*, p. 100.   91 Ibid., p. 75.

Dunne's acknowledgement that 'We were part of a vanished world'[92] gives the force to Barry's theatrical demand for its recognition. The dramatic memorialisation of 'that fled time'[93] after which 'All the traditions [were] broken up and flung out'[94] is rendered with an absoluteness of conviction through Dunne's location as the dramatic focus of the play. His grief over the loss of his son and estrangement from his family, above all the charged vignettes of childhood, humanise the man to the extent that when he recalls his meeting with Michael Collins they are presented to the audience as a dynamic alternatives to what, in *Our Lady of Sligo*, is described as 'The mewling, puking death grip of de Valera and all his lousy crew'.[95] Albeit that the Ireland moulded by de Valera provided the disputed template for modern Ireland, it is that which is lost, abandoned, and rejected which is Barry's concern. This is not simply to continue the fashionable pastime of denouncing de Valera but, more constructively, to allow all Irish histories their allotted space; even those whose desired outcomes ran counter to that of dominant national desire.

Consequently, while *The steward of Christendom* charts the final days of one whose allegiance was to the lost days of a British monarch who 'built everything up and made it strong',[96] *Our Lady of Sligo* presents other consciousnesses whose relationship with the overall trajectory of history is marginalized; this time that of those who, while feeling that 'We were going to make our mark in the new world of Ireland' live only to atrophy in 'the sheer boredom of Ireland, the sheer provincial death-grip this lies upon the land' and lament the passing of 'those lives that lay in store for us, in store like rich warm grain.'[97]

As with *The steward of Christendom*, *Our Lady of Sligo* never reduces the human dimension of the drama so that it becomes a bloodless thesis on alternative histories. Mai of *Our Lady of Sligo*, even more than Thomas Dunne of *The steward of Christendom*, is a flawed human being whose life and losses are vividly captured as she, like Dunne, relives past experiences; he in the mental instability of his old age, she in the morphine-induced reveries of her terminal cancer. But what both render with an absolute conviction is the fact that their 'other' lives, his with those who served the crown in the pre-Free State era, hers among people who desired lives more cosmopolitan than those on offer, are also worthy of record. And as both are captured in 'the bleak hours of this dying time'[98] audiences stand as confessors to memories of lives which, for all their imperfections, are also representative of those who 'always had a boat to row across the dark waters of the Irish story'[99]

Both *The steward of Christendom* and *Our Lady of Sligo* are elegiac works, their centre-stage focus on the dying consciousness of Thomas Dunne and Mai

92 Ibid., p. 78. **93** Ibid., p. 92. **94** Ibid., p. 95. **95** Barry, *Our Lady of Sligo*, p. 24. **96** Barry, *The steward of Christendom*, p. 82. **97** Barry, *Our Lady of Sligo*, pp 22–4. **98** Ibid., p. 45. **99** Ibid., p. 21.

respectively creating a sense of loss, wasted vitality and unharnessed energies. But in *The only true story of Lizzie Finn*, Barry presents a protagonist who refuses to succumb to the imperatives of her historical moment and, indeed, liberates both herself and her husband from the downward trajectory to which he is doomed as a member of the increasingly impoverished Ascendancy. Unlike the dying moments of both *The steward of Christendom* and *Our Lady of Sligo*, *Lizzie Finn* closes on the characters' exit into a future which they will determine with the observation 'Better go off now while the going's good.'[100]

Lizzie Finn's story is the complete antithesis of conventional histories of the diasporic Irish female in England since she triumphs as a music hall dancer in late-nineteenth century Weston-super-Mare, finally falling in love with, and marrying, a renegade son of the Ascendancy who, having gone to South Africa in the British Army, fights on the side of the Boers. Barry is then concerned to break with the categories and class histories his characters suggest and focus on their individual stories. As with *The steward of Christendom* and *Our Lady of Sligo*, *Lizzie Finn* resonates with the force of memory, but unlike the other two plays it presents a character who refuses to follow the prescribed path on which her background appears to have set her. The quality of lament which distinguishes all of Barry's work is still present, but in *Lizzie Finn* it is moderated by the democratically resolute assertion of Lizzie's husband, Robert, that 'We are all very much equal under the clothes history lends us'[101] and her own determination to repair the ruined finances of his family by returning to the music hall. When she states 'We'll just walk out the blessed door and turn the old key in the lock. Why not?',[102] she embodies Barry's own commitment to the ever-present opportunity of Ireland's individuals simply walking 'out the blessed door' of the closed rooms of history and embarking on narratives which, as his conclusion to *Lizzie Finn*, has no end other than those yet to be determined.

While competing histories of the nation state have occupied historians for the last several decades, Tom Dunne has noted that 'The most fundamental "revisionism" to date is being forced by hitherto undervalued areas of common life and experience, like the history of women and of locality.'[103] The implications of this diversification into what David Lloyd terms 'the superseded and overlooked residues of history'[104] resides in the effective threat to nation-state exclusivity of identity which is effected by the acknowledgement of other histories, whether these be of class, gender or religion. While the state's concern with self-preservation and advancement has tended to effect the

---

100 Sebastian Barry, *The only true history of Lizzie Finn*, in *Three plays by Sebastian Barry* (London, 1995), p. 65. **100** Ibid., p. 35. **102** Ibid., p. 65. **103** Tom Dunne, 'New histories: beyond "Revisionism"', *Irish Review*, 12 (1992), p. 2. **104** David Lloyd, 'Nationalisms against the state: towards a critique of the anti-national prejudice', in Timothy P. Foley, Lionel Pilkington, Sean Ryder and Elizabeth Tilley (eds), *Gender and colonialism* (Galway, 1995), p. 264.

marginalisation of contesting histories, as state formations are themselves threatened by the global economic forces to which they have subscribed, rather than succumbing to the vacuum and vacuity this can usher in 'it may be possible to locate in the marginalized forms of lived social relations the contours of radical imaginaries'.[105] And as the serious plurality of alternative histories are recognised theatre becomes the conduit through which those multiple narratives find their imaginative public expression. History remains a prime preoccupation of Irish theatre, however its future may be distinguished by the recognition that while it is still 'politics by other means' these are now the politics of multiple experiences, rather than those of narrow and competing nationalisms.

105 David Lloyd, 'Discussion outside history: Irish new histories and the subalternity effect', in Shahmid Amin and Dipesh Chakrabarty (eds), *Subaltern Studies X: Writings on South Asian history and Society* (Delhi, 1996), p. 277.

Ireland's Celtic heroes

D. GEORGE BOYCE

When Arthur Freed, the producer of the film *Brigadoon* (in which an American searches for and finds a mysterious disappearing and reappearing village in Scotland) visited Scotland, he said that he 'found nothing there that looks like Scotland'.[1] It is possible to surmise what Freed had in mind: loughs, glens, kilts perhaps- certainly not the streets and buildings of Glasgow and Dundee; and it can be deduced from his disappointment that he was repelled by such 'non-Scottish' places. Of course the highlands, loughs, glens and even kilts do exist, and to postulate a distinction between imagination and reality is too obvious and oppositional. These too are real things. But the point is that one concept of place, of its topography, its character, its ambience, is taken, not only to represent the whole, but to stand for it, to constitute its essence.

W.H. Greenleaf, in his study of ideologies, warned against the search for 'essences'. He preferred to use the notion of 'character' and 'tradition' to encompass, for example, that wide variations in ideas that comprise conservatism, or liberalism or socialism. Far from these labels telling us anything much about the ideologies they purport to describe, they obscure the distinction within, say, liberalism between the individualistic, anti-state liberalism of James Mill, and the collectivist variety espoused by L.T. Hobhouse. The search for essences or cores is therefore, Greenleaf argues, a fruitless one.[2] Yet the search for essences was on, certainly in the nineteenth century, across Europe. This was a quest for the essential, defining characteristic of nations. It might be, and usually was, language; there were also folk tales, fairy tales, customs, even clothing, for in the nineteenth century 'national dress' was codified; or, rather, peasant dress was taken as the true national dress, as representing the essential Hungarian, Romanian, German people. This dress did really exist: but nationalists created a sanitised, cleaner, more acceptable version, appropriate for the middle classes who would be obliged to wear it.

Europeans in the nineteenth century were conscious that they were living in an age of unprecedented change. Industrialisation, the spread of communications, the increase in population, all caused them to take heed of their present, their future and – paradoxically – their past; or pasts, for there were

---

1 Quoted in Ian Rankin, *The hanging garden* (London, 1999), preface. 2 W.H. Greenleaf, *The British political tradition:* vol. 2, *The ideological heritage* (London, 1983), pp 7–15.

different versions of the past, depending on the perspective of the observer. If social, economic and political change were to be managed and controlled, then it was necessary to look to history to offer guidelines; and not only guidelines. History could also offer persuasive arguments and an agenda for those who sought actively to control and shape the future. The way forward was to make a nation state (or 'discover' one) as the best means of directing change and ensuring that the nation did not fall behind its rivals in economic or political power. But for the nation that had no state, nor the liklihood of making one in the foreseeable future, the making of a distinctive national culture, the setting out of markers and symbols, the defining of what it was that made that people unique in the world, must be a preliminary to any political action. Johann Gottfried Herder (1744–1803) pointed the way. Herder was born at Mohrungen, an enthusiastic child of the Enlightenment; but he asked what 'progress' was, and answered that it need not be seen as linear. Society was a unique distillation of a particular way of life, of cultural awareness, of language, shared traditions and myths. A state with its bureaucratic machinery could trample on or ignore the distinctive cultures of local communities. Enlightenment thinkers tended to adopt an abstract, generalising vocabulary, blind to subtle distinctions and nuances embedded in local cultural traditions. In many European countries in Herder's day (and afterwards) writers were encouraged to express themselves in an idiom or style derived from France. People were thus becoming divorced from their roots, and the only way to halt this process was to foster local awareness of folklore, songs and the 'national' pastimes of unsophisticated cultures.[3]

But there was at least one serious obstacle to the project of recovering distinctive ways of life; this process must come from the educated classes, and yet these same educated classes were the very people who were most attracted to the modernising cultures of their time, of which the great exemplars were France and England. It was important to educate these people in the appreciation of their own cultures – if indeed they were any longer their own. The Hungarian Academy was created in 1825, and sought to encourage a revival in the use of the Hungarian language; in Russia, writers such as Aleksander Pushkin began to encourage the Russian elite to abandon French for Russian.[4] Leon Tolstoy, in *War and peace*, conveyed this in the episode of Natasha's visit to 'Uncle', who began playing a folk-dance on his guitar.

> 'Now then, niece!' he exclaimed, waving to Natasha the hand that had just struck a chord.

3 B.A. Haddock, 'Shifting patterns of political thought and action: liberalism, nationalism, socialism', in Bruce Waller (ed.), *Themes in modern European history, 1830–1890* (London 1990), pp 213–31, at p. 221. 4 T.Baycroft, *Nationalism in Europe* (Cambridge, 1998), p.14.

Natasha threw off the shawl from her shoulders, ran forward to face 'Uncle', and setting her arms akimbo, also made a motion with her shoulders and struck an attitude.

Where, how, and when had this young countess, educated by an emigree French governess, imbibed from the Russian air she breathed that spirit, and obtained that manner which the pas de chale would, one have supposed, long ago effaced? But the spirit of the movements were those inimitable and unteachable Russian ones that 'Uncle' had expected of her.

Tolstoy then points out the significance of this 'slim, graceful countess reared in silks and velvets ... who yet was able to understand all that was in Anisya: in Anisya's father and mother and aunt, and in every Russian man and woman.[5]

So the search was on for authenticity. But it was not an easy one, for while peasant ways might appeal to some, they were at odds with, for example, the ambitious, thrusting middle-class lawyers who followed the banner of Daniel O'Connell in the early nineteenth century. Yet there could be found in traditions, in folk lore, in poetry and song a heroic appeal. The Finns had their epic, *Kalevale* ('land of heroes'), a poem of some fifty cantos, first published in 1835, and in a second edition in 1849. This was refurbished by a contemporary writer, Elias Lonnrot (1802–84) who used classical forms to shape the material which he had collected among the peasants of eastern Finland and Russian Karelia. A people seeking to mark a distinction between itself and its Swedish or Russian masters would see an outlet in a work which stressed heroic struggle against a formidable foe, as the hero 'sailed away to loftier regions'.[6] In another small country, cheek by jowl with a larger one, Wales, writers such as Iolo Morganwg (Edward Williams, a stonemason of Glamorgan) adopted ideas of the English as well as European romantics, creating an order of Druids in 1789, and composing poetry, and romantic history, and above all the National Eisteddfod ('session'), which was of medieval origin, and which, having been relaunched in the late eighteenth century, was revived after the Napoleonic wars. Four provincial societies were founded to promote Welsh culture and hold Eisteddfods between 1819 and 1821. Significantly, Iolo Morganwg wrote about Wales in English, and yet his order of Bards was incorporated into the Eisteddfod in Carmarthen in 1819.[7]

This points up a paradox in the nineteenth century search for authenticity in culture: those who were in the vanguard were often obliged to adopt modern methods, such as the newspaper press, to spread their message, and to use a 'foreign' language through which to launch and sustain their quest for a

5 Leon Tolstoy, *War and peace* (Oxford, 1992 ed.), p. 546.   6 Norman Davies, *Europe: a history* (London, 1997), p. 818.   7 Prys Morgan and David Thomas, *Wales: the shaping of a nation* (Newton Abbot, 1984), pp 202–3.

traditional way of life. [8] Thomas Davis is a good example of this, with his Anglo-Irish background, his fine grasp of the English language, and his desire to repudiate both– or, rather, to ensure that both could be incorporated into a wider Irish patriotism. This desire to belong and yet to lead was not confined to Ireland. In Germany, the middle classes, 'profoundly dissatisfied with their world' were confronted with the 'tension between their desire to preserve their status and their equally fervent desire to radically alter society'. They hoped to resolve this tension 'by the appeal to a spiritual revolution which would revitalise the nation without revolutionising its structure – a revolution of the soul'. [9] This search to preserve and yet revitalise, to launch a revolution, not of society but of the soul, drew its Irish seekers into the world of Celtic Ireland, into a search for authenticity, that has endured form the early nineteenth, into the twentieth, and is by no means over yet: for just as the Germans of Tacitus were the 'Germans in their youth' [10] so were the Celts of Ireland the modern Irish nation in its youth.

What was it – is it – about the Celts that fascinates? Their appeal is expressed in jugs and mugs, books and art, and – not least – in politics. It is necessary as a preliminary to ask who or what were the Celts that they exercise this appeal. James MacKillop, in his *Dictionary of Celtic Mythology* tells us that the Celtic peoples did not call themselves 'Celts' until comparatively recent times. The word 'Celt' has no counterpart in Old Welsh and Old Irish. The word is found in English usage in John Milton's *Paradise Lost* (1667) and was fixed in the English language by around 1707. The pronunciation of the word Celt is debatable: the Greeks used a hard 'c'; the French a soft 'c'; thus Glasgow Celtic are hard Celts , though not Celts in any racial sense. Now the concept is associated with New Age culture and a certain mysticism; [11] 'Irish dancing' is also an inescapable part of Sinn Fein Ard Feish. The appeal is undiminished.

That appeal is most commonly associated with Irish nationalism, though Irish nationalism has not always regarded it as essential to its character. The appeal of Celtic Ireland, and its heroes, is wider than that, and encompasses the three main groups of people whose interaction has shaped the modern history of Ireland: Protestant, Catholic and Dissenter. These groups have existed, not always in instability or violence, but certainly in insecurity; and insecurity pushes people in the direction of a search for roots, for ways of staking their claim to an identity that will preserve, or gain, or recover, their political social and cultural status. And this search seems to require heroes, exemplars who will inspire the troubled peoples and restore their confidence and self-respect.

8 John Connolly, 'An analysis of six issues of the Nation', MPhil thesis, University College Cork, 1997, p. 58; Niall O Ciosain, *Print and popular culture in Ireland* (London, 1997), pp 186–9. 9 George L. Mosse, *The crisis of German ideology* (London, 1966), p.7. 10 Ibid., p. 67. 11 James McKillop, *Dictionary of Celtic mythology* (Oxford, 1998), pp xiii–xvi.

Unsurprisingly, in the recent history of Ireland, Celtic Ireland and its heroes still stalk the land – or some bits of it at least.

This heroism assumed several manifestations. There was the hero figure, setting an example to his descendants; there was the resurrection of Celtic Ireland itself as a kind of hero, as the cradle of values and ideals that must be revived, and then emulated; there was the hope that Celticism might provide ways of uniting the people of Ireland, and resolving their insecurities; there was even the possibility that a Celtic revival might unite the Celtic peoples of the British Isles, and offer a kind of cultural federalism. All these strategies and possibilities surfaced as the Celts gained and held a grip on the imagination of many in the nineteenth and twentieth century.

The starting place for any discussion of Celtic Ireland must be the work of Thomas Davis, for here is an example of Celticism as a means of healing the divisions between the religious groups in Ireland. Davis sought to portray the Celts as the foundation people of Ireland, whose nobility of character and pre-Christian mentality must (necessarily) exclude sectarianism and at the same time offer an example of a great civilisation to poor, violent, faction-ridden Ireland. To embrace the Celtic past was to begin to create a glorious future: one in which the Irish nation need have no feeling of insecurity about its large, rich and powerful neighbour. Davis' Celtic Ireland would be anti-materialistic; more to the point, it could be led by the Anglo-Irish, if they could be brought to see where their interests as well as their ancestry lay, for whether they were Danish, Norman or even Saxon in origin they could find common pride in Celtic culture. Celtic Ireland was an aristocratic society, and Davis and his people could identify with that society and offer leadership; and thus would an O'Connellite Ireland, English speaking, pursuing the false gods of English Materialism, dominated by the Catholic Church, be transformed into an Ireland that would be a safe haven for Protestant Ireland.[12]

Although Davis had his sights on materialistic England, his ideas were derived from what might be called a wider British culture. In particular, Thomas Carlyle in his 'Signs of the times' (1829) declared that 'were we required to characterise this age of ours by any single epithet, we should be tempted to call it, not a Heroical, Devotional, Philosophical or Moral Age, but, above all others, the Mechanical Age'.[13] Moreover, the 'mechanical genius of the time' had 'diffused itself into quite other provinces. Not the external and physical alone is now managed by machinery, but the internal and spiritual also. Here too nothing follows its spontaneous course, nothing is left to be accomplished by old natural methods'.[14] We no longer worship the Beautiful and the Good: but a calculation of the Profitable'.[15] Carlyle hoped for a spiritual rebirth,

12 D. George Boyce, *Nationalism in Ireland* (London, 3rd ed, 1995), pp 154–61.
13 Thomas Carlyle, 'Signs of the times' (1829) in *Collected works: miscellaneous essays, vol. II* (London, Chapman Hall, n.d., 1895?), pp 56–82, at p. 59.   14 Ibid., p. 60.   15 Ibid., p. 74.

of which self-renunciation was an essential part;[16] the people would look up to the hero, and be led by the strength and wisdom of the few.[17] In this way he could be said not only to have paralleled Davis, but to have anticipated Patrick Pearse.

Carlyle's influence was even more marked in another enthusiast for Celtic Ireland, Standish O'Grady. This was noted by a writer in the *Irish Book Lover* in 1920. O'Grady was 'of those who grew up about the feet of Ruskin and Carlyle'. 'A wind of prophecy, a Cassandra-blast, blows through his pages as through theirs'.

> His great kindred spirit led him to the great clouded figures of the earli-
> est Irish literature, and he released them from the pages of scholars'
> books and stamped them as they passed to liberty with his own seal, so
> that, rightly or wrongly, they have entered Anglo-Irish literature with
> divine or magical attributes, with that famous Celtic glamour which
> bewitches the coteries and causes Irish scholars mildly to blaspheme.[18]

O'Grady reclaimed the Celtic hero from an antiquarian, fustian past to a romantic and political present. He was profoundly influenced not only by Carlyle, but by Benjamin Disraeli, and (the rather unlikely) figure of Lord Randolph Churchill. O'Grady wanted to use the Celtic aristocrats as exemplars for the Irish landlords, who were in danger of being pushed aside from their natural seats of power by the Land League. In his *Toryism and the Tory democracy* (1880) he eulogised Disraeli as the 'first amongst our public men honestly to acknowledge the political and social transformation effected by the rapid advance of Democracy in the present age'.[19] In 1885 in the *Dublin University Review* he set out his strategy, derived from his notion of Celtic and Aristocratic society. 'Until recently', he wrote, 'there has been in this country one class to which reformers might address themselves with at least some chance of success. By the nature of their position, by inherited right, by defined law, the territorial proprietors were Ireland's rulers, and with some prospect of success might have been approached by a strong reformer within or without their own ranks, and summoned to fulfil their function, and called upon to rule well, and with a strict eye to the national welfare.'[20] They had the 'faculty of command born with them or bred in them', which enabled them to control the 'wild, tameless democracy'

---

16 R.W. Hudson, *Introduction to Carlyle*, 'On heroes and hero worship'; and 'Sartor Resartus' (1841; London, Dent, 1967 ed.), pp ix–x. 17 Ibid., p. xiv. 18 'Prominent Penmen', in *Irish Book Lover*, xi (Mar. 1920), 76–7. 19 Standish O'Grady, *Toryism and the Tory democracy*, quoted in D. George Boyce, 'Trembling solicitude: Irish conservatism, nationality and public opinion, 1833–86', in D. George Boyce, Robert Eccleshall and Vincent Geoghegan (eds), *Political thought in Ireland since the seventeenth century* (London, 1993), pp 124–45, at p. 141. 20 Standish O'Grady, 'Irish Conservatism and its outlook', in *Dublin University Review* (Aug. 1885), pp 4–15, at p. 5.

and lead it to 'higher and ever higher stages'. If the landlord were to do this, 'he will find plenty of men willing to enrol themselves under him and work for him, as they did for many an Irish landlord in the old times'.[21]

This was O'Grady's political agenda; but he also had a spiritual one, that deeply reflected the influence of Carlyle. Just as O'Grady described the pagan as 'very much in earnest about his religion', with a 'reverential feeling towards Nature',[22] so did Carlyle describe pagans as 'in their own poor way true and sane!'[23] The world, 'which is now divine only to the gifted, was then divine to whosoever would turn his eye upon it': 'All was Godlike or God'.[24] Out of paganism – a 'perplexed jungle' of beliefs; lay the root of hero-worship (the deepest root of all).[25] Hero-worship was indestructible; 'the one fixed point in modern revolutionary history'.[26] For the Norse people, Odin was a hero; the Norse religion was a 'consecration of valour'.[27] O'Grady likewise looked to the great hero figures of the past, who were at one with nature. In the *Irish Review* in April 1912 O'Grady published an article on 'Paganism: Greek and Irish'. He described how the son of Nial, king of Ireland was baptised and converted to Christ, but his belief in the old gods did not therefore expire: no, it remained with him until his dying day: 'Grim, honest, whole-hearted old Pagan! You were at least no Hypocrit.'[28] It was the duty of the governing classes to revert to the gods of nature, to get Ireland's 'unemployed, under-fed multitudes out from these seething cities of want and discontent' to 'cultivate the good earth', and thus lift the 'monstrous delusions of the Past … like a mist from the mind of these countries'. The 'hounds of Destiny begin to give tongue': Ireland must return to the countryside, to the 'sane and wholesome country', and thus would the Irish people fulfil 'your glorious Destiny'.[29]

O'Grady is the most intriguing of the great Anglo-Irish figures who stalked Ireland in the Victorian age; but there was also an infrastructure of societies and organisations to give a more down to earth and popular appeal to the Celtic past, and to this past as an example for the present and future generations. For these ideas to have any hope of realisation, they had , as George Mosse argued in his *Crisis of German ideology*, to move from the elites to the masses.[30] And those who wished to popularise their ideas must move from the position of an ideology which was only vaguely relevant to the real problems confronting the people to that in which the ideology became 'normative for the solution to those problems'.[31] To pursue this analysis it is necessary to turn to some of the less known figures and organisations that sought to make the Celtic idea 'normative' to the solution of Ireland's problems.

21 Ibid., p. 14.   22 Standish O'Grady, 'Paganism – Greek and Irish', in *Irish Review*, 11 (Apr., 1912), pp 56–67, at p. 61.   23 Thomas Carlyle, *Heroes and hero worship and the heroic in history* (1841; London, 1904 ed.), p. 7.   24 Ibid., p. 9.   25 Ibid., p. 11.   26 Ibid., p. 15. 27 Ibid., p. 41.   28 Standish O'Grady, 'Paganism – Greek and Irish', pp 60–1.   29 Ibid., pp 66–7.   30 George L. Mosse, *Crisis of German ideology*, p. 61.   31 Ibid., p. 9.

There were, to be sure, some favourable signs for the Celticists. In the mid-nineteenth century the designs and motifs of older societies were much admired, and not only in Ireland; here again there is a British dimension. In Great Britain jewellers drew upon Celtic designs for their work, using for example the Conan brooch. The Tara brooch found in 1850 also proved an inspiration. This was not merely a question of fashion; it was comforting to the Irish middle classes to think that they were the descendants of the high kings of Tara.[32]

And so around the middle of the nineteenth century various societies were founded to study the Irish past, all of them deeply influenced by the Irish present. That present was one of deeply held and bitterly contested political ideas; of poverty; famine; a kind of national degradation. This not only troubled Catholics; it also perturbed Protestants, who were indeed caught in an unhappy predicament. They were under attack from the Catholics and yet found no champions to defend them in their sister kingdom England. In 1848 Sir Samuel Ferguson spoke bitterly of the 'unworthy manner in which this ancient Kingdom, this loyal, great and peaceable people- have been spoken of by English representatives in the House of Commons'.[33] One of the most troublesome issues for Protestants was the Church of Ireland's vulnerability in the face of Catholic (and English radical) attacks. The Church of Ireland was not only a state church; its very existence was bound up with the Act of Union itself, which declared that the churches of England and Ireland were now united in one body. This was more apparent than real; and the Irish branch of the Anglican church had to gather together some good arguments in its defence. It had two modes of counter-attack: it represented tradition in religion, and its tradition was firmly founded on the original Celtic church in Ireland. In 1888, some twenty years after disestablishment, George Stokes DD, Professor of Ecclesiastical History in Trinity College, Dublin, wrote in his *Ireland and the Celtic Church* (London, 1888) that the Danes 'paved the way enabling the Church of Rome to overthrow our ancient national customs and independence'. Irish national independence and Irish ecclesiastical independence terminated practically together; hence his desire to trace the 'history of the Church of Ireland during its period of Celtic independence'.[34]

Long before the disestablishment battle was lost and won, Church of Ireland clergy were active in ransacking Celtic Ireland for a heroic defence of its privileges. In the Irish Archaeological Society there were to be found, not only Anglicans, but fervent evangelicals, anxious to save the souls of their neighbours, especially of their Roman Catholic neighbours: the reverend Caesar

32 Elizabeth McCrum, 'Commerce and the Celtic Revival: Victorian Irish jewellry', in *Eire-Ireland*, xxxviii, no. 4 (Winter, 1993), 35–52, at 36–8. 33 Quoted in Boyce, 'Trembling solicitude', in Boyce et al., *Political ideas in Ireland*, p. 135. 34 George Stokes, *Ireland and the Celtic church* (London 1888), pp 343, 348.

Otway, founder of the *Christian Examiner*, was one such.[35] This society was founded in 1840, and was followed by the Celtic Society in 1845 and the Ossianic Society in 1853. The members of these societies did not use them for sectarian purposes; they were genuinely interested in scholarly pursuits (as was the Gaelic League of the 1890s). But like the Gaelic League, they paid particular attention to aspects of the past: the Irish Archaeological Society selected documents that would bolster its claim that Protestants were the authentic possessor of the Irish church tradition before the Normans. The Celtic Society was also non-sectarian in its composition. It merged with the Irish Archaeological Society and retained a Protestant-Catholic balance on its management council. Likewise the Ossianic Society strove to avoid a sectarian taint, concentrating on Irish folklore and poetry, including bardic poetry, and once again Protestants, especially clergymen, were among the leading editors of manuscript publications.[36]

Yet the search for the past led these societies into mythology; and mythology is, after all, a chief component of nationalism. The Ossianic Society concerned itself with folklore. It was a less exclusive organisation than the archaeological and Celtic societies, which were mainly supported by the gentry and middle classes. The Ossianic Society rules declared that all council members should be Gaelic scholars (which few of the nobility were) and charged a lower membership fee.[37] The society concentrated on publishing material on the culture of the Gaelic-speaking peasantry, especially the Fianna, that legendary band of warriors whose leaders were chosen by merit, not birth.[38] The largest part of its membership was drawn from the clergy, with the legal profession, merchants, civil servants, publicans, booksellers well represented, and from the lower middle classes, policemen, shopkeepers, and even land agents.[39] Only one member, William Smith O'Brien, was from a gentry background, and, ironically, he was of a genuine Gaelic aristocratic ancestry.[40] Moreover, the Ossianic Society's main purpose was not primarily to publish historical materials, but to publish work that would halt the decline of Irish, which, after the Great Famine, was accelerating rapidly, especially in Connaught and Munster. The Society gained much support from the Irish overseas, especially in the United States of America, where Irish language names were adopted by political organisations such as Clan na Gael.[41] Thus did the Ossianic Society move into the attempt to create a national identity based on the Gaelic language and culture, especially folklore; the Archaeological Society, by contrast, with landlords of a conservative/unionist disposition well represented, concentrated on ecclesiastical and noble history, and the relationship between church, state and landlords to preserve the social order.[42]

---

35 Damien J. Murray, 'Romanticism and Irish antiquarian societies, 1840–1880', PhD thesis, National University of Ireland, Maynooth, 1997, p. 63. 36 Ibid., p. 89. 37 Ibid., p. 114. 38 Ibid., p. 115. 39 Ibid., p. 116. 40 Ibid., p. 117. 41 Ibid., p. 143. 42 Ibid., p. 153.

Of course, the events that these societies were seeking to bring about were events of long gestation; Ireland in the 1850s was not the Ireland in which the Gaelic League of the 1890s found such a receptive audience. But they were the essential forerunners to the later success of the League. Likewise, Sir Samuel Ferguson had not the materials to hand to create the literary revival of the 1890s. But, again, there were lesser man and lesser women too who were anxious to give the Irish people what they needed: a sense of their history, a pride in their past, an appreciation, in particular, of Celtic Ireland.

One of the most important figures in directing attention to a study of the Irish past was Patrick Weston Joyce (1827–1914) historian, linguist and collector of music. He was born in Co. Limerick, and educated at hedge schools. He taught at the Model School, Clonmel, and in 1850 was one of fifteen teachers selected and trained to reorganise the National Schools system. He went on to take a degree in Trinity College Dublin in 1861, and to become principal of a teacher training college in Marlborough Street, Dublin, in 1874–93.[43] Joyce was a most prolific writer, publishing dictionaries of the Irish language, books of Old Celtic romances, histories of Ireland (including the celebrated *Child's history of Ireland* in 1903) and works on Irish place names. He was a member of the Society for the Preservation of the Irish Language. It is hard to overestimate his influence on the materials taught in Irish schools, and his contribution to changing the curriculum of the national schools, from one of bland, British and Imperial centred instruction to the study of Irish history and the Irish language, an influence that continued into the Irish Free State. Irish children were taught that they were members of a British nation, albeit one that encompassed England, Ireland, Scotland and Wales: their books of lessons explained that 'the island of Great Britain, which is composed of England, Scotland and Wales, and the island of Ireland ... form the British Empire of Europe', and that to the east of Ireland 'is England where the Queen lives' and that 'many people who live in Ireland were born in England, and we speak the same language and are called one nation'.[44]

Joyce sought to instruct them in appreciation of their Irish national history. He was, however, no xenophobe: in his *Child's history of Ireland* he specifically set out to 'foster mutual feelings of respect and toleration among Irish people of different parties', and to teach them 'to love and admire what is great and noble in their history, no matter where found'.[45] Occasionally he used the description 'Irish people' to refer exclusively to the Catholics, as for example when he wrote that the 'Irish people' resisted the projects of plantation and

---

43 These details are taken from Henry Boylan, *Dictionary of Irish biography* (Dublin 1978), pp 163–4. 44 Vanessa Rutherford, 'Aspects of childhood in Ireland, 1800–1926', PhD thesis, National University of Ireland, Maynooth, 2002, p. 46. 45 P.W. Joyce, *A child's history of Ireland* (Dublin, 1903 ed.), p. vi. 46 Ibid., p. 210.

reformation.[46] But he was at pains to give as much praise to the heroic defence of Derry in the Williamite wars as to the deeds of Patrick Sarsfield.[47]

But where Joyce transcended the usually more prosaic style of his history was when he wrote of Celtic Ireland. His books are filled with the most striking images of Celtic art and design;[48] and in his *Smaller social history of Ireland* (1906) he declared that:

> From the account given here, and from the evidences adduced in this and in the larger work, we may see that the ancient Irish were as well advanced in civilisation , as orderly, and as regular, as the people of those other European countries of the same period that – like Ireland – had a proper settled government; and it will be shown further on that they were famed throughout all Europe for Religion and Learning.[49]

He went on to explain that the writer who endeavoured to set forth his subject in 'words of truth and soberness' was sure to encounter the disapproval or hostility of those who held extreme opinions on either side. 'In regard to my subject', he went on, 'we have, on the one hand, those English and Anglo-Irish people - and they are not few - who think, mainly from ignorance, that Ireland was a barbarous and half-savage country before the English came among the people and civilised them'. Joyce also castigated those of his countrymen who had an 'exaggerated idea of the greatness and splendour of the ancient Irish nation'.[50] Above all, he believed that 'irrespective of personal considerations, it seems to me very desirable that a good knowledge of the social condition of Ancient Ireland, such as is presented here, should be widely diffused among the people: more especially now' , he concluded, 'when there is an awakening of interest in the Irish language, and in Irish lore of every kind, unparalleled in our history.'[51]

This was a fair claim; the 1890s did witness just such an 'unparalleled' interest in things Irish. This was reflected, not only in the great work of the Literary Revival, but in a kind of lesser literary revival that took place at the same time, and was almost certainly inspired by, and possibly even helped transmit, the ideas of the great revival. Arthur H. Leahy transmitted the message in poetic form, in his *Heroic romances of Ireland*:

> 'Tis hard an audience to win
> For lore that Ireland's tales can teach
> And faintly, 'mid the modern din
> Is heard the old heroic speech

47 Ibid., Ch. xlix. 48 For example, the cover of his *A child's history of Ireland*. 49 P.W. Joyce, *A smaller social history of Ireland* (London, 1906 ed.), pp vi–vii. 50 Ibid., pp vii–viii. 51 Ibid., p. ix.

Think not a dull, a scribal pen
Dead legends wrote, half-known and feared:
In lettered lands to poet men
Romance, who lives today, appeared.

For when, in fear of warrior bands,
Had learning fled the western world,
And, raised once more by Irish bards,
Her banner stands again unfurled;

Not as in Greece aspired their thought,
They joined in battles wild and stern;
Yet poetry once to men they taught
From whom a fiercer age would learn.

Their heroes praise a conquered foe,
Oppose their friends for honour's sake,
To weaker chieftains mercy show
And strength of cruel tyrants break.

In forms like these men loved of old.
Naught added, nothing torn away,
The ancient tales again are told,
Can none their own true magic sway?[52]

The attempt to make their 'true magic sway' a modern generation gathered force. Two examples are of particular interest. One is a book written by Sophie Bryant (1850–1922) who was born in Dublin of English parentage, and whose childhood was spent mainly in Co. Fermanagh.[53] Like Joyce, she played a key role in the Irish National education movement, and in 1913 published *The genius of the Gael: a study of Celtic psychology and its manifestations.*[54] Her purpose was to 'show how the observed characteristics of Irishmen, in so far as they differ from others, may be explained by the prevalence in them of a certain psychological variety, structural, or functional, or temperamental, which is the fundamental quality of the Celtic mind'. She began her book with a quotation from Thomas Davis: 'It (the nation) must contain and represent the races of

52 Arthur H. Leahy, *Heroic romances of Ireland in two volumes: Irish Saga Library No. 2* (London, 1905), pp xxi–xxv. 53 Details from *Who was who, 1916–1928*. 54 Sophie Bryant, *The genius of the Gael: a study in Celtic psychology and its manifestations* (London, 1913).

Ireland. It must not be Catholic, it must not be Saxon. The Brehon Law and the maxims of Westminster, the cloudy and lightning genius of the Gael, the placid strength of the Sassenach, the marshalling insight of the Norman – these are the components of such a nationality.'[55] From this process, Sophie Bryant asserted, 'of mixed hereditary and education the race emerges'.[56] There were 'foster-children and natural children', but a 'well-blended and composite people emerges'.[57] Nevertheless, it was the 'Gaelic race" which 'forms the nucleus of the Irish nation and breathes into Irish nationality its all-pervading and most expansive spirit'.[58] In most strong men there was 'underlying the Christian conscience, something more primitive, derived from an older ancestral past or acquired from early pagan literary influences'. The land that grows heroes, she concluded 'will yield a good crop of saints'. She quoted with approval Standish O'Grady's eulogy on the 'Irish bards and that heroic age of theirs which nourished the imagination, intellect and idealism of the country'.[59] And when Christianity and the Gaelic mind synthesised then the blend was a most dynamic one, of which Sophie Bryant quoted an example:

> Do god deeds without lie or falsehood,
> Do without lies good deeds on earth here,
> That is the one straight road to follow:
> That is the road and not go off it.

'This' she added, 'might equally well pass for a Fenian utterance or for an instruction of St Patrick.'[60] It is not too fanciful to add that it might pass for that mixture of Fenian and saint, Patrick Pearse.

The next example is Eleanor Hull (1860–1935), who, like Bryant, was of Anglo-Irish origin.[61] She was born in England, of parents from Co. Down, and read 'Celtic Studies' under Kuno Meyer and Robin Flower. She contributed to various literary journals and with the help of Professor F. York and various Irish friends she founded the Irish Texts Society for the publication of Irish manuscripts in 1899. She published various works on Irish literature, including Gaelic poetry. Her *Pagan Ireland: episodes of Irish history, volume 2*,[62] was read by P.W. Joyce, whose educational net was thrown wide. This book recounted the story of 'Donn-Bo' who fell fighting for the king of Erin. His head was found by the king's men and put on a pole. It began miraculously to sing. The head was taken back to the body and the neck joined itself with the shoulders. 'The old King-stories that Donn-Bo loved have been forgotten by Erin's children,' lamented Eleanor Hull. 'Even the few of them to whom the tales of Finn and of Cuchulainn are not quite unknown, know little of the old romances of

55 Ibid., p. 8.   56 Ibid., p. 14.   57 Ibid., p. 15.   58 Ibid., p. 20.   59 Ibid., pp 24–5.
60 Ibid., p. 257.   61 Details from the *Dictionary of Irish biography*, p. 154.   62 Eleanor Hull, *Pagan Ireland: episodes of Irish history*, vol. 2 (Dublin, 1908).

Cormac mac Airt, or of Niall of the Nine Hostages, or of Conn of the Hundred Fights …' If 'on the Plains of Heaven an Irish King wearied for the stories of his ancestors, why should not the children of Erin care to hear them in the valleys of Earth?'.[63]

The part played by people of Anglo-Irish descent in the recovery of the Celtic past will not have gone unnoticed. Their insecurity – significant at the time of O'Connell; important again at the time of the disestablishment of the Church of Ireland and the Land War – crystallised by the last decade of the nineteenth century and played no small part in the foundation of the Gaelic League by Douglas Hyde, and the Literary Revival by W.B. Yeats and others. But it also caught the mood of Catholics, especially the middle classes who, as D.P. Moran put it, would no longer be trodden on with impunity.[64] What gave the Celtic idea its power was this identification of the past with the advancement of Catholics that had taken place since the 1840s, but was still by no means complete: and was least complete in the matter of what might be called the psychological dimension. The search for status, social and economic, was closely related to the recognition of Home Rule as the nation coming out of bondage. Even the pragmatic politicians, William O'Brien, told the Cork National Society, of which he was president, in 1892 that

> The Celtic spirit is the saving of a materialistic age. Celtic hearts in our own days have carried the fire of divine faith into the depths of the New World as bright as the night it was kindled by St Patrick on the Hill of Slane.

He pointed out that 'Celtic ideals' did not find 'satisfaction on the English tongue- that they … feel an alien chill and discomfort in their English garb'.[65] But there was still the possibility that the Celtic idea could play some part in uniting, rather than dividing, the peoples (or at least the Celtic peoples) of the British Isles- that it could inspire a kind of 'pan-Celticism' on the lines, perhaps, of the pan-Slavic movement in Russia in the 1880s. After all, some of the chief proponents of the Celtic past – Ferguson, O'Grady – were unionist in politics; and indeed Sir Samuel Ferguson's widow, Lady Ferguson, in her *Story of the Irish before the Conquest: from the mystical period to the Invasion under Strongbow*,[66] tested the waters of unity, when she praised Cuchulainn, 'the preux chevalier of Irish chivalrous story',[67] but at the same time praised the

63 Ibid., preface. 64 Shane O'Neill, 'Politics and culture in Ireland, 1899–1910', DPhil thesis, Oxford, 1982, p. 126. For a full discussion, see Senata Paseta, *Before the revolution: nationalism, social change and Ireland's Catholic elite* (Cork, 1999). 65 William O'Brien, 'The influence of the Irish language', in Lady Gregory (ed.), *Ideals in Ireland* (London, 1901), pp 63–4. 66 Lady Ferguson, *The story of the Irish before the Conquest: from the mystical period to the invasion under Strongbow* (3rd ed., Dublin, London, 1903), pp vii–viii. 67 Ibid., p. 51.

'rough and tedious process of transition' (the Norman Conquest) which was the means of 'our admission to a larger sphere of citizenship, to a share in many peaceful as well as warlike glories, to the general use of the noble language in which all the genius of science and all the highest utterances of modern poetry and philosophy have found a worthy expression'.[68]

The greatest figure in the resurrection of Celtic heroism is Patrick Pearse; his praise of the Cuchulainn spirit is too well known to need much detailed description.[69] Pearse, like some of the Anglo-Irish Celtic enthusiasts, believed in education as a means of spreading the heroic ideal. Denis Gwynn told how he was chosen to play the part of Cuchulainn , despite his belief that he was 'far from being a figure for heroic parts'. But 'after the second performance attended by W.B. Yeats, Lady Gregory (possibly) Padraic Colum, and the celebrated author himself (O'Grady), Pearse was ready with a speech in which he so clearly drew comparison between the play and the present, that he left no doubt that he considered Ireland was in a similar mood of dejection and despair awaiting a deliverer'. O'Grady, 'seated in the audience with his grey hair and piercing eyes' was asked to reply and stated that, like Pearse, he noted the play's symbolic meaning: 'He hoped that it might presage a new age in which the young men and women of Ireland would once again lead the lives of free people on the mountains.'[70] Desmond Ryan put it more succinctly: at St Enda's, Cuchulainn was 'an invisible but important member of the staff'.[71]

But there was another Pearse, the dabbler in pan-Celticism and the admirer of unionists – or at least of what he called the Orangemen who were prepared to fight and die for their beliefs. This Pearse contrasted with the Gaelic League enthusiast, the reverend Eugene O'Growney, who claimed that Protestants and foreigners had taken an interest in the Irish language, yet it was the repository of one of the richest Catholic traditions in the world, and its preservation could save Ireland from the evil spirit of materialism which found expression in the English language.[72] Pearse would have agreed with the second part of this statement; but he had a broader outlook when it came to the question of Protestants. In 1898 the Irish Committee of the Pan-Celtic Congress was established in Dublin, with Protestant luminaries such as George Sigerson, AE (George Russell) and Standish O'Grady there, all under the inspiration of Lord Castletown.[73] In May 1898 the Irish Pan-Celts proposed sending a 'United Gaelic deputation' to the Welsh National Eisteddfod in Cardiff;[74] but the Gaelic League disapproved.[75] Yet Pearse did attend on behalf of the League and

68 Ibid., p. 331. 69 For which see Patrick Rafroidi, 'Imagination and revolution: the Cuchulainn myth', in Oliver MacDonagh and W.F. Mandle, *Irish culture and nationalism, 1750–1950* (London, 1983), pp 137–48. 70 Denis Gwynn, 'Standish O'Grady', in *Old Kilkenny Review*, 22 (1970), 11–14. 71 Patrick Rafroidi, 'Imagination and revolution', p. 142. 72 Shane O'Neill, 'Politics and culture', p. 38. 73 Ibid., p. 72. 74 Ibid., p. 74. 75 Ibid., p. 79.

disapproved of those who insisted that the other Celts in the British Isles were of a different religion from the Irish Celts, and spoke a different language and that, as the Revd Patrick Forde put it, there was an 'intrinsic connection between religion and national character'.[76] Hyde dubbed the Pan-Celts as 'Imperial federationists',[77] but Pearse did not so regard them. And Pearse's gift for invective found its most interesting expression when he scorned the Home Rulers for anticipating that 'Orange boys and Orange girls' would be forced to learn Irish, though he acknowledged that, however unrealistic, 'the prospect of the children of Sandy Row being taught to curse the Pope in Irish was rich and satisfying'.[78]

This was long before Pearse moved towards the concept of the Cuchulainn hero figure, purged of his paganism, and closely identified instead with the Christ-like example of self-sacrifice for the love he bore – as Pearse transformed it - to the Gael. Pearse hoped to create a nation cast in the heroic mould, but also a society in which people would abandon self-seeking materialism and help eachother. This was a truly revolutionary vision, on a par with that of the Jacobins after 1789 and the Bolsheviks after 1917: mankind would be made anew, and utopian visions would – must – come to pass.

The new Irish Free State, equipped with the works of P.W. Joyce, set out to cast Irish education in the Celtic mould. Michael Collins spoke of the imperative need to build up Gaelic traditions to the exclusion of all others: games, pastimes, cultural pursuits, all must shape this Gaelic mind.[79] De Valera also pursued the recovery of the hidden Ireland: a small, frugal independent nation was the descendant of a great race, a great tradition, that of the Celts, and, by following their example would be great again: not in terms of power and wealth, but in moral values.[80] Of course all this was vulnerable to ridicule, and it was ridiculed. Eimar O'Duffy in 'King Goshawk and the Bards' (1926) satirised the Cuchulainn legend:

> You should have seen Cuchulainn playing tennis with the gentry and ladies of the Bon Ton suburb. He learnt the whole art and skill of the game in ten minutes, and straightway beat the champion of all Ireland six-love, six-love and six-love. Never had such strength and agility been seen before. He could cross the court at one leap, he never served a fault, and none but the champion ever returned his service. He would take any stroke on the volley; and at the net his smash invariably burst the ball.[81]

More recently, in an Ireland in which tribunals inquiring into government scandals are now an unofficial part of the Irish constitution, Jonathan Philbin

76 Ibid., p. 80.   77 Ibid., p. 100.   78 Ibid., p. 107.   79 Michael Collins, *The path to freedom* (Dublin, 1962 ed.), p. 18.   80 D. George Boyce, *Nationalism in Ireland*, p. 351. 81 Patrick Rafroidi, 'Imagination and revolution', p. 144.

Bowman told the story of how 'newly illuminated manuscripts reveal that Cuchulainn accepted cash payments from the berry, hawthorn and cowhide trader Ben Dunne. Later it emerged that Cuchulainn may be only one of a number of mythological figures who accepted cash from the tradesman.' For years these allegation had been circulating, said 'storyteller Fintan the Tool, but heretofore they have been hidden by the Celtic mists of time. The discovery of these manuscripts certainly casts a new light on Cuchulainn, who for years led a lavish lifestyle, keeping a cellar of fine vintage mead, and reportedly enjoying the company of the mythical queens Maeve, Barbara, Anne, Trudi, Eimar, Finulla, Anne again, among other maidens. Cuchulainn also kept horses.'

While the nation was shocked, 'a recent poll reveals that many of the populace now believe that Cuchulainn may have taken other tokens of esteem from visiting dignitaries, and there were murmurings about the beautiful ox-hide handbag he had presented to one of his maidens'. 'A shocked nation awaits the next tribunal with interest'.[82]

So the Cuchulainn myth has now become a sword wielded, not as Pearse and his like hoped, to carve out a new , moral, heroic nation, but to satirise its inheritors. This must be healthy, and speaks of a more relaxed Ireland, secure at least in its ability to see its Celtic heroes in a rather different perspective. But the Cuchulainn myth is not yet dead; nor have the Celts, or some variety of them, yet fully served their purpose. Insecurity breeds the need for myths, as it did for the declining Anglo-Irish and the rising – but at least partially blocked – Roman Catholics. Now, in the cockpit of Northern Ireland politics, the intermingling of Protestant, Catholic and Dissenter, so close spatially, so apart politically, and engaged in a struggle for survival or supremacy, depending on the point of view, has called forth a renewal of the Celtic myth. For Celtic Ireland, and Cuchulainn, the Ulster Prince, are, as the England team's fans' football song put it 'coming home' : home to Northern Ireland.

The extraordinary events of the last thirty years; the collapse of the unity of Ulster Unionism; the rise of Irish Republicanism (in its peculiarly local form and character); the war of the paramilitaries: all have brought forth atavistic sentiments: and myth thrives on and feeds atavism, which in turn feeds myth. It is not surprising that Cuchulainn should re-emerge as the champion of the reunification of the four Provinces of Ireland; it is not altogether astonishing that riverdance and revolvers should find themselves in curious, but understandable, company. What is more surprising that Loyalist Paramilitaries in July 1992 ('Ulster's only legal defenders') should depict themselves with flag and shield, with above it the dying Cuchulainn.[83] The Young Unionist Council reminded unionists that Cuchulainn was 'the mythical hero of the earliest inhabitants of Ulster, the Cruthin. He lived – and died – defending his

82 John Philbin Bowman, 'Hero hounded by torc of a golden circle', in *Sunday Independent*, 3 Aug. 1997. 83 *New Ulster Defender*, 1, no. 2 (July, 1992).

kingdom from the men of Ireland who sought to invade. Ancient legend records that when mortally wounded, he fastened himself to a hugh rock that he might die standing and not at the feet of his enemies. Today a statue of this legendary hero of Ulster can be found in the GPO in Dublin, where it commemorates the rebels of the 1916 Easter Rising'. The unionists concluded that 'Neglect of an ancient heritage resulted in republicans being able to steal the legend of Cuchulainn from us.'[84]

Modern Ulster unionism found its own Standish O'Grady in the figure of Ian Adamson, who, inspired by the loss of confidence in their identity by Ulster Protestants, set out to research and rewrite the ancient history of Ulster and Ireland. Adamson discovered that the earliest inhabitants of Ireland were not the Gaels, but the Cruthin – a people closely related to the Scottish Picts. The Cruthin took refuge in Scotland, seeking relief from an aggressive, expansionist, imperialist Irish Gaelic people. Therefore it is conclusive that some at least of those who moved from Scotland to Ulster in the sixteenth and seventeenth century were descendants of the original inhabitants of Ulster: 'Pressurised by Southern Gaelic expansion into Scotland earlier in the Christian era, they had at last returned to the lands of their ancestors.'[85]

Protestant, Catholic and Dissenter: these are the people whose interaction make up the history of Ireland. Adamson gave his Celtic legend a peculiarly Dissenting dimension. Those who had 'returned to the lands of their ancestors' had 'in every sense of the words [*sic*] remained loyal and true. They had maintained the authority of Charles I, had refuted that of Cromwell's Parliamentarians, and had protested against the execution of the King. They had defended Derry and Enniskillen. They had saved Ireland for the British Crown and if Ireland had fallen, so too would Scotland and perhaps even England as well'.[86]

Yet, 'all this passed for nothing'. The eighteenth century saw the application of penal laws to Dissenter as well as Catholic, such as the Test Act, which 'although ostensibly passed to further discourage Catholicism' had at its real object 'to place the Presbyterians on the same plane of impotence'. Mindful of the need for Protestant unity, Adamson was careful to explain that 'most bishops of the Church of Ireland were especially tolerant in an age of bigotry'. The 'most unkindest cut of all was selling of land in Ulster. One plot of land which had been drained and cultivated by a thrifty "Scotch-Irish" family was sold to two or more Catholic families who could only continue to live there at mere subsistence level'.[87]

84 Young Unionist Council, Discussion Paper 2 (July, 1986).   85 Ian Adamson, 'The identity of Ulster: the Scotch-Irish', paper delivered at the Irish Historians in Britain conference, University of Sussex, 1982, p. 7; see also Graham Walker, *Intimate strangers: political and cultural interaction between Scotland and Ulster in modern times* (Edinburgh, date) pp 4, 176. 86 Adamson, 'Identity of Ulster', p. 7.   87 Ibid., pp 7–8.

Thus did Ian Adamson seek to create a distinct Ulster identity, in contradiction to the Irish nationalist idea of the Gael, like Tacitus' Germans, as the
nation in its youth. This identity would be complementary to a wider British
identity. Adamson spoke for the Dissenter, and so the cycle is completed: the
Celtic Hero could be conscripted by the competing groups in Ireland, and used
to identify both themselves, and the group in its relationship with England.
Adamson was anxious to stress that his history was written to display the
complex origins of the people of Ulster, though his work found its most
favourable reception among Loyalist political and indeed paramilitary groups:
it is perhaps significant that one of the earliest manifestations of this use of
Celticism as a Loyalist support myth were the 'Tara' gangs of the early 1970s.
The idea that Adamson's work seeks to popularise - that there could be a
Unionist identity and a British identity that were complementary was more
attuned to the times than the old unionist slogan that 'Ulster is British'. This
was vital in an era when the whole United Kingdom set of nations was redefining its culture and its mutual relationship; and Adamson hoped that his history
would re-legitimise Ulster unionism at a time when Dublin, London, nationalists and republicans in Northern Ireland are seeking to de-legitimise it.

This use of the Cuchulainn myth did not quite work for Ulster unionists.
Perhaps the problem was epitomised in the aside made as a collection of
Adamson's books was being loaded on to a lorry for transmission to its reader-
ship: one of the helpers picked up a copy and observed, 'it is awful Fenian-
looking'.[88] The Celtic myth could not displace that of the heroic age of Ulster
Protestantism, the seventeenth century; perhaps it was not necessary; perhaps
Ulster Unionism's claim to be the progressive and modern element in Ireland
demanded a modern, or at least an early modern context. The search for roots
has developed in more popular directions, in the founding of Ulster-Scots
associations, the publication of the first grammar of Ulster-Scots, the re-
naming of streets in that idiom, as a counter to the republican re-naming of
streets in Gaelic.[89] Just as the Irish cultural enthusiasts turned in on themselves
when they perceived that Ireland was becoming the most westerly province of
the British Isles, and found a ready response in the uneasy, but ambitious
middle class Catholics, so the Ulster-Scots cultural enthusiasts have made
some progress in a part of United Kingdom whose government seems anxious
to be rid of them and which is eager to support financially what Dr Clifford
Smyth, author of Ian Paisley's biography, described as 'a kind of Riverdance
culture'.[90]

The search for Celtic Ireland has of course attracted scholars, antiquarians,
historians, linguists, archaeologists as well as those with a more overt political

88 Personal information.   89 Daniel Hannan, 'Swamped by Riverdance', in *Spectator*, 13
Dec. 1997, pp 21–2.   90 Ibid., p. 22.

agenda. The political agenda derives its strength from the search for roots: for a legitimising principle in an island whose political and cultural life was marked by a conflict of nationality. The presence of three distinct people in Ireland – Protestant, Catholic and Dissenter – gave what was a general European phenomenon a particular intensity, a special appeal. The Protestants, a minority in an age of democracy and mass political organisation, must seek for a time in history when an elite, albeit a cultural elite, played a leading role in shaping the values and traditions of their people. They were losing power – economic, social, religious, political – and they must save themselves from the consequences of minoritisation. Celtic Ireland seemed to offer an escape from this fate. It only hastened it.

The Catholic nationalist, disillusioned, even disgusted with the Home Rulers and their Anglicised ways, critical even of the great Daniel O'Connell and his instruction to learn English and abandon Irish, sought Celtic Ireland as a means of reviving the national spirit, of creating a nation that was demonstrably un-English. They too were in danger of becoming a minority: an Anglicised minority in the English dominated British United Kingdom. The Roman Catholic middle classes, dispossessed of their roots, clerks, civil servants, teachers, seeking firmer and morally superior ground, sought and found solace in Celtic Ireland; but, more radically, in Gaelic Ireland, by which was meant the Ireland that suffered the Reformation, rather than the Pagan Ireland beloved by the Literary revivalists. The Irish Free State, some have argued, was founded by and for the petty bourgeois whose representatives adopted and supported this project. But this too caused difficulties: for the bulk of the Irish people, though certainly not English in their ways of life and thought, could not shake off English influence, cease reading or listening to or watching the English and London based media, take on the Irish language,[91] live frugally, or – even – live the lives of Cuchulainn-type heroes, never telling a lie, never having falsehood imputed to them – as Jonathan Philbin Bowman so brilliantly satirised in his 'Tribunals' article.

Modern Ulster unionists, seeking to find a new sense of legitimacy, especially in the light of their 'betrayal' – or (as they would see it) betrayal – by successive British governments, have moved beyond the heroic era of Protestant resistance to Catholic power, the seventeenth century and its culmination in the great delivery of 1690, to a new origin myth. But the work of Ian Adamson has not gained resonance, and looks more like a desperate attempt to dislodge republican self-glorification than an engagement with the Ulster Protestant past, or a version of it. Moreover, Adamson's leap from the Cruthin to Ulster Presbyterianism only emphasises the distinction between Ulster's Presbyterians

91 R.B. MacDowell, *Crisis and decline: the fate of the Southern unionists* (Dublin, 1997), pp 195–6.

and Anglicans, a distinction which Ulster unionist leaders have always sought to play down. For the same reason, the Ulster-Scots project might divide, rather than unite, the unionist people.

Nonetheless, these are Ireland's Celtic heroes: valuable, at times even indispensable, to the contending peoples of Ireland, Protestant, Catholic and Dissenter. The Celtic myth bears witness to the divided and troubled history of Ireland, in the end dividing still further rather than healing. And so perhaps the last word can be given to an eleventh century writer, who (for his own good reasons), declared that

> These stories did not happen at all as they were told, but it was to ingratiate themselves with the rude Ulster race that the smooth-tongued poets invented their lying fables.[92]

92 Francis J. Byrne, *Irish kings and high kings* (London, Batsford, 1973; reprinted Dublin, 2001), p. 106.

Index